JOHN TAYLOR'S VILLAGE STORIES

VOLUME 6

STANTONBURY
&
NEW BRADWELL

JOHN A TAYLOR

JOHN TAYLOR'S VILLAGE STORIES

6 STANTONBURY & NEW BRADWELL

Published by Magic Flute Publishing Ltd. 2023

ISBN 978-1-915166-13-5

Magic Flute Publishing Limited
231 Swanwick Lane
Southampton SO31 7GT
www.magicflutepublishing.com

A catalogue description of this book is available from the British Library

MAGIC FLUTE
PUBLISHING

CONTENTS

ACKNOWLEDGEMENTS

In compiling this book I have been able to source the Buckinghamshire Archives, the Northamptonshire Archives and the resources of the Milton Keynes Central Library.

Several individuals have made valuable contributions and I would like to thank Martin Baggott, Jennifer Broadbent, Graham Crisp, Bryan Dunleavy, David Farron, Sammy Jones, Audrey Lambert, Sylvia Mead, Brian Newman, and John Salmon.

John Taylor
April 2023

Although these photographs were taken in the early 20th century they recall a time before 1850 when New Bradwell as such did not exist. The lone Stantonbury farmhouse (shown above), some wharf cottages, the New Inn and the Windmill house and associated cottages were the only signs of life to be found.

In the photograph above the New Inn mooring is just beyond the Bradwell Road bridge on the left.

The only evidence today that there was once a village in Stantonbury is the ruin of the 12th century church. The village at Stanton Low was never large and was mostly depopulated in the 16th century. A handful of cottages were clustered around the church, the last being demolished in 1946.

The two photographs above date from the early 20th century.

THE EARLY VILLAGE

At a time when the gravel pits at Linford were extending towards Stanton Low, on Saturday, January 12th 1957 from being a keen member of the local archaeological society Robert Harris of Western Road, Wolverton, a student at the local Technical School, whilst delving in the spoil thrown up by an excavator discovered Roman tiles, hypocaust flues, a coin and pottery pieces, indicative of a Roman building. He took the specimens to Charles Green, who represented the Bucks County Society, and on examining the site on the Sunday it seemed the bulldozer had bitten into the east side of what was possibly the headquarters of a sizeable farming estate, lying on both sides of the river. The finds were then exhibited during the month at a meeting of the Wolverton and District Archaeological Society at New Bradwell.

Of more certain times, after the Norman invasion William the Conqueror bestowed the manor of Stanton to Miles Crispin, it being assessed at the Domesday survey at 5 hides with a worth of £6. Included was a mill and meadow sufficient for four plough teams. As for the ensuing manorial history, this is copiously told in the several learned published works and the equally learned 'on line' academia. Therefore suffice to say that during the 13th century the manor became associated with the Barry (or Barre) family, so accounting for the morphing into Bury as an addition to the name. They held ownership until the late 14th century and seemingly houses of the early community lay in the field north of the church, situated between two village streets running east to west.

Then during the ownership of Nicholas Vaux came a devastation of the village by his policy of turning the acreage from arable to pasture. This stemmed from the profitability of, probably, sheep grazing, and 40 people were thrown out of work. He died in 1523 and the estates then passed to his son Thomas, who sold Stantonbury in 1535.

By 1563 only three households remained and in 1653 Stantonbury was acquired by Sir John Wittewronge. His family seat lay in Harpenden although he is said to have built a substantial house at Stantonbury for his eldest son John. (Allegedly this was destroyed by fire in 1743, with evidence of the location indicated by extensive foundations southwest of the church, between the churchyard and the canal.)[1] In 1727 the estate was sold to Sarah, Duchess of Marlborough, who settled it on John Spencer, her grandson. Thereon it became the property of the ensuing Earl Spencers of Althorpe, in Northants., and in 1736 only four farms and a few cottages remained in the parish. However regarding the situation a while later, in the 1950s a member of a local historical society said that his wife's grandfather had heard from a very old man that he could remember houses in the village, including an old blacksmith's shop and a dovecote. That would be around 1790 and indeed in the 14th century is mentioned a dovecote as well as a water mill. The completion of the Grand Junction Canal at the beginning of the 19th century brought local opportunities for trade, and in April 1817 Messrs. Harrison, Oliver, and Kitelee relinquished their business of coal merchants to John Scrivenor.[2] Indeed the Scrivenor family would become local farmers, as mentioned in 1845 when was advertised:

> 'The Manor, or reputed Manor of Stantonbury on the turnpike road between Newport Pagnell and the Wolverton Station on the Birmingham Railway.
>
> Messrs. Driver have received instructions to offer to public competition at the auction mart on Tuesday, May 27th at noon in one lot the above estate comprising 750 acres of rich grazing and productive arable land producing £1,434pa arranged into 2 farms, one of them with a farm residence and homestead in perfect order, and 458 acres of arable and pasture land including 16 acres of woodland in the occupation of Messrs. Scrivenor. The other a grazing farm of 203 acres of rich fatting land with farmhouse and homestead in the occupation of --- Bailey Esq, and sundry other lands including some ozier beds in the occupation of Mrs. Higgins; together with the Manor or reputed Manor of Stantonbury comprising the whole parish in the county of Bucks., most conveniently situate , adjoining the Turnpike road leading from Newport Pagnell to Stony Stratford, two miles from the former and four miles from the latter, both excellent market towns, and within two miles of the Wolverton Station on the London and Birmingham Railway. The above property is held by the vendor under a lease granted by the late John Earl Spencer to Richard Harrison, Esq., for a term of 200

years, from the 2nd of November, 1831, provided three lives therein named, of the then ages of 49, 33, and 14, should so long live, at the reserved annual rent of £148.'

With the coming of the railway Wolverton from its situation mid way between London and Birmingham was chosen as the location for the main engine works, so causing a need for extensive housing for the employees. When the available land at Wolverton was exhausted the Radcliffe Trustees refused to sell any more, and so the railway company, the London and North West Railway Company, purchased a portion of the Stantonbury and Bradwell estates. Indeed a poster circulated at the time read: 'An estate purchased on the Newport Pagnell road, March 20th 1854. Plans and specification at the Radcliffe Arms.' As for the original Stantonbury, with regard to Mr. Scrivenor in September that year an observer of the agricultural scene wrote that he was one of those farmers of the first magnitude, 'who have grown as great a weight of Swede turnips per acre as I ever saw grown in any county in England. The said parties graze some good oxen; and they are well aware that the root crops are the mainstay of all good farming.' Then in June 1859 was penned 'Stantonbury proper, as we may call it, the old original Stantonbury, lies about a mile from the usurper of its name. At present there is only a farm house here and there; one not far from the church, and which in its day has been of some pretensions, is occupied by labourers. The affix Bury has not in this instance the meaning usually assigned to it. It is a corruption of Barry - the manor having been anciently in a family of that name. We would suggest, now that the name has been transferred to a new site, that it should resume its proper orthography.' In 1862 was announced: 'Sale by Samuel S. Dudley of the leasehold estate of Stantonbury at the Mart, near the Bank of England, London, on Wednesday. To be sold pursuant to a decree of the High Court of Chancery made in the cause of Buchanan v Harrison with the approbation of Vice Chancellor Wood in two lots at 1pm on Wed. March 26th 1862 at the auction mart near the Bank of England, London, the leasehold estate of Stantonbury, situate close to Wolverton Station and midway between the market towns of Stony Stratford and Newport Pagnell; consisting of 775 acres of fine land, comprising grazing pastures and arable land, with an excellent farm residence and agricultural buildings, and two other homesteads, yards, and buildings bounded on the north by the River Ouse. The Grand Junction Canal runs through the estate, upon which there is a wharf, with a house, storehouses, sheds, etc. It is tithe free.' 'Also, two policies of assurance in the Guardian Office for £2,674 and £589 2s, together with additions thereto amounting to £51 11s. The estate may be viewed on application to the several tenants.'

As for those employed on the estate, in November 1862 a single man was needed as a shepherd, 'steady, industrious, and with a good character.' With lodging available on the farm applicants were to contact 'Mr. Selby, Stantonbury.' Then in February 1870 Thomas Selby required 'a steady, intelligent, industrious man to act as foreman on a large farm. A cottage on the farm. Also a man to catch moles.' However in January 1875 it was not only moles that were in need of catching but also 20 year old Joseph Innwood. He was a miller and labourer who on the 23rd had stolen from Thomas at Stantonbury a sack and four bushels of wheat. He was sentenced to a month in prison with hard labour. Then in 1877 on Friday, February 23rd on the instructions of Earl Spencer an auction was conducted by John Macquire of oak, ash, elm, oak saplings and rangewood; 'standing, numbered and blazed on the farms of Mr. Selby and Mr. Johnson. Some of the oaks are very large and fine. The company is requested to meet the auctioneer on the canal bridge, on the road leading from Wolverton to Newport Pagnell, at 10.30am, on account of the extent of ground to go over.' At Stanton Low Pastures in 1881 at noon on Thursday, October 6th an auction of farm stock and implements was conducted by George Wigley on the premises by the direction of Mrs. Johnson. She was relinquishing the occupation of the farm at Michaelmas. However Mr. Selby was still farming but for his employee Joseph Fennemore in 1886 on December 2nd when feeding the horses one of them turned on him and bit his nose off. In fact with surgical precision level with his face, and Dr. Rogers of Newport Pagnell was swiftly summoned. In 1903 on Thursday, March 12th at Stantonbury Hall the death occurred of Mrs. Selby, with the interment taking place on the Monday at Stanton Low. Thomas died at Northampton in 1913 and in the succeeding years much gravel excavation took place on the Stantonbury acres. Indeed by the late 1950s even Stantonbury Farmhouse had succumbed to the excavations.[3] In 1956 it became inevitable that the site of the village would be engulfed by a pit being worked westward by the Bletchley Concrete Aggregate Company. In consequence the recently formed Wolverton Archaeological Society decided to excavate at least one house platform, but no progress could be made due to the intransigence of the manager of the pit and the tenant farmer. With the continuing extractions in 1960 Thomas Roberts (Westminster) Ltd., who had planning permission to take gravel between Stanton Low and Haversham Mill, applied to the County Council to divert the existing unclassified road near Stanton Low Farm to approximately follow the course of the river to join the existing road at Haversham Mill. No objection was raised by Newport Pagnell RDC with Mr. R. Dunbabin, the clerk, saying that possibly the only comment they could make was that the new road would be no lower than the existing one, as the area was liable to flood. Thus when in the spring of 1966 the workings encroached on the village site the destruction commenced, and the method of working rendered any useful archaeological investigations impossible. Farming came to an end in 2007 and in consequence much of the pastureland developed into meadows and rough grassland. Presently the Parks Trust manages these fields through a combination of carefully controlled cutting and livestock grazing. However each year some areas are left uncut to provide continuous cover for wildlife.

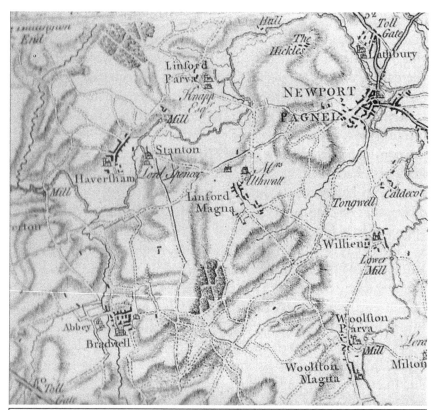

This map was drawn in about 1768, before the canal and before the railway. Stantonbury and what became New Bradwell was mostly pasture and meadow land and was very sparsely populated. At the time of the map there was a mansion house, a church and a few cottages at Stanton Low.

After the canal was opened in 1800, the district attracted new buildings, including the New Inn, shown here in the 1920s.

A NEW TOWN

In 1833 on May 6th an Act for the London and Birmingham Railway was given Royal Assent. From its halfway position the small village of Wolverton was chosen as the site for the main locomotive repair works, which opened in 1838. Then in 1846 it was enlarged to construct locomotives, and once all the available land at Wolverton had been exhausted the township of Stantonbury ('New Bradwell') was developed for the accommodation of the hundreds of employees. Ironically during the development of this new settlement evidence was discovered of an earlier community, when in 1879 during drainage works a bronze founder's hoard of 16 worn out implements was discovered. This comprised a palstave, a broken sword, two broken spear heads and 12 socketed celts, 3 of which were broken.

With the expansion of the railway works at Wolverton the need arose for more housing to accommodate the increasing number of employees. However as owners of the most convenient land the Radcliffe Trustees refused to sell any further acres. Therefore the railway company had little option but to investigate elsewhere, and found that about a mile eastwards of Wolverton arable fields could be had at Stantonbury. Here in 1852 they purchased 15 acres, mainly the site of gravel pits, between the canal and the turnpike road to Newport Pagnell. Also - all at £150 an acre - some 4 acres of meadow adjoining Bradwell Brook and the road, and within a year some 116 houses, a pub and several shops had been built. Such developments continued apace, and in 1858 at 3pm on Monday, July 19th an auction of 95 lots of valuable freehold building land adjoining the L&NWR building estate, and 'situated within 10 minutes walk of the Wolverton Station', was conducted by Mr. S.C. Harrison at the New Inn, Bradwell. As described this came with 'valuable and extensive frontages to the Newport Pagnell Turnpike Road, and to the New Streets which have been judiciously laid out and well drained.' 'The situation is well adapted for the erection of moderate sized houses and business premises, for which there is a constant and increasing demand.' Thus for the embryo community the secular aspects were being addressed, and in consequence the need arose for religious and educational provision. In 1857 the district known as Bradwell had been added to the ecclesiastical

After 1856, three streets of terraced houses were built below the canal, known as Top Street, Middle Street and Bottom Street. They were later re-named as Bridge Street, Spencer Street and High Street. The top photo shows the distinctive 3 storey houses at the end of each block.

parish of Stantonbury, and - with the Rev. C.P. Cotter having been appointed as vicar to Stantonbury with New Bradwell - in 1858 on Monday, May 24th the Marquis of Chandos, chairman of the London & North Western Railway Company, laid the foundation stone of St. James' Church. Building commenced to the designs of Mr. G.E. Street of London (architect of the Strand Law Courts) with the construction entrusted to Mr. J. Mills of Stratford-Upon-Avon. Indeed the area had been transformed from its rural past, and regarding this change in November 1858 an observer wrote; 'Only a few years ago, the very ground on which New Bradwell now stands consisted of ploughed fields. Instead of green hedges, tall trees, and luxuriant corn crops, we now behold a new church and schools in erection, a Baptist Chapel, respectable shops, an accommodating inn, and about 120 newly built houses, the property of the London and North Western Railway Company, and occupied by the artisans employed at the engine works, Wolverton.' As for the naming of this new community, in June of the following year was penned;

'Stantonbury - The new village, or rather the new town which has sprung up since the establishment of the railway between Wolverton Station and Newport Pagnell, and which used to be called New Bradwell, has lately been re-christened, and rejoices now in the name of Stantonbury. You are informed of the fact by a large board upon which characters are inscribed which "he who runs may read." Stantonbury is therefore the new name. Its houses are all of one date and one pattern. However you will find that these apparently unattractive dwellings are thoughtfully contrived for the convenience and comfort of the class of persons for whose occupations they were designed; that they are all well arranged with reference to sanitary considerations, and that they are probably the nucleus of a large and handsome town. The great central space is of inestimable value and we are glad to see that it is irrecoverably devoted to the public by an erection within in it of a very handsome range of schools, and a new church. Let us hope that the rest of the inclosure will be planted ornamentally.'

The need for housing continued, and in September 1860 the L&NWR advertised for contractors and builders to tender for the construction of cottages at Stantonbury. Then in 1861 at the L&NWR half year meeting of the proprietors, held at Euston Station, the directors asked for a vote for £6,500 for houses for the company's workmen at Stantonbury. Indeed in mid September that year 36 more houses at Stantonbury were tenanted by workmen of the 'Wolverton Engine Works,' built by Mr. Dunkley of Blisworth.[4] In fact 'Houses are springing up in all directions.' Whilst the layout of the new streets was linearly efficient it seems from Wolverton the road access was anything but, prompting 'J.L.' to write in a letter to the local press;

A Stantonbury (later New Bradwell) terraced house from the 1850s

'Let any person take his stand on the canal bridge at Wolverton Station and look straight in the direction of Stantonbury new church, he will see what a distance would be gained by having a new road straight through, leaving Stone Bridge House (Mr. Radcliffe's) on the left instead of the right. And if he will turn in the direction of Haversham and Castlethorpe, he will see what a gain it would be to have a short straight road by the end of the Radcliffe Arms to the Haversham Arch. What I would suggest, then, is this, to make a straight road from the Stantonbury new church to the canal bridge at Wolverton, and another short road by the end of the Radcliffe Arms to the Haversham Arch, and thus do away with the old crooked road altogether. I think it will be readily admitted that such a plan would be a very great improvement both to Wolverton and Stantonbury, as well as the neighbourhood round, which must of necessity be benefited by having a straight road to the station.'

Apart from housing, for many of the occupants an area on which to grow vegetables would be beneficial, and in September 1861 Charles Aveline, 'builder etc., Wolverton Station', advertised 22½ acres of productive arable land to be let from Michaelmas. With a frontage to the turnpike road this was 'next to New Bradwell with Stantonbury and between that place and Wolverton station with frontage to the turnpike road. ... The situation of the land in this populous neighbourhood renders it exceedingly well adapted for occupation as a market garden, or for underletting in garden allotments, which would be readily taken.'

As for prospective builders, in 1861 at the Royal Engineer, Wolverton, various sites were auctioned on December 10th. These included a close of pasture land of 8a 2r 18p, 'more or less', called 'The Furzen Leys' situated in the parish of Bradwell near to Wolverton station. This had a frontage to the turnpike road, and 'N.B. This lot, from its situation between the populous and rapidly increasing places of Wolverton and Stantonbury forms a most eligible site for building. Immediate possession can be had. The apportioned rent charge on this lot is £2 10s 6d.' Mr. Durham was the auctioneer, but it would be Mr. Foxley who at 6pm on October 22nd 1863 auctioned freehold building land at the County Arms;

Lot 1. All those 4 building lots situate and having a frontage to School Street marked and numbered in the Railway Company's

Plan 37, 38 and 39 each having a frontage of 16 feet.

Lot 2. All those 4 building lots situate and having a frontage in School Street, marked out and numbered in the Railway Company's Plan respectively 45,46,47 and 48 with a frontage of 16ft 1in to each lot.

Lot 3. All those 3 building lots situate and having a frontage in Newport Street in the Railway Company's Plan respectively 79,80 and 81 with a frontage of 17 feet to each lot.

Lot 4. All those 4 building lots in Bradwell Street marked 61, 62,63 and 64 with a frontage of 16ft 2ins to each lot.

The whole to be subject to certain regulations laid down by the L&NWR to be produced at the time of the sale.

For many of those seeking employment the railway works seemed an attractive alternative to the otherwise poorly paid and mainly agricultural roles in the rural district. Not only were those from the immediate area enticed but also from further afield, including Robert Wylie who came from Scotland. However of an entrepreneurial flair he soon realised the potential of the local housing developments, and leaving his railway employment set up as a builder, with the building of three houses in Church Street, Wolverton, as his first contract.

However he soon became more associated with New Bradwell, advertising in November 1863 a draper's shop and premises for sale. These were namely No. 1 corner of Bradwell Road and North Street, and, 'occupied by respectable tenants,' two newly built houses with butcher's shop, gardens and premises at the bottom of North Street, Stantonbury. He might have perhaps been interested in the brick making equipment of Mr. James Craddock, brick and lime merchant, which, since he was leaving the district (having been resident with his wife at the Queen Victoria inn at Old Bradwell), came up for auction that year on Thursday, September 24th. No doubt of additional interest would have been the facilities of Mr. J. Collier, who in November purchased the 'stone quarries etc.' adjoining Bradwell wharf. Having commenced the burning of lime he could supply a large quantity of building stone, road stone and lime stone - 'Fresh burnt lime in any quantity on most economical terms.'

Yet for Mr. Smith he was now 'leaving for a distant county,' and in 1863 having let the County Arms Inn instructed Mr. J.W. Reader to auction on the premises the household furniture on Saturday, November 28th.

Meanwhile Mr. Wylie was establishing a family at Stantonbury, where as one of their many children in 1864 on April 1st his wife gave birth to a son. In March 1865 on the vacant space adjoining the County Arms, formerly the site of gravel pits, contracts were enacted to build 18 houses. Also, comprised 'of large dimensions', a new club room for the inn by Mr. Wylie. However one Saturday morning during the digging of a deep foundation trench a partial collapse buried George Stanton, of Newport Pagnell, and when hurriedly dug out by his workmates he was found to have injured his right shoulder. In April 1865 a description of the local scene read 'several pieces of building ground have been lately occupied at Stantonbury, and cottages for the accommodation of the workmen have sprung up in a short space of time. Many other plots are also stumped out for immediate occupation by the builder. A site for a new chapel has also been decided upon, to be erected in the summer.' Apart from builders the local potential had also been realised by land speculators, including 'M. Bromwich' of Newport Pagnell, who that year could offer for sale, 'or let on building lease,' a valuable piece of building ground at Stantonbury on the corner of School Street and Newport Street.

Then in December 1865 'in a neighbourhood where houses are in great demand' freehold building land was for sale by private contract in about 220 convenient plots. All were situated within 5 minutes of Wolverton Works, and prices, conditions of sale etc. could be obtained at the houses of Messrs. Culverhouse and Aveline, of Wolverton, where a plan of the locations could be viewed. Also they could be seen at New Bradwell at the house of Robert Wylie, who on Saturday, December 23rd gave his workforce of over 40 men their annual dinner. Afterwards in addressing the company he hoped their trade would continue to prosper and that his men would stay with him, 'as he didn't like change.' Then in speaking of Mr. Wylie, Mr. Dix said that having known him for a number of years he'd always found him frank and affable, and no doubt his men found him honest and straightforward. Various entertainments followed, and Joseph Reynolds, better known as 'poetical or rhyming Joe,' caused much amusement with his wit and comicalities. By May 1866 around 90 of the advertised plots had been sold. Then on the 15th of the month by the instructions of Mr. W. Pearce an auction at the Anchor Hotel, Newport Pagnell, was conducted by Joseph Redden. This included a newly erected freehold house and premises at New Bradwell 'with attractive corner shop and appurtenances' which, at a rental of £20pa, was in the occupation of John Sykes, tailor and postmaster. Also an adjoining private residence in the occupation of Dr. Miles at a rental of £12pa. On Friday, August 17th he again featured, when on the instructions of 'the proprietor' at 6pm at the New Inn he auctioned:

'Lot 1. A freehold house and baker's shop with yard, buildings, etc. in School Street in the occupation of David Edwards at a rental of £20. The 2 freehold houses adjoining, let at £23 8s pa with pump and well of water.

Lot 2. A freehold house and premises and well near to the above producing a yearly rental of £11 14s, all recently built.'

By the direction of the trustees of the will of the late William Gilbert, in 1867 on Friday, July 12th a property auction was conducted by Mr. Durham at the Cuba Hotel.

Lot 1. 6 brick and slate houses in Church Street, Stantonbury, in the occupation of John Jones, Thomas Rigby, Mr. Shackleford, Mr. Forster, Edward Meacock, John Childs. Each at a rent of 5s a week and each house with a parlour, sitting room, and 3 bedrooms. There is also an open yard with coal house, wood house, and closet. Also a well of good water and pump.

Lot 2. Three houses, one having a shop, with cellar beneath, parlour, and 3 bedrooms to each, adjoining the Cuba. The house and shop are in the occupation of George French grocer at a rent of £22pa. The other two are occupied by Mr. Edge and Mr. Edwards at 5s a week.

PIONEER BUILDERS

For those of business acumen the arrival of the railway and the consequent building of Wolverton Works presented a lucrative opportunity to set up as builders, constructing houses for the hundreds of workers. Richard Dunkley of Blisworth was prominent in the early years, constructing most of the railway workshops, mills, and sheds of the Works and 72 cottages for the workmen. His life and work needs no mention here, as the story is comprehensively told on line in 'Richard Dunkley, Railway Builder and Businessman.' However there were others who were contemporarily involved, and their lesser known story is the subject of this chapter.

ROBERT WYLIE

Robert Murray Wylie was born in 1837 on October 14th at Gallowlee, Ochiltree, Ayrshire, to William Wylie, a master joiner, and Elizabeth Murray. (Gallowlee was a portion of the highest part of the village.) He and two sisters, Marion and Agnes, were baptised on February 2nd 1839, and it seems it was that year that their mother died.[5] Robert served his apprenticeship to the trade of a carpenter and builder, and in 1859 moved to New Bradwell to seek employment at the Wolverton railway works.

Whilst toiling in the pattern making shop he soon became aware of the prospects to be had in the burgeoning building trade, providing local housing accommodation for the hundreds of workers. Leaving the railway works he duly set up as such, and in October 1862 as 'Robert Wylie builder etc. Stantonbury' posted thanks for the patronage he'd received since commencing his business. He had now moved to more convenient premises and could additionally offer 'Mouldings, Mahogany, and all sorts of sawn boards kept on hand for sale.' 'Estimates given for general repairs.' Also that year he was appointed overseer of the parish. Robert had now established a solid enterprise and included among his contracts would be the mill at Olney. Indeed it's said that during this construction he walked night and morning the 8½ miles from and to Stantonbury, to work a full day with his men from 6am.

In 1863 at Loughton on July 21st he married Sarah Emily Adnitt, born at Floore, Northants. His business continued to prosper and in February 1867 he purchased the Stone & Lime Works, New Bradwell, thereby being able to supply lime, stone, slate, & timber. Also cement, chimney pots, paving bricks etc., lime stone at 1s 4d per ton, road stone at 1s 6d per ton, building stone at 1s 9d per ton., and lime at 2s 6d a quarter.

His first houses were seemingly 1 & 2 Newport Road, Stantonbury, in the first of which his son, Charles Ernest Wylie, was born in 1870 on July 3rd. Many other children would be subsequently born. In 1871 Robert is recorded as a lime merchant but also as a land owner, employing 10 men and 4 boys. On a chance occasion in Old Bradwell he met Col. William Duncan of Shenley Park, Bucks.[6] The Colonel was looking for a tenant for the Home Farm and thought Robert would be ideal. However Robert was initially disinterested but he took the farm in 1876, although a mention occurs in 1874 that he was 'formerly a builder at New Bradwell.' Whatever the lineage, employing 19 men and 11 boys in 1881 he was resident with his family at Lime Cottage, New Bradwell, as not only a lime merchant but also a farmer. In fact in 1883 on November 6th one of his heifers gave birth to 3 female calves. Of his agricultural acres, one of his fields lay opposite St. James' Church, which he often allowed for the use of local festivities. In farming he proved as equally adept as in building, and in 1886 on Wednesday, December 8th at the Newport Pagnell Christmas Fat Stock Show he was awarded 2nd prize for Shorthorns, the prize for Best Fat Maiden Heifer, 2nd prize for Best Pen of Five Fat Ewes, and 2nd prize for Best Pen of Five Fat Tegs. By now he was a well respected resident, and in November 1888 in seeking membership as a County Councillor included in his hopeful credentials; "I have had twenty-six years experience in the management of parochial affairs; and should you do me the honour to elect me your representative, I will use my best endeavours to promote the economical and efficient administration of County Business." In 1889 on the evening of Monday, January 7th a meeting in support of his candidature was held in the schoolroom at Stantonbury. Here the Rev. C.P. Cotter said that he thought Mr. Wylie was the best choice. They wanted a thorough businessman on the Council, not a politician, but one who would take an interest in the rates being reduced. It seems this was the aspiration of many and Mr. Wylie would be duly elected.

In 1891 he and his wife were resident at Lime Cottage, New Bradwell, with - as listed per the census - their offspring Bruce, 26, a civil servant, Ronald, 19, a draper's assistant, Annie, 18, 'a farmer's daughter', and John, 16, Mary, 14, and Robert, 10, all born at Bradwell. Also from the relevant records in 1894 the homestead and acreage at Old Bradwell was let to him at an annual rent of £85. The following year with two others he was a councillor for Bradwell and Bradwell Abbey on the Newport Pagnell Rural District Council, being also a member of the Newport Pagnell Board of Guardians. Indeed he was now well embedded in public life and public offices, with further examples to include being one of the nominations in 1896 as a candidate for the Newport Pagnell Board of Guardians and Rural District Council. Then in 1899 as one of the four persons nominated for the three seats on the RDC. In fact he topped the poll with 201 votes.

In 1901 Lime Cottage was still the residence of himself and his wife Sarah plus several members of their extensive family - Bruce, 35, a civil servant; Ernest, 30, farmer's son; John, 26, farmer's son; Robert, 20, a chemist's assistant; Mary, 24, mother's help. Sadly Sarah died on June 7th 1906. The funeral was held on the Monday at the church of St. Lawrence, Old Bradwell, with numerous floral tributes and a large attendance of family and friends. Then at the meeting of Newport Pagnell Board of Guardians and RDC, in speaking in tribute the chairman said he had known Mrs. Wylie from her early years and 'He could say with absolute truth that the union of Mr. and Mrs. Wylie had been a very well assorted one, and Mrs. Wylie, as a good wife, had been one of the greatest blessings to her husband.'

That year Robert acquired from Earl Spencer the Stanton Low Farm. This comprised some 376 acres (on the fringe of which stood St. Peter's Church) with the pastures acknowledged to be some of the finest in the country for bullock feeding. In late 1907 Robert married Arabella Louisa Anne Greaves, born at Haversham, the widow of William Greaves. He had been a farmer at Haversham and in 1901 Arabella in continuing as a farmer and employer was resident at Haversham with her brother in law and also her daughters. By 1910 to include one of Arabella's daughters, 16 year old Dorothy, Robert and Arabella were living at Stantonbury Park Farm where that year on the afternoon of Monday, May 16th a valuable cow was killed by lightning in front of the house.

Robert continued to be active in council matters, indeed attaining the status of Alderman, whilst in farming matters in 1916 he purchased Home Farm at Old Bradwell. In other activities in the following year as a school governor he gave 15 lime trees to be planted in front of the school. Together with his sons Robert would farm the Abbey farm at Old Bradwell. However this they relinquished in 1919, in which year Robert died on April 10th. Many representatives from the public bodies attended the funeral at Old Bradwell on the Monday, and with effects totalling £28,319 19s 8d probate was granted to Bruce Murray Wylie, civil servant, and also Archibald Frederick Wylie, Charles Ernest Wylie, and John Alexander Wylie, farmers. Arabella died in 1922 and as Wylie Bros. the farming was continued by the partnership of John Wylie and his elder brother Charles.

Then in May 1941 their retirement from farming was announced, with the freehold farms known as Stanton High, Stanton Low, Greaves and Home Farms, situate at Stantonbury and Bradwell, scheduled for auction at the Swan Hotel, Newport Pagnell, on Wednesday, June 25th. This was to be conducted by Mr. P.C. Gambell but prior to the auction he was able to sell them by private treaty to Mr. G.E. Bond (Messrs. Bennett, Sons and Ward, Buckingham). In this he was acting for Mr. Thomas Roberts of Bletchley Aggregates, owners of gravel pits in the locality, who acquired the farms for the purpose of investment. Also included at the intended auction were the 5 houses known as Melbourne Terrace, overlooking New Bradwell railway station. These had been built by Robert Wylie in 1871 but failed to find buyers, the bidding having risen to £290. With the farms now sold, an auction was held on Wednesday, September 24th 1941 of the agricultural implements, machinery and horses at Home Farm, Old Bradwell. Then of the cattle and sheep at Stantonbury Park (near Newport Pagnell) on Friday, September 26th 1941.

RICHARD WHITE MUNDAY

Richard White Munday was born in 1840 to John Munday, born at Haddenham in 1815, and, born at Buckingham, his wife Sarah (nee White).[7] In 1841 with his father in occupation as a bricklayer he was living in Bridge Street, Buckingham with his parents and his maternal grandmother Catherine (Kitty) White. Then in 1851 the family were resident in Elm Street, Buckingham, comprised of his father, who was now a builder employing 6 men, his mother, aged 39, his sister Rebecca, age 4, born at Buckingham, and Kitty White. (Rebecca died in 1858). In 1861 as a bricklayer he was living at Chandos Road with his father, (who was now employing 17 men and 3 boys), his mother Sarah, and sister Esther, age 9, born at Buckingham. In 1865 at Buckingham parish church he married Elizabeth George. She was born at Launton, Oxon., in 1844 and in 1869 Richard began in partnership with her brother Esau George as a builder at Stantonbury (New Bradwell). Indeed it was as a builder, employing 12 men and 5 boys, that in 1871 he was living at Bristle Hill, Buckingham, with his wife, his son Harry, age 3, born at Buckingham in 1867, and son John George, age 1, born at Buckingham. (He died in 1872). That year a daughter, Martha, was born at Stantonbury on September 23rd. In April 1872 Richard successfully tendered for the construction of Newport Pagnell Police Station and Petty Sessions Room, this being for the agreed sum of £1,377 6s 3d with the work to be completed by November.

However it seems few other contracts were forthcoming, and in April 1874 notice was given that the partnership between Richard White Munday and Esau George, 'builders and carpenters at New Bradwell,' was dissolved by mutual consent on March 25th. His career now took a new direction (in other activities he would hold the rank of Colour Sergeant in the Buckingham Company of Volunteers) and in 1875 on Saturday, May 15th at the meeting of the Board of Guardians he was appointed Inspector of Nuisances for the Buckingham Union. This was in place of Mr. Matthew Simmons, who had recently resigned. Then in 1876 on the evening of Monday, March 27th in the Council Chamber at Buckingham a special meeting of the Town Council of Buckingham considered applications for the appointment of surveyor. These included one from Richard, 'of Brackley Road', who was duly appointed to be the surveyor for the parish for 12 months. This would be at a salary of £50. In 1877 he was Inspector of Nuisances for the Rural Sanitary Authority Buckingham, yet it was as a builder that in 1881 he was initiated into the Grenville Lodge of Masons on February 22nd. However in the census of that year he is recorded as the borough surveyor, resident at 6, Chandos Road, Buckingham, with his wife Elizabeth, and son Harry and daughter Martha. Of that address in 1883 he was surveyor to the borough and inspector of nuisances to the urban and rural sanitary authorities. In 1885 he was reappointed as Sanitary Inspector for 12 months, being also the surveyor, and in 1889 served as a trustee of the Buckingham Mutual Loan Society. However he and his family now left Buckingham and in 1890 he was the licensed victualler at the Horn Hotel, Braintree, Essex. In April the following year he visited William Gough, keeper of the White Hart in the Market Square, Buckingham, leaving his wife Elizabeth to tend the Horn Hotel with her unmarried daughter Martha and unmarried son Harry. In 1892 on the evening of Thursday, October 20th a meeting was held at the hotel to form a Licensed Victuallers' Protection Society. Harry was elected secretary and at a meeting in 1894 Richard would be elected president. Then in November that year at their annual meeting and banquet he was instituted as Worshipful Master of the St. Mary Masonic Lodge, No. 1,312. In August 1896 Martha suffered the loss of a gold diamond ring, stolen by one of the hotel waitresses. The theft was all the more traumatic from having taken place two days before Martha's marriage, held on August 20th at the church of St. Michael the Archangel, Braintree, to William Beard Lake.[8] After several weeks of illness Richard White Munday died of dropsy in 1896 on December 26th with the will proved by George George (it is a double George!) He was buried in Braintree cemetery. Aged 69 his widow, Elizabeth, died in 1911 on November 29th. She was also buried in Braintree cemetery and is commemorated on the gravestone of her husband.

ESAU GEORGE

Born at Shalstone, Bedfordshire, to William George, a dairyman, and his wife Mary Ann, Esau George was baptised in 1848 on

October 29th. In 1851 he was living at Shalstone with his parents and siblings, and likewise in 1861 at Hill Farm House. In 1869 he began in partnership with Richard White Munday as a builder at Stantonbury (New Bradwell), and in 1871 was lodging in Newport Road with William Adnitt, a retired wheelwright, and his family.

In 1872 as a road contractor at Wolverton he was charged on June 14th at Stony Stratford Petty Sessions with having obstructed the highway at Wolverton on May 25th. This regarded leaving piles of lime, bricks and stones, and giving evidence police constable Thomas Port said he saw a quantity of 'rubbish' lying on the road opposite the school at Wolverton Station. He spoke to Mr. George who said he'd ordered some of his men to put it there, being the materials needed for their work on the footpath. He also put some there himself, keeping watch for two nights until 11pm to prevent any accident. His partner in the work had also kept observation for one night until 9pm. However on the Saturday night when taking the corner too sharply a horse and cart driven by Mrs. Hawley ran up the kerb and turned over on running into the heap. Seeming restive the horse was out of her control but the chairman said it was evident that the obstruction should have been attended. A fine was imposed of 10s with 2s costs.

In 1874 by mutual consent the partnership of Richard White Munday and Esau George as builders and carpenters at New Bradwell, 'under the style and title of R.W. Munday & Co.,' was dissolved on March 25th. With a capital of £400 Esau would continue the business at New Bradwell, and the following month on April 22nd at the church of St. George the Martyr, Wolverton, he married Elizabeth Graham, the youngest daughter of Mr. Graham of the Royal Engineer, Wolverton. In 1875 on July 19th he was initiated into The Scientific Lodge of the Masons at Wolverton, and continuing in occupation as a builder in 1878 tendered for taking down and rebuilding the Swan Hotel at Fenny Stratford. Bids had been invited by Mr. Gotto, of Leighton Buzzard, but at the opening on Tuesday, May 21st Esau's tender of £1,308 proved too high.

Perhaps he thought that opportunities now lay elsewhere, for in 1880 it was announced that on Tuesday, June 8th J.P. Goodwin was to hold an auction at Stantonbury of a builder's stock in trade, 'as Esau George was leaving the area.' Also on the same date on Esau's instructions an auction was to be held at the Railway Tavern, Stantonbury, at 7pm. 'Subject to such conditions as will be then produced.' This was 'All that valuable plot of building land situate in the Gravel Field, Stantonbury, and having a frontage of 196 feet 6 inches in Harwood Street, and 120 feet in Thompson Street.' Viewings were on application to Mr. George, Stantonbury.

However the following year he was still a contractor at New Bradwell, living at 28, Newport Road, with his wife and now children. Also accommodated was William George, age 73, 'retired farmer.' In 1881 on the afternoon of Wednesday, February 23rd Esau's wife when driving home in her own conveyance from Wolverton was in collision near the railway bridge with a fly belonging to Mr. Hawley of Stony Stratford. With the wheels detached by the crash she was thrown from the trap, the remains of which were dragged for some way by the bolting horse. Much shaken she was conveyed to her home, to rest in a serious state.

Despite the earlier notice, in September 1882 Esau was still resident at New Bradwell, where for making about 150 yards of road, excavating a quantity of earth, and erecting a cart hovel, fence etc., his tender of £98 10s 6d was accepted. Indeed in 1883 he was listed as a builder at New Bradwell, and as such on Thursday, May 10th an auction was conducted by J.P. Goodwin at the Victoria Hotel, Wolverton, at 6pm of 13 newly erected brick and slate houses and premises at Wolverton and Stantonbury. Also a large plot of building land at Stantonbury in the owner's occupation. For viewings applicants were to contact the tenants or 'Esau George, builder, Stantonbury.' As for other offerings, that month he advertised for sale seed potatoes, ash leaf kidneys and 'early rose.'

In 1883 in September there was only one tender for scavenging the parish of Bradwell. This was from Esau George, the former contractor, but since it proved £20 more than the previous year the Board of Guardians decided to arrange the work themselves. Perhaps this finally prompted Esau's move elsewhere, for by November 1883 he and his family were resident at Woburn Sands. However it was at Buckingham that year on Wednesday, November 28th that the death occurred of his father William George, and then in 1884 at

Woburn Sands on May 15th that of Esau's wife, Elizabeth Sarah, at the age of 34. Then in 1885 on Tuesday, December 22nd at the parish church of Aspley Guise he married Annie Elizabeth Whitman, the daughter of George Whitman, a tailor/employer. The best man was Mr. Richard White Munday, and in the afternoon the newly weds left for a honeymoon at Torquay.

Thereon Woburn Sands would be their home where in 1886 on the night of Friday, December 10th a fire was discovered on the premises. This adjoined the property of Arthur Kent, a wheelwright, with the discovery made around 7.30pm by his wife. Seemingly some trusses of straw had caught alight and the blaze was soon put out with water thrown by Mrs. Kent and others. Adding to Esau's now extensive family, in 1886 at The Terrace, Woburn Sands, a son was born.

Yet not so thriving were his commercial matters for in 1887 the first meeting of his creditors was held at the County Court Buildings, Northampton, on Friday afternoon February 4th. His debts and assets were examined, and he attributed his failure to losses on building contracts, depreciation in the value of his stock, plant and house property, the death of horses, bad debts, and the expenses incurred in attending illness. In view of the bankruptcy, on the instructions of Mr. A.C. Palmer, the trustee, on Thursday, March 3rd 1887 at 11am Messrs. Durham, Gotto & Samuel auctioned the stock in trade and plant of a 'contractor and builder in an extensive way of business.' Also all manner of building materials and plant, a bay cart horse, a black cob, and a light dog cart with lamps and cushions complete. Catalogues had been available from Messrs. A.C. Palmer & Co., Chartered Accountants, Northampton, Leicester, and 7 & 8 Railway Approach, London Bridge, London. Again, on the instructions of Mr. A.C. Palmer, in 1887 on Thursday, May 19th at the Swan Hotel, Woburn Sands, Messrs. Durham, Gotto and Samuel were to auction at 5pm two recently erected freehold villa residences. With gardens and stabling these adjoined the public road 'in the centre of this greatly increasing neighbourhood', and 'The Houses are of elegant and expensive design, and are fitted throughout with pneumatic bells and all modern conveniences.' 'Woburn Sands as a health resort is well known, and tenants will be readily found as the summer advances.' Viewings could be arranged by applying to Esau George. In 1888 on April 4th another daughter added to his family at Woburn Sands.

However by 1891 Esau and his family had moved elsewhere and following a couple of migrations, during which more offspring were born, had settled at Sparkhill, Birmingham. That year with Esau in occupation as a carpenter he and his family were resident at 70, Madeley Road, Birmingham. Sadly by 1904 he was a widower, and as a carpenter and joiner by 1911 had moved to 50, Norman Road, Sparkhill Road, Birmingham, resident with a son and a daughter. He died at the Infirmary, Middlesex, in 1918 on November 22nd and with the body brought from Brentford he was buried in St. Michael's Churchyard at Woburn Sands, the gravestone commemorating himself and his first wife Elizabeth Sarah.

The Newport Road at the corner of Glyn Street. Development in the south side of the street started soon after the first phase of Stantonbury, as it was then known.

THE TOWN'S DEVELOPMENT

Thus within a few years a prospering community had arisen; builders were building, speculators were speculating, and shopkeepers were keeping up a good business, attending to the needs of the hundreds of Wolverton Works employees - that is until from 1865 the railway company began transferring all locomotive work from Wolverton to Crewe. Nevertheless there were social and recreational needs and at the Cuba Hotel in 1866 on Saturday, July 14th a new lodge of the National Independent Order of Odd Fellows, called 'The Philanthropic,' was opened by the official of the Birmingham district. There were over 70 members and at a dinner given by the hosts, Mr. and Mrs. Harding, many toasts were proposed with several entertainments contributed by the members.

Then the following year on the evening of Monday, April 1st the 'Wolverton and Stantonbury Philharmonic Company' gave a concert of vocal and instrumental music in the Infant School Room. Afterwards a burlesque was performed entitled 'The Six Magnificent Bricks,' and as one observer penned "Of all the grotesque figures I ever beheld on a platform, the Six Magnificent Bricks beat all for originality and comicality of appearance. … The scene was, as described on the programme, truly unique, beautifully so, and the company, male and female, were well up in the various parts they had to perform."

Indeed such festivities would be greatly welcomed in view of the depressing depletion of hundreds of employees from Wolverton Works, not least in early 1868, for 'trade at Wolverton in consequence of the removal of some hundreds of men from Wolverton Works has become very dull, trade lessened, and a great many houses are untenanted. Near the Corner Pin Inn in a row of 18, 14 are unoccupied. Trade is affected at Wolverton, Stantonbury, Newport Pagnell, and Stony Stratford.' Perhaps in view of this downturn in 1868 at 6pm on Thursday, July 30th an auction was conducted by Joseph Redden of the freehold brick and slate The Old Elm Tree Tavern at New Bradwell. The sale was on the instructions of the mortgagees, and as per the advertisement also comprised the large piece of garden ground and appurtenances near the railway station and canal; 'Bar parlour 21ft by 12ft; commodious bar, tap room 24ft by 18ft; kitchen, 3 bedrooms, club room 21ft by 20ft, excellent cellarage, stabling, pump and never failing supply of good water. Present rent £35pa. To view apply to tenant John Mitchell. Possession at Michaelmas next.'

As for the Foresters' Arms, in 1869 on August 25th at Newport Pagnell Petty Sessions the renewal of the licence was refused. Mr. Copson would reapply but only to be again refused. Possibly due to the gloomy outlook, that year John Sykes left the neighbourhood and to include a child's crib all his household furniture and effects were auctioned on the premises at the Post Office on Monday, October 25th.

Yet for those seeking improvements in the town a group of young men had asked for the use of the Baptist Schoolroom to start a Mutual Improvement Class. This was readily granted but not so pleasingly mine hosts at the Cuba Hotel were left out of pocket when a company travelling as 'Cambel's Christy Minstrels' 'bunked off' without paying their bill for lodging.

In February 1870 by large posters they announced they would give two entertainments in the Science and Art Institute, Wolverton, on the evenings of Friday and Saturday, February 18th and 19th. However on the Friday the attendance proved less than 50, then on the Saturday none, and so shortly after 8pm they swiftly disappeared into the night! Seemingly aided by the lack of street illumination, for it was not until October 1870 that the L&NWR erected gas lamps, 'which are now regularly lit along the roadside between Wolverton and Stantonbury.'

Also on brighter matters, in 1870 with the Rev. Cotter presiding the first in a series of intended fortnightly entertainments, 'readings and music entertainments,' was held on the evening of Saturday, December 10th. The chairman said that last year they had great success at the former part of the season, but the latter part suffered from the nuisance of 'noisy boys.' As for the present contributions, 'Mr. Whittle with his comic song appeared to please the younger part of the audience, but we think it was not so much admired by those advanced in years.'

In 1871 it seems the Sykes family were back at the Post Office, for on February 16th at St. James' Church the marriage took place of Charles Frederick Sykes, the Post Master (also a tailor), and Emma Paybody. She was the youngest daughter of the late Thomas Paybody, of Newport Pagnell, and on December 13th a son was born. (Emma died in July 1941 at the age of 90 and was interred in the same grave as her late husband at New Bradwell cemetery.)

Also that month on Wednesday 20th at the Swan Hotel, Newport Pagnell, an auction by Joseph Redden took place. This was by order of the Trustees under an Assignment for the benefit of creditors made by George Goff, late of Newport Pagnell, merchant, and included a baker's shop in the occupation of Mr. F. Moore, baker, in School Street, two adjoining tenements in the respective occupation of Mr. Goff and Mr. Quinney, they being weekly tenants at 3s 6d each per week, and a plot of ground at Newport Pagnell near the Grand Junction Canal, 'as now stumped out.' This had a frontage to the canal of 90 yards and a depth of 20 yards, and 'The above plot of ground is eminently adapted for a wharf, being immediately contiguous to the canal, or is equally eligible for building purposes.'

Also available was the Foresters' Arms in the occupation of John Edge for this was advertised in March to let; 'Apply to Messrs. Rogers and Co, Newport Pagnell Brewery.' Then in 1872 at the Petty Sessions on Wednesday, September 18th an application by Mr. Hipwell, 'beer shop keeper' of New Bradwell, and Mr. Harding, of the Cuba Hotel, was heard for permission under the New Licensing Act to open their houses at 5am instead of 6am. This was to provide for the men employed in Wolverton Works since many had to walk some miles to start at 6am. The Bench duly ruled that the men were travellers, and therefore as such could be supplied with refreshment.

On the evening of Monday, May 19th 1873 with the Rev. Cotter in the chair at a meeting in the National schoolrooms it was resolved to memorialise the Postmaster General to grant an improved postal accommodation. Presently there was only one delivery and one despatch each day, the latter at 5.50pm, and instead of being forwarded direct the letters reaching Wolverton for Stantonbury were sent to Stony Stratford, 2 miles away. There they were kept for nearly a day before being returned to Stantonbury for delivery. By now accommodation sufficient for the employees of

Wolverton Works had been mostly built, and it was no doubt due to the diminished demand that some builders were investigating opportunities elsewhere.

The railway line to Newport Pagnell opened in 1864.

Indeed in April 1872 Richard White Munday, of New Bradwell, had successfully tendered for the construction of Newport Pagnell Police Station and Petty Sessions Room. A welcome contract but it seems there were few others, and in April 1874 notice was given that the partnership between Richard White Munday and Esau George, as builders and carpenters at New Bradwell, was dissolved by mutual consent on March 25th. Esau would then continue the business at New Bradwell, where in 1876 a daughter would be born to his wife on June 27th. During the initial 'building boom' in some instances perhaps less than adequate attention had been paid to the required standards. Manifest towards the end of 1874, when a meeting was held of the Newport Pagnell Sanitary Board to seek a meeting with the estate agent of the L&NWR. This regarded alleged 'nuisances' on the company's property at Stantonbury and New Bradwell, for it transpired that as a result of investigations much illness had been prevalent among those families in occupation of company houses. Such instances were 'characterised by febrile symptoms, simulating in a few instances those significant of typhoid fever', and it was subsequently discovered that the cesspits connected with the affected properties were 'radically bad.' Also one of the wells was subject to constant pollution from road wash containing excreta, and the whole system of the sub drainage was ineffective and injurious to health. At length a resolution was passed 'That, having heard the statement of the Medical Officer and Inspector of Nuisances, and of Mr. Tinsmith (the Estate Agent of the Company), this Authority is of opinion that the mode of sewage disposal at New Bradwell is extremely defective and a nuisance dangerous to health, and requires immediate attention on the part of the company to remedy it.'

In consequence the company prepared a plan, for the consideration of which in 1875 on Monday, January 18th a meeting of the Newport Pagnell Sanitary Authority was called at the Anchor Hotel, Newport Pagnell. The scheme had been prepared by Mr. Braunston, the sanitary inspector, but after a prolonged discussion the Sanitary Authority decided not to countenance any scheme of drainage, as the L&NWR 'were disposed to do that which they were desired to do for the removal of the nuisance complained of.'

Realising £1,850, in 1875 at 1pm on Monday, February 8th the Cuba Hotel was auctioned at The Mart, London, by Alfred Thomas, the brewery auctioneer. This was due to the failing health of the owner, and in April the licence was transferred from William Harding to John Child. Then in August 1876 the Foresters Arms' was advertised for let with yard, garden and outbuildings; 'Apply Allfrey and Lovell, Newport Pagnell Brewery.' That year in December floods due to recent snow and rain rendered the district around Wolverton and Stantonbury reminiscent of a lake. However for any builders still having commercial aspirations, in March 1877 several plots of freehold building land were available at Stantonbury 'by private contract, as whole or in one lot.' Application could be made to D. D. Millward, Railway Tavern, Stantonbury. However prospective house buyers might have been dissuaded on reading a letter to the local press in October 1877:

'Will you please allow me to draw attention to the streets in New Bradwell, commonly called Stantonbury (although not in Stantonbury parish). I am not certain who the surveyors are, but I cannot conceive where their consciences are to allow the streets to be in the condition they are. They are so full of natural gutters that it is very dangerous to man and vehicle to go above walking pace in many parts. Let anyone drive at a sharp trot on the road in the gravel field or on the street that runs up from the Cuba Hotel, or several other places, and he will be lucky to escape without being pitched out, or have the springs of his trap broken. It is decidedly the worst piece of road I travel on.

I am, yours truly,

THOMAS BROOKS

Great Linford

Oct. 22nd, 1877.'

Yet there was better news in June 1878, when the Rural Sanitary Authority of the Newport Pagnell Union advertised for tenders for the construction of glazed pipe sewers, man holes, air shafts 'and other work connected therewith at New Bradwell.' Plans and specifications could be obtained from Mr. G. Branson, the Inspector and Surveyor to the Authority, at his office No. 91, High Street. Newport Pagnell. At the National School on the evening of Friday, August 30th the Stantonbury Mutual Improvement Society Class assembled for a presentation to their secretary, Mr. J.E. Smith. He was leaving for an appointment at Doncaster and the testimonial consisted of a large photographic album with the inscription 'Presented to Mr. James Edward Smith, by the Stantonbury Mutual Improvement Class, in testimony of their respect for him, as founder of the class, and their appreciation of the zeal and ability with which he has supported it during the past ten years. C.P. Cotter, M.A., president, 30th August, 1878.'

Also leaving the scene would be the Radcliffe Arms and in consequence of it having to be pulled down J.P. Goodwin received instructions to auction on Monday, January 6th 1879 all the household fixtures, fittings and trade utensils, including a bagatelle board. At the meeting of the Board of Guardians in 1879 on Wednesday, October 1st the tender of £70 of Robert Wylie, of New Bradwell, was accepted to empty the earth and ash closets. Also to clean out the gullies for storm water, plus the sewers outfall in the parish of Bradwell. However the acceptance was hardly surprising, since his was the only tender!

Indeed it seems by 1880 the boom times of residential development had passed, and on Tuesday, June 8th it was advertised that J.P. Goodwin was to auction all the extensive stock of Mr. Esau George, builder of Stantonbury. Allegedly he was leaving the neighbourhood yet nevertheless retained a local interest, for in October 1881 it was advertised that Mr. Esau George, 'builder Stantonbury and Stony Stratford,' had the need for a few good bricklayers. Then the following year in September his tender of £60 for scavenging at Bradwell was accepted.

Additionally at the Victoria Hotel, Wolverton, in 1883 at 6pm on Thursday, May 10th J.P. Goodwin auctioned 13 newly built brick and slate houses and premises at Wolverton and Stantonbury. Anyone interested was to apply 'to Esau George, builder,' with those at Stantonbury comprised of 3 brick and slated cottages and premises in School Street, adjoining Mr. Edwards, baker, in the occupation of Messrs. Haynes, Skeen and Burgess; 'There is a capital well of water on the premises.' The tenants each paid 4s a week and hopefully prospective purchasers wouldn't be put off by the 'nuisance' experienced when travelling from Wolverton to Stantonbury and back due to the state of the brook. As per a local ratepayer in November 1884; "From the farmhouse to the Morning Star, the foul stench fills the air, as dangerous to health as it is unpleasant to the nose." Indeed the writer hoped it would soon be abated, 'before The Corner Pin is turned into a fever den.' As for Mr. George he would pursue interests elsewhere, with it stated in September 1886 that 'Esau George who went from Stantonbury to Woburn Sands now has large contracts on Aspley Heath and elsewhere, and employs many men.' (In contrast at Stantonbury in May 1887 there were 250 houses.)

Indeed that area was now becoming very popular through increasing renown as a picturesque health resort. Also picturesque was the second annual show of the Stantonbury Horticultural Society held in 1886 on Saturday, July 24th. A popular event, and music by the Newport Pagnell Church Institute Brass Band and the local Drum and Fife Band helped the occasion to blossom. Then in September a Draught and Chess Club was started at Stantonbury, to be held in the schoolroom on Tuesdays and Saturdays.

A branch of the Women's Liberal Federation was formed at Stantonbury in May 1889, in which month on the 29th at the meeting of the Sanitary Authority of the Newport Pagnell Board of Guardians complaints were reported by Mr. Hailey regarding the water. This was obtained from the Wolverton public supply but a sample sent to Northampton for analysis by Mr. Bingley was subsequently deemed 'fairly good' and suitable for use. Yet that month in his report the Medical Officer of Health stated that Mr. King's foreman at Wolverton had told him that when the well was previously examined a broken drain was found nearby. This carried off the sewage of 14 cottages, and as a result contamination had soaked the contiguous ground. No effluent was found in the well although possibly the water might have been polluted at times. The drain pipe had since been repaired and on being sent a sample of water from the well Mr. Bingley had pronounced it to be pure. In fact the matter was hopefully at an end, as it seemed the well was not to be used again, as the supply was now being obtained from another source (as distinct from the river) further from the town.

Definitely an improvement, but on matters of health in January 1890 over 500 of the town's population had influenza. On the instructions of the Rev. W.M. Miller, with the consent of the Bishop and Patron and the Governors of Queen Anne's Bounty, in 1890 at the County Arms on Monday, September 1st an auction was conducted at 6pm by Durham, Gotto & Samuel. Being the property of the Commissioners of Queen Anne's Bounty this comprised 27 plots of freehold building land which, with 33ft frontage to the road leading to Bradwell, were staked out adjoining the public road from Wolverton to Newport Pagnell. All were sold and acting on behalf of the Stantonbury Liberals one of those attending the sale bought a plot for £53 on which to erect a Liberal Hall. Not surprisingly other plots were acquired by local builders.

For prospective house buyers there was now the Wolverton and District Model Building Society, which that year on the evening of Monday, September 22nd held their prize draw for £100 in the Public Room at Newport Pagnell. As the lucky winner Master George Percy Sykes, the son of the Stantonbury Post Master, Charles Frederick Sykes, thereby secured a most useful deposit for when the need arose to purchase a house of his own.

32

Opportunities for local builders continued, and noted as 'The Stantonbury Estate' in August 1891 building land in convenient plots for cottages was advertised for sale; 'Apply to the owner Thomas Cosford, Connaught Street, Northampton, or his local agent George Tranfield, 2, Aylesbury Street, Wolverton.' For policing the growing community police constable Cox, 'a smart young officer,' was stationed at Stantonbury but in 1893 on Wednesday, July 19th he died after a short illness. Despite trying to continue his duties his suffering from a severe attack of inflammation of the brain and a long standing kidney disease occasioned his death. He left a widow and young family, with the funeral taking place on Saturday, July 29th at Twyford. That month sixteen houses in Wallace Street, numbered 1 to 16, were offered for sale by private treaty. The rental produced £162 10s annually and prospective purchasers were to apply to Hart and Norris, solicitors, Peterborough.

Hopefully they wouldn't be put off when during the month a comment appeared on the dangerous state of footpaths in the streets. Kerbing and a large portion of the pavement had broken away, with bricks lying in all directions. Sanitary matters were hardly much better and on Wednesday, October 11th it was stated at the sanitary authority meeting of the Newport Pagnell Board of Guardians that a deputation from Stantonbury had called to present a memorial. Signed by 234 inhabitants, to include 25 property owners, the two doctors, and the vicar, this called the Authority's attention to the 'unhealthy and undesirable' conditions in that parish, and regarding the concerns the meeting resolved that the matter should be adjourned until the next occasion, when Mr. Branson could provide a general report.

In 1894 on February 17th the Stantonbury Social Workmen's Club opened in a small rented cottage in Queen Anne Street. The clubmen had purchased the furniture and fittings and also paid all the initial expenses. Presided over by the Rev. Woodhouse in 1894 on the evening of Monday August 27th a public meeting was held in the schoolroom to discuss forming a branch of the National Anti Gambling League. In his opening remarks the Reverend pointed out the need for measures to prevent the problem of betting and gambling 'now so prevalent in the district.' Also to adopt some means of rescuing the young from the perils. Deputations from various denominations were present and in conclusion a resolution was proposed by the Rev. J. Matthews, the Baptist minister, 'That this meeting having duly considered the subject feel it desirable to form a united society, including Wolverton, Stantonbury, and Stony Stratford.' It was suggested that the chairman being representative should write to the communities mentioned to ask that a joint meeting might be held at Wolverton.

New Bradwell Silver Band in the early 1900s. This photo is from the book 'Wired for Sound' by Sammy Jones, which gives an interesting history of the band.

In 1895 on the evening of Tuesday, April 30th a fire nearly destroyed the New Inn. It was in the occupation of Thomas Harvey who had secured and left the pub at 10pm. His tenancy had expired that evening with the licence, on the application of the owners, Messrs. Allfrey and Lovell, brewers of Newport Pagnell, having been transferred to Horace Brown. The blaze was first noted at about 11pm and despite the attendance of the Newport Pagnell Fire Brigade the outbreak was not mastered until the roof had burnt through. Caused by the fire and the water the damage amounted to over £400, and with the cause unknown it was uncertain if the premises had been insured. In 1895 on the evening of Monday, May 20th a general meeting of members of the social working men's club was held on the premises to form a games club. This would be named the Stantonbury in Buckinghamshire Whist and Cribbage Association and submitted by the secretary, Mr. R.D. Williams, a code of rules was unanimously adopted.

In 1895 on Thursday, September 26th the local authorities began clearing out the brook which passed through Stantonbury. Then in October the Medical Officer of Health, Mr. Hailey, reported another case of typhoid in the town. This made 8 cases during the last two months and on speaking to some of the Stantonbury residents about the brook they said a great deal of the sewage came from Wolverton, which largely contributed to the nuisance. They thought the present cleaning out would only prove a temporary remedy but the nuisance might be further alleviated by taking the sewage to the river further from the houses. Here there was more water to carry it off. However Mr. Hailey thought the only satisfactory remedy was to buy a piece of land where the sewage could be irrigated, as in other places. Indeed in May the following year he said that on receiving complaints of bad smells from the brook he had visited the location and found it in a worse state than the previous year. The effluent flowing into the brook from the Wolverton sewage works was very impure and certainly contaminated the brook more than the Bradwell drainage.

Not surprisingly at the meeting of Newport Pagnell RDC in 1896 on Wednesday, September 9th the Medical Report mentioned that a person living in St. Mary's Street, Stantonbury, was ill with typhoid. She had been living in Newport Road and therefore it seemed the disease had originated there. The drinking water was obtained from a well which supplied several other families, and on being sent a sample the analyst had found it quite unfit for use. In consequence the well had been closed as was another in Newport Road which supplied 5 families. There had also been cases of scarlet fever, and in 1897 at the meeting of Newport Pagnell RDC on Wednesday, October 6th the Medical Officer's report stated that Mrs. Gregory, living at the Morning Star, had been suffering from fever following her confinement. The doctor who attended her had reported the matter to him as he attributed her illness to the smell of the sewage in the brook, which ran at the back of the house. In fact Mr. Gregory had frequently complained about this, saying that after the second heavy rains the bedroom windows had to be closed because of the smell.[9] Fortunately Mrs. Gregory was now recovering but a child of Mrs. Brownsell in the High Street, Stantonbury, was ill with typhoid. The drinking water was obtained from a shallow well in the garden at the back of the house and a sample had been sent for analysis. Yet since the Company's water main ran at the back of this street a supply could easily be laid on to all the houses. It would be a good thing if the Council would give their permission for a rough analysis to be made of water in all the wells in the street, and to close those found to be contaminated. That would then force the owners to have the Company's water. He was certain that it was because the houses were close together that the shallow wells were polluted. As for the stated rough analysis the council gave permission for a dozen samples to be taken. These were at a cost of 5s each and it would be subsequently found that of the 20 taken from Stantonbury 18 were bad and the other 2 'doubtful.'

In 1897 on the evening of Saturday, October 30th the Stantonbury Working Men's Club in St. James' Street was opened. The ground had been purchased with money loaned from the members, with the building erected by money loaned by 'an anonymous lady.' The premises included a library, bar and smoke room on the ground floor, concert room, billiard and bagatelle room on the first floor, with an adjoining cottage for the steward. In performing the opening ceremony Mr. Hall, secretary of the Working Men's Club and Institute Union, Clerkenwell, congratulated the company on the building, and with Mr. Freeman at the piano the evening was spent with songs etc.

As for another happy occasion, in 1898 at the church of St. James' on Thursday, July 28th the wedding took place of Florence May, the daughter of the postmaster Mr. C.F Sykes, and Mr. G.S. West, the eldest son of Mr. G. West of Beechwood, Dunstable. In 1899 on the afternoon of Saturday, October 14th the Liberal Hall on the Newport Pagnell Road, on the site previously purchased at auction, was opened by the Rt. Hon. Lord Carrington. A building committee had been formed about a year ago and with monies raised from donations and shares the construction to plans by Mr. A. Wilson, of Stantonbury, was undertaken by George Tranfield for

£208. Designed for seated accommodation of 300, and measuring 50ft by 25ft, the corrugated iron and wood structure was lined with felt with a match board interior, and behind a convenient platform was an ante room 25ft by 10ft. (The Bradwell Liberal and Radical Club was formed in 1906.)

Whilst not on the scale of the previous decades, at New Bradwell the new century saw continuing building activities and transactions. Among the first was an auction on the evening of Friday, May 25th 1900 at the Victoria Hotel, Wolverton, where Mr. T.C. Woods of Messrs. Woods and Co., Northampton, conducted the sale of 17 houses in the coincidentally named Wood Street. Attracting a good attendance numbers 4,6,8,10,12 made £630, numbers 14,16,18,20,22, 24 made £705, and the remaining six £735.

Then again at the Victoria Hotel, in 1901 on the evening of Thursday, July 11th an auction of freehold building land at New Bradwell was conducted by Messrs. Durham, Gotto and Samuel of Stony Stratford and Newport Pagnell. With the consent of the Bishop and Patron and the Governors of Queen Anne's Bounty the vendor was the Rev. J. Light, the incumbent of Stony Stratford, and the extent comprised 5 acres 23 poles in two lots, namely 3a 16p and 2a 7p - 'as staked out, adjacent to the public road from Wolverton to Newport Pagnell.' 'The present is an excellent opportunity of acquiring a considerable extent of ripe building land in the centre of a thriving district, where there is an undoubted want of further house accommodation, which can thus be supplied advantageously.'

Yet despite the hype there was only a small attendance with Mr. Geo. Garside of Leighton Buzzard purchasing Lot 1 for £500, and Lot 2 for £330. March 1902 saw the plans submitted for three cottages for Mr. Freeman of Wolverton in St. Giles Street, and one house in Thompson Street for Mr. Sharp, referred to the Parochial Committee at the Council meeting. As for ready built property in January 1907 ten adjoining freehold houses in School Street were offered for sale 'in good repair.' 'For details apply Mr. G. Booth 112, Cambridge Street, Wolverton.' However perhaps potential residents might be put off by a doctor's report, ending Lady Day 1907, which contained 'Enteric Fever is endemic in New Bradwell; there were 12 cases in 1902, 3 in 1903, 7 in 1904, and 3 in 1905. All cases this year (1907) received water from the London and North Western Railway Co.'s mains. This water had been repeatedly condemned by the Medical Officer of Health of Wolverton.'

The following year, 1908, by order of the mortgagees an auction was conducted on the evening of Friday, June 19th at the County Arms of numbers 1,3,5,7,9,, St. Mary's Street. Being brick and slate cottages all were occupied but with only a small attendance only number 9 was sold, to James Holland Stairs for £175. Numbers 1&3 were withdrawn at £300 and numbers 5&7 at £305. However there was greater interest in 1910, when on the evening of Friday, March 18th at the County Arms an auction was conducted by Geo. Wigley & Sons of nine cottages. With a plot of building land these were 2-18 High Street, bringing in gross yearly rentals of £107 18s, and at £670 the purchaser was Mr. W.C. Kemp of Stantonbury.

There was a large attendance, as also in 1911 on the evening of Wednesday, August 23rd when a ceremony of great interest to the residents of Stantonbury took place in the playground of the Council Schools. This was a presentation to Miss Grant, the leader and organiser of the Girls' Club, who on the Friday next would sail to Winnipeg to be married. She had served her teaching apprenticeship at the Stantonbury schools and was subsequently appointed to a post at a school in Basingstoke, Hants. However she then returned to Stantonbury some six years ago to nurse her invalid mother. After her mother's death she continued to look after the home for her father, who would accompany her to Canada.

In 1913 a plot of building land came up for sale in June in Queen Anne Street. Not that everyone thought the town an ideal situation, as manifest at a meeting of Newport Pagnell RDC. Here consequent to a report by a special committee it was considered with regard to Castlethorpe that since the population mainly consisted of railway workers the demand for housing could be more satisfactorily met at New Bradwell. This was adopted and seconded but a member then moved an amendment that the report be referred back, saying that with respect to Castlethorpe and Hanslope the suggestion was to drive the workers into "such a miserable place as New Bradwell."

On the instructions of the executors, on Friday, November 2nd 1917 an auction was conducted by Woods & Co. at the Railway

Tavern of a brick and slate shop at the corner of Glyn Street and School Street. This was in use as a Post Office and Telephone Call Office and, together with an adjoining cottage tenanted by Mrs. Tarry, was in the occupation of Mr. C.F. Sykes at a yearly rental of £23. However it was withdrawn at the sale, and to perhaps enhance the potential at the meeting of Wolverton UDC in 1919 on Tuesday, May 13th the suggestion that the name be changed from Stantonbury post office to New Bradwell post office was adopted.

No doubt due to the world war at this period the property market had greatly slackened, and in 1924 at the meeting of Wolverton UDC on Tuesday, April 1st the house for which plans were presented would be the first in the area for many years. Yet there were encouraging signs, for at the meeting of Wolverton UDC on Tuesday, September 28th 1926 a letter from the Ministry of Agriculture and Fisheries was read, wherein consent was given to the appropriation of allotment land at New Bradwell for housing purposes. The 12 houses proposed would be of the parlour type and built in pairs, and with application to be made to the Ministry of Health for a loan of £7,643 the anticipated completion date was March 31st next.

As for other locations, at the meeting of Wolverton UDC in March 1927 a letter from the Rev. E. Steer, vicar of Stony Stratford, stated that regarding the site in Bounty Street the Governors of Queen Anne's Bounty were not prepared to quote a price for the land, even as a basis for negotiations. However from acting as agent for Wylie Bros., in a communication from Mr. P.C. Gambell a price was quoted for a field on the Old Bradwell road, for which they were prepared to negotiate. The council proposed to use the frontage for houses and the rear as a sports ground, and the letter would be forwarded to the District Valuer. The matter was then further considered in 1928 at the meeting of the council on the evening of Tuesday, July 3rd. Here it was reported by the deputy clerk that no reply had been received from the Ministry of Health, and since procedures would have to be involved for both housing and sports a provisional order would need to be made. With one member saying that nothing would be gained by delay the only thing to do was to acquire the land by compulsory purchase order. This was seconded with an amendment carried to adjourn for a month. Such matters were again the subject at the meeting of the council in October. At this with regard to negotiations towards acquiring the proposed site for the New Bradwell Housing and Sports Ground it was stated in a letter from Mr. P.C. Gambell that Messrs. Wylie Bros. were not prepared to accept the council's offer of £950. Nor were they prepared to negotiate further. They had required £1,150 and it was carried that the council should again contact the District Valuer. On receipt of his reply a special meeting would then be called to finally settle the matter. Also at the meeting a letter was read from the Minister of Health approving the council's proposal to build the 12 houses on the site of the Newport Road allotments at New Bradwell. However application would have to be made to the Minister for his formal consent to appropriate the land for building purposes. Also, before any tenders could be invited they would need to wait for the District Valuer's report. Once this had been received a meeting of the Housing Committee would then be called. On a less positive aspect the Minister of Health had received a letter of objection from Dr. Miles, claiming the unsuitability of the land from being in a low lying part of New Bradwell. Indicating the ground to be saturated it seemed that 5 of the 6 trial holes had filled with water and the doctor said he was opposed on the matter of health, with the location being close to the river bed, covered with water weed, and poisoned by gases from the sewage farm. However a member claimed it was untrue that the holes were full of water. They had a special interview with their own Medical Officer of Health and were satisfied with their procedure. In consequence it was resolved that the Council would reply to the Ministry that they were satisfied with the location, and that any difficulties regarding damp would be obviated by concreting over the whole site.

With the possibility of having its own aerodrome, during June 1929 New Bradwell was host to Sir Alan Cobham's 'air campaign.' This aimed to promote public awareness in aviation, and accessed by a temporary foot bridge across the river from the old bathing place the location was a large meadow opposite the Newport Road recreation ground. On the day of arrival Sir Alan and his team flew in at around 11am and having greeted the aviators the chairman of

Wolverton UDC and the council members were taken on a free trip, being afterwards briefed about the possibilities of aviation and the importance of establishing a local airport. Then as chosen by a popular school vote schoolchildren Evelyn Godfrey, Margery Kightley and Jim Cook were given a 7 minute circular flight over Stanton Low and Haversham. Of their experience they then wrote an essay, being each rewarded with a photo of the aircraft autographed by Sir Charles Wakefield (who had paid for some 10,000 schoolchildren to have free trips) and Sir Alan Cobham. However with Col. L.C. Hawkins saying it would only be used for forced landings the council turned down the chance to have an airport at Bradwell. Perhaps in hindsight the best decision, for it might well have heightened the chances of New Bradwell becoming even more of a target during WW2, as with the other local airfields.

As an advocate of healthy living & accommodation, Dr. Charles Henry Miles inspired by the Garden City of Stevenage had these houses, named West View, built in the 1930s. Two were named 'Garden City Villas.'

During 1929 a start was made on council housing at New Bradwell, and in January 1930 for the New Bradwell Housing Scheme the clerk of Wolverton UDC was authorised to apply to the Public Works Loan Board for two loans - £2,316 for 40 years, and £2,375 for 60 years. 43 applications had been received for the 12 council houses under construction along the Bradwell Road, opposite the vicarage, and with these complete by April 1930 the first tenants would be Mr. and Mrs. Sapwell, who moved into number 2 that month. As for the existing housing stock, in June 1930 having failed to find buyers at auction four semi detached brick and tile freehold properties, 1,2,3,4 Garden City Villas, abutting on the Old Bradwell Road, New Bradwell, were offered for sale by private treaty. Also the three bed roomed 2,5,12, West View, New Bradwell, occupying 'a high and commanding position' on the Old Bradwell road at New Bradwell.

In September 1930 loan sanction for £4,900 was received regarding the second group of 12 houses of the New Bradwell Housing Scheme, and by the end of the year 24 houses had been completed. In February 1932 it was reported to Wolverton UDC that the agents of the late Dr. Miles estate had accepted the council's housing committee offer of £700 for the purchase of a field at West View, Bradwell. This was to develop as a housing site albeit dependent on the consent of the Minister of Health.

At New Bradwell the town's water was not laid on to the houses along the Newport Road west of the church, to St. Mary's Street, most of the houses in St. Giles, Queen Anne, Wallace and Wood Streets, or Caledonian Road. All flushing had to be done by buckets of water pumped from shallow wells which, rarely more than 20 feet deep, had to be lowered during the drought of 1921. Many people had to access a spring in Bounty Street to collect drinking water but in 1932 the LM&SR Company laid down new mains to all these properties, complete with fire hydrants. A factor perhaps contributory to the brisk bidding that year on Tuesday, November 22nd for six brick and slate freehold properties in St. Mary's Street. At the Victoria Hotel, Wolverton, these were put up in pairs, with 43 & 45 bought by a solicitor of Buckingham for £332 10s; 47 & 49 by Mrs. West of New Bradwell for £350; and 51 & 53 by Mrs. Law for £320.

That month with a Wolverhampton firm as the contractor work began on 60 houses. Local labour was employed and with the properties linked up with water and gas by September 1933 several families had moved in, there having been 198 applicants; 'Trail after trail of furniture and truck after truck of oddments caused much good humoured amusement to the passers by. The north country dialect indicated some of the Manchester men have at last secured homes which will put an end to their long journeys to the North every weekend.'

One of the council villas.

Even in September 1935 the council still had 140 housing applicants and therefore decided to erect a further 30 houses on their New Bradwell housing estate. These would all need interior decoration, and for carrying out that of the staircases and landings for the twenty two Council houses at East View, New Bradwell, the tender of £36 17s from Messrs. E.C. Turvey & Sons was accepted at the meeting of Wolverton UDC in January 1936. Regarding the additional thirty houses on the Bradwell Road Estate, for which tenders had now been invited, it was pointed out there would be four elevations. Some would have plaster all the way down; some to the ground floor windows; others plaster up to the bedroom window ledge; others all brick, and by such variations it was considered that the lay out of the estate would be improved.

Then in June 1936 the tender of £10,170 from Mr. J.C. Tarry of Newport Pagnell was formally accepted for building 30 non parlour houses at New Bradwell - it being decided to apply to the Ministry for sanction of an additional loan of £1,150, repayable over not more than 60 years. With the new housing being established (presently some 200 with a further 120 contemplated) there came an associated need for social facilities, and at the meeting in 1937 of the Buckinghamshire Licensing Committee, held at Aylesbury on Monday, May 10th, the removal of the licence of the George in Stony Stratford High Street to the centre of the Bradville Estate at New Bradwell was approved. By November that year (1937) there were now 1,064 houses at New Bradwell.

This was for a population of 3,700, of which some would be moving to new addresses, for in 1938 at the meeting of Wolverton UDC on Tuesday, April 19th the Housing Committee recommended that these applicants, in the following order, should be offered houses in Bradwell Road as they became vacant; Frederick Jordan, Lodge Farm Cottage, Castlethorpe; Alfred Chambers, 22, Thompson Street; Frederick Cooke, 22, Glyn Street; William Townsend, 24, Thompson Street; Bertis Newman, 34, Cambridge Street; Richard Gayton, 61, Newport Road. As for the new housing 'over the hill', the Housing Committee reported that Messrs. Edward Culff & Co. had sent a letter asking if the council would care to acquire the remainder of the undeveloped land on the Bradville Estate, New Bradwell. This would be as it was or with the roads completed to specification but the Committee recommended that in view of the council's undeveloped land on the Bradwell Road Estate, plus their other housing commitments, the matter should not be entertained.

As for the properties on the Bradville Estate, where shops were now in the course of construction, semi detached modern freehold houses were advertised for sale that month at £550, 'deposit £25, balance 14s 4d per week NOT A PENNY MORE.' No road charges or legal costs were applicable and particulars could be obtained from the representative on site, Mr. Thompson, Plot 13, or from Edward Culff and Co., estate agents, surveyors, and auctioneers of Westminster Chambers, 92, St. Mary Road, Walthamstow. Then in June two modern flats on the Bradville Estate were advertised, 2 rooms down, 3 up, 'two of which have a delightful outlook … Built in wardrobes in each room, electric light, hot and cold water, w.c. up and downstairs. 'Write: Plot 26.'

With regard to other activities, on Thursday, July 28th 1938 at the quarterly meeting of Bucks County Council, held at Aylesbury, the Highways, Bridges, and Boundaries Committee reported receipt of a tender of £19,414 16s 2d from G.F.X. Hartigan Ltd., Newport Pagnell. As the lowest this was for the diversion of the Wolverton to New Bradwell road near Stonebridge Farm, requests for this to be done having been made for several years to Wolverton UDC, with representations frequently forwarded by the Council to the County Authority. At the meeting of the council on October 18th 1938, at which concerns were expressed regarding the continued flooding of houses at East View, New Bradwell, another letter had been received from Edward Culff and Co., this time offering to sell 35 houses and 112 building plots on the Bradville Estate. The reply would be the same as to their previous missive. Apart from housing and shops, also being erected on the Bradville Estate was a pub which, fronting the New Bradwell to Loughton road, after six months of construction opened its doors on Friday, October 28th 1938. It had been at the meeting of Wolverton UDC in January 1938 that the Highways & Sanitary Committee reported approval of the plan from Northampton Brewery Company for licensed premises on the Bradville Estate. However this was subject to the piping of the ditch on the north side of the council's housing estate by large field pipes. Also that the fence to be erected was of a type approved by the council, and that section 17 of the Restriction of Ribbon Development Act 1935 be applied with regard to the service roads and entrances - 'after consultation and to the satisfaction of the County Highway and Police authorities.'

Houses on the Bradville Estate on the Bradwell Road at the corner of Althorp crescent.

With Mr. L.B. Baillon ARIBA as the architect the contractors were the firm of Mr. F.A. Hedges of Syresham, near Brackley, with the electrical installation undertaken by Mr. E.W. Butler, electrical engineer, of 20, Oxford Street, Wolverton. Extending the width of the building, a feature at the rear was a winter garden with a glass roof. This had access to a spacious lounge, and additionally provided was a separately heated outdoor department. In the following month new houses 'with every modern convenience' were advertised for rent on the Bradville Estate at 12s a week; 'The sum of £25 to be allowed to each tenant, off the first year's rent, as deposit on purchase entirely at tenant's option.' Details could be had from Mr. Thompson, 'Silverdene,' Abbey Way, Bradville Estate, or Edward Culff and Co., estate agents, surveyors, and auctioneers Westminster Chambers, 92, St. Mary Road, Walthamstow.

Yet there were still no facilities for purchasing postage stamps etc., and at a meeting of Wolverton UDC in October 1938 a letter was read from Major Whiteley MP; "I understand your council have recently applied for a sub post office to serve the new estate at New Bradwell. I am told that this request has not been granted. In my view your council was justified in making this request and I shall be only too ready to take up the matter with the Postmaster-General." All the details would then be forwarded to the Major, and subsequently a pillar box would be erected in Stanton Avenue.

Perhaps vindicating the concerns of Dr. Miles, many years

before, in October occupants in the newer houses of Newport Road experienced flooding of their properties to a depth of several feet. Water had also entered houses in Caledonian Road and also Newport Road in the vicinity of Queen Anne Street.

Being on higher ground the residents were more fortunate on the Bradville Estate where in November came the need for a 'barmaid general' at the Bradville Hotel. It was perhaps due to this recent competition that the County Arms had now sought permission to carry out certain alterations. Indeed it seems no objections were raised, for at Stony Stratford Petty Sessions on Friday, December 23rd 1938 Superintendent F. Bryant said that if carried out as proposed the plans would make the house a credit to the owners. Also at the Sessions the full transfer of the licence of the Bradville Hotel was granted to Eric Harry Bailey, this being consequent to the application by Horace Clarke, the Northampton Brewery Company's representative. In fact the transfer of the licence from the George in Stony Stratford High Street had been agreed at the annual Licensing Meeting of the Stony Stratford Petty Sessional Division in February last. This was later confirmed by Bucks County Licensing Committee and in consequence quite a number of persons, including many regulars of many years custom, spent the last evening of the pub on Thursday, October 27th 1938. As for the

Stantonbury St. Peter's Football team.

hosts, Mr. and Mrs. Harry Bridges, they would now leave for the Cherry Tree at Little Broughton, Market Harborough.

The story of the town during WW2 is deserving of a separate book. However there needs to be mention of the alarms wrought by enemy action and these are told in the Weapons and War chapter. In July 1941 a new sub post office on the Bradwell Road, New Bradwell, was opened. This need had been long requested by Wolverton UDC and the facility would be under the charge of Miss Stimpson, who was previously engaged in the New Bradwell office in the High Street. Eight weeks after that of his wife, the death occurred of 68 year old George Thomas Foxon in 1942 on Saturday, June 6th at 3, Melbourne Terrace, New Bradwell. Beginning at New Bradwell station in 1913 he would be the office porter for 21 years but retired at the age of 60 through ill health. (The story of the branch line from Wolverton to Newport Pagnell, with the intermediate stops at New Bradwell and Great Linford, is told in other books of this series. Suffice to say that in 1865 Andrew Williamson had been appointed as station master at New Bradwell, being transferred in 1880 to that at Farthingoe, near Banbury.)

Throughout the country enemy bombing destroyed countless houses and as a means of intermediate accommodation in early 1945 Wolverton UDC were fortunate to be granted an allocation of 90 'pre fabs.' Not least their request had been favourably viewed from already having a prepared site, which was a tribute to their clerk, Mr. Cussons, who had the foresight to advise the council to purchase Messrs. Culff's undeveloped estate at New Bradwell. On temporary foundations the pre fabs would form Abbey Way, Bradvue Crescent, and Bridle Crescent, with the first tenant moving in on June 1st 1946. Regarding conventional housing, at the meeting of Wolverton UDC on Tuesday, February 19th 1946 a tender of £39,034 for the construction of 30 three bedroom houses at Althorpe Crescent, New Bradwell, was accepted. However due to road charges, fencing etc. the actual cost per house would increase from £1,301 to £1,380. Ranging from £39,034 to £45,864, seven tenders had been received, and from being the lowest that of Messrs. Gilbert Cole and Co., of Northampton, was recommended and would be sent to the Ministry of Health for approval. The costing was based on a superficial area of

877ft per house but at the meeting in December last the council had approved an increase to 925ft, 'or thereabouts,' in accordance with a suggestion from the Ministry of Health. Therefore on the priced bill of quantities the tender would need to be revised upward.

Despite difficulties in the procurement of interior fittings, some 4 or 5 of the 90 pre fabs were now in the course of construction, with the rent as fixed by Wolverton UDC to be 12s per week plus rates. Already there was a list of some 140 applicants and where possible preference would be given to members and ex members of the Forces and their families, who would benefit from the provision of a fridge and economic household running costs.

Indeed a welcome accommodation although regarding one of the first tenants there would tragedy in 1947, when on the morning of Friday, January 24th their 14 month old baby died in a fire at their pre fab, 45, Bradvue Crescent. The child was Robert Douglas Cameron Pointer, the son of Mr. R. Pointer DFC and his wife, who said that on finishing her ironing, and pulling out the plug, she left to go to the butchers. Having fastened the baby in his high chair she took her 4 year old daughter to the next door neighbour and would be gone for no more than 15 minutes. Then on her way back she was met by the neighbour, Mrs. Parker of 47, Bradvue Crescent, who told her to rush home as the pre fab was on fire. While minding the daughter Mrs. Parker had heard the crackling noise of the blaze, and knowing the baby was inside helped to smash the bedroom window. At the time Sidney Heel, a Wolverton council labourer, was emptying bins on the Bradvue estate and on hearing his mate raise the alarm he rushed to the pre fab to find the kitchen in flames. The fire had yet to reach the front but the back bedroom was filled with smoke. A neighbour then said there's a baby in a cot, at which he hurriedly went round again and although seeing a cot and a pram despite entering the blaze three times he couldn't find the child. On opening the door there was a mass flames and so a chain of buckets was formed until the firemen arrived. One of their part time members then found the baby lying among the debris on the floor. At the subsequent inquest the father said they'd occupied the bungalow since 1946. A fire in the living room heated the water and the rest of the building by hot air through air ducts in the roof. Electric points were provided in all the rooms and until the cold weather they hadn't used the hard fuel heater. This initially worked efficiently until about a week ago, when it didn't seem to heat the water and there was no hot air issuing from the ducts. When asked about a bang or explosion, as reported by one witness, the Wolverton UDC Surveyor, Arthur Baker, said he thought this would have been the asbestos sheeting cracking in the blaze and falling to the ground. The cause remained a complete mystery and in consequence a verdict of death from misadventure was recorded.

Perhaps confirming that between warring nations there seems little real enmity among the majority of the populations, coerced by the oppressions of a minority, in January 1948 two marriages took place in New Bradwell of German brides at the church of St. James.

The newly weds would live elsewhere whilst as for the town at the meeting of the Wolverton UDC on Tuesday, February 17th 1948, after hearing of the slow rate of building on the New Bradwell housing estate a councillor asked for a railway carriage housing site to be considered. The chairman replied that the lack of progress was due to a shortage of materials and labour, and he didn't think they wanted to 'clutter up' the district with railway carriages. However Mr. Frederick Billingham, who occupied a converted railway carriage at New Bradwell, told the meeting that the coaches made nice homes and were preferable to the standards of accommodation being experienced by many waiting applicants.[10] Yet despite the shortages by November 1949 all but nine of the houses were complete on the Wolverton UDC estates at Furze Way, Wolverton, and also Althorpe Crescent, New Bradwell.[11]

In March 1950 a tenant hopefully advertised to exchange a pre fab at New Bradwell for a council house or bungalow at Wolverton. Wishful thinking perhaps!

Also in August that year part of Stanton Avenue extending in a northerly direction at New Bradwell was renamed Althorpe Crescent, where consequent to the liquidation of the original contractor the costs of employing a council watchman, and for clearing up the area, was reported as £248 19s 9d.

As for one of the pioneers of New Bradwell housing, after an illness of 8 days in 1953 on Wednesday, January 7th the death occurred of William Charles Kemp at his home of 39, Newport Road, Woburn Sands. He was 93 and his sister, Miss P.S. Kemp, had resided with him. For many years he had been a builder at New Bradwell, also supervising the building of Wolverton Social Club and carrying out work for the railway company and the Radcliffe Trustees. Some 38 years ago he retired from active business and in 1933 moved from Newport Pagnell to Woburn Sands. In 1955 at the March meeting of the Wolverton council the chairman of the Cemeteries and Recreation Grounds Committee, Mr. E. Moore, welcomed the agreement of the council to buy the open space opposite the County Arms at Corner Pin from the County Council. For too long it had been considered an eyesore, and the cost as per the figure of the district valuer was £75. It would still be an open space but the terms of the agreement allowed for the provision of car parks. For the past nine years the council had rented the land at £1 a year by which they had little incentive to carry out any improvement.

With houses, shops and a pub now established on the Bradville Estate the need remained for a centre for social functions. Funds were being raised by the Bradville Estate Social Committee, and their Christmas Fayre in the Labour Hall in December 1957 enabled them to top the £200 mark. Meanwhile much needed accommodation was still being provided at New Bradwell by the 90 'temporary' pre fabs.

Albeit lessened by one when, with only the walls left standing, 28, Bridle Crescent, was destroyed by fire on the afternoon of Sunday, January 11th 1959. Together with their children Linda, age 4, and Tony, age 3, this had been the home of Mr. and Mrs. Leslie Wilson who, having married 6 years ago, had lived in rooms in the 'little streets' at Wolverton until securing the pre fab some seven months ago. It seemed the fire had started when the daughter in moving a pushchair knocked over an oil stove. Three of the family made dramatic escapes and a neighbour rescued the boy. However with no insurance the family lost all their possessions and in recounting the incident the father, a milkman for the Co-op, said that being asleep at the time "I awoke with a start and heard Linda screaming. Then I saw flames right up to the ceiling. I jumped out of the bedroom window as I was and ran to call Reg. Clark, the next door neighbour.

When I ran back through the snow the back door was locked so I got in through the window. The smoke was then so thick that I could see nothing." Mrs. Wilson said that whilst in her living room she heard Linda scream - "I ran into the passage and saw a wall of flame. Linda had run into the airing cupboard and I ran and snatched her up and got her out of the bathroom window... Linda was black with smoke and hysterical when I got her out. It seems that she must have pushed the pushchair and it knocked over an oil stove." Reg. Clark had been watching television when Mr. Wilson burst in, and rushing to the pre fab he shouted if any one was in. When Tony replied he then crept in through the smoke and rescued him. Within minutes a crowd of neighbours ran to help and when it seemed for a while that the fire might spread to the Clark's pre fab they threw buckets of water onto the blaze, and furniture was moved out of two rooms. Neighbours soon brought children's clothes and Mr. Clark went to Wolverton to fetch clothing for the parents. Not least for Mr. Wilson for having been asleep he was only in his vest and pants. He was additionally given a suit and raincoat by the WVS.

In the aftermath of the tragedy at the meeting of Wolverton UDC on Tuesday, February 24th 1959 it was decided to fit all the pre fabs with a fire extinguisher at a cost of 43s 6d each. The charge would be made to the Housing Revenue Account, and also at the meeting the chairman, Councillor T.H. Haseldine, said that his fund for the Wilsons had now been closed at £55.

At 165, Newport Road, New Bradwell, on the morning of February 24th 1959 the death suddenly occurred at the age of 84 of Mrs. Florence Osborne. A widow for 39 years she had been a long standing newsagent, being succeeded in the business by her son, Jim, from Glyn Street. On his death his widow then continued the business for a time, later selling it to Mr. G. Martin.

In 1961 on Saturday, February 25th around 20 houses at New Bradwell bore the initial impact of a violent whirlwind and hail storm that just after 11.30am passed through North Bucks. Described by one resident as far worse than the bombs in WW2, the aptly named Norman Rainbow of 51, Althorpe Crescent, claimed it was due to a fireball which he saw skimming the roofs of the houses; "It seemed to come from over the main railway line, and there was this terrific bang which coincided with the gust of wind." Ray Meakins and his wife of 65, Bradwell Road, also saw a blue flash, with the explosion raining plaster down onto their bed.

In 1963 on Thursday, September 19th at the age of 83 the death occurred at his home of 3, Moon Street, Wolverton, of Frederick Robinson. A native of Winslow he was early apprenticed as a trimmer at Wolverton Works but in 1911 he left to become licensee of the Morning Star. On leaving the pub he and his family went to live at Glyn House, Stantonbury, where he stayed for 17 years. However for the past 16 years he and his daughter, Mrs. Pansy Hepher, had lived in Moon Street. During WW1 he served in the RFC and when later transferred to the Royal West Kent Regiment served in France. During WW2 he had been a special constable at the Newport Pagnell station. By 1965 there were intimations that a new city was to be built in this part of North Bucks.

However for New Bradwell changes were already underway, for at a meeting of Wolverton UDC in March 1965 it was recommended to accept the tender of £771 by Arthur Sanders Ltd., of Rushden, for the demolition of the compulsorily purchased Wood Street houses.

Then the following year on the evening of Friday, June 3rd at the annual meeting of Buckingham Conservative Association, held at Bletchley, the treasurer, Mr. W.S. Johnson, reported that Bowyer Hall (named after an MP) had been sold. It was to have been bought by the trustees of New Bradwell Methodist Church for youth work but a higher offer was made and after his purchase Mr. C.P. Hiorns, of New Bradwell, who had a building and decorating business, received planning permission to turn the hall into a large DIY and fireplace showroom. Indeed he had begun manufacturing fireplaces in his workshops, and intending to open shortly after Christmas said "We hope to have the largest showroom for fireplaces in North Bucks. The building will have a complete new front, we are going to give it a proper 'face lift' and bring it up to date. It is something that is really required in the town. We will be giving the place a new slant again."

This book finishes where the development of the long rumoured New City begins. However to set the scene regarding New Bradwell perhaps a few mentions might be of interest; not least when at the meeting of Wolverton UDC in March 1977 the question was asked by Councillor Ed Baines as to when the borough housing committee would demolish the six remaining prefabs at New Bradwell. The decision to demolish all the pre fabs had been taken the previous month, and in reply the Housing chairman, David Lee, said that bearing in mind the problem had been 'hanging about' for many years they would proceed as quickly as possible. As for other accommodation, in April 1977 it was announced that the facelift scheme for New Bradwell's controversial 24 ex railway cottages would cost £186,072. For carrying out the conversion, repair, and modernisation, Milton Keynes Development Corporation had let the contract to the Rushden firm of Robert Marriott Ltd., the cottages having been at the centre of a local row for many years.

Indeed the previous year over 1,500 residents at New Bradwell had signed a petition in a last ditch attempt to persuade the Environment Secretary, Peter Shore, to demolish the properties and reverse the decision of an earlier public enquiry. In the event it was ruled that the 24 listed dwellings must be kept, whereupon the borough council sold them to MKDC for modernisation, with a suggestion that local people should be given first option for accommodation. In the week beginning Sunday, April 17th 1977 the Corporation said work had already started at the Spencer Street site, with an expectation that the first tenants would move in next spring. The houses, to accommodate some 84 people, would be brought up to modern standards having partial gas fired central heating, new kitchens and bathrooms. The rear lean-to's would be demolished but the original ambience of the terraces would be kept. With the intention to provide a nearby car parking area the street would be fully pedestrianised, and following negotiations with the Corporation the Rainbow Housing Co-operative was formed. Subsequently the first tenants arrived in 1978 in May but seemed not entirely welcoming of the local press, with one reporter's cheery greeting of "Nice day" met with "It was, until you ******s came along." Not that a local van driver on his rounds was surprised, saying "They're a very strange bunch in there. But at least they'll give us something to laugh about."

The official opening took place later that year with the Corporation's Housing Director, Ben Affleck, unveiling the street's new name plate and planting a tree. With one cottage kept vacant for use as a meeting place, a workshop, an office, and library of pooled books, this was Milton Keynes first housing co-operative, and under the scheme tenants were to maintain and manage the 24 cottages, carry out landscaping in the traffic free street, and grow food together on nearby rented land. As for the occupants, one tenant said "I like the feeling of neighbourliness you get living in Spencer Street, It's marvellous how friendly everyone is in New Bradwell." At the official opening Mr. Affleck said it was encouraging to see a group of people willing to come together and work hard to bring about such a scheme. A great deal of negotiations with Rainbow had taken place, and they agreed that local people could be admitted here. Including New Bradwell's very own 'White Witch,' Mrs. Dorothy Horspool, who on being forced to leave 8 years ago, when the cottages were under threat of demolition, was moved to St. Peter's Way, New Bradwell; "But I loved living here and when I heard about the Rainbow scheme I rushed to put our names down. Now we're back and it's wonderful. … I feel I've come home again, but to a much better one!"

Some years before the Morning Star had been badly damaged by fire, and in January 1983 came rumours that despite the refusal for planning permission it might be pulled down to make way for 9 houses. The 'vividly painted' derelict pub was owned by Manns Brewery and consequent to their lodging an appeal against the refusal the matter would now be considered by the Secretary of State for the Environment. As for the Borough Council's decision, they deemed it was within the flood plain, meaning floods elsewhere. Also the houses would be out of keeping with the open character of the northern edge of the city.

Then in June 1983 members of the planning committee were told that an appeal against the decision had failed, and that a Department of the Environment inspector had agreed that the development could not go ahead. As stated by the Planning Director, Ed Follows, "It should form a reasonable transition between the open part of the city and the newer developed part. We have been in discussion with the company and it is now up to them to take that initiative. Obviously they wanted to pursue their original plans as it would give them more property, but I think what we are asking would be perfectly profitable for them." The Inspector had considered the visual impact of the development proposed, and the kind of activity it would create, would be inappropriate on this site. Thus on the condition that the derelict building should be demolished the one acre site was put up for public auction in 1983 at the County Arms at 6.30pm on Wednesday, November 23rd. Mr. Neadon of the auctioneers Howkins and Co. had said a reserve price wouldn't be fixed until just prior to the auction but the anticipated sum would be between £30k and 40k. In fact the actual pub site was about 3/5ths of an acre but was made up to an acre since also offered for sale was an additional piece of land running down to the river, 'where there is an impressive walnut tree and several other interesting trees.' Indeed it was hoped a prospective developer would make this an attractive landscaped site, and eventually 4 houses would be built. The arrival of the New City has wrought many changes to New Bradwell but despite the closure and eyesore of derelict pubs the community still continues to thrive - but that's a story for another time.

THE BRADVILLE ESTATE
The Post War Years

An aerial view of the Bradville estate in the 1950s, showing the single storey pre-fabs in the foreground. (Courtesy David Farron)

As told in the Town's Development chapter, the Bradville Estate was commenced in the mid 1930s, and for readers seeking more in depth information the Buckinghamshire Archives hold interesting documents relating to those beginnings (Ref. D-X925, and D-X925/1.) The developers were Messrs. Culff & Co. of Walthamstow, and on the evening of Friday, December 4th 1936 a dinner and social for the men employed on the Bradville Estate was given by the firm at the Craufurd Arms, Wolverton. This was presided over by the principal, Edward Culff, with the arrangements for the evening having been made by Mr. G. Bunyan, a director of Midland Roadways Ltd., who were laying the sewers and roads on the estate. Inevitably the population of New Bradwell would increase and with the development of the Bradville Estate, plus the growth of council houses on the Old Bradwell Road, in June 1937 a new bus stage was granted by the East Midland Commissioners. This would be for a 1d stage fare from the Bradwell Road turning from the Newport Road to Stanton Avenue. As for another consequence, the first meeting of the newly formed Mothers' Club was held, appropriately, at the Labour Hall.

Regarding the development of the Bradville Estate, in March 1945 at the meeting of Wolverton UDC the proposals for the provision of more housing accommodation, as contained in their Housing Committee report, were studied; "The Clerk reported that after protracted negotiations with various Government departments the district valuer had now issued his valuation for the purchase of the 11½ acres (approximately) of freehold building land at Bradville to be £5,000, the acquiring authority to pay vendors' solicitors costs, and that these terms are agreed by the owner, subject to formal contract. Application has been made to the Ministry of Health for formal consent to the purchase by the Council, and when this is received the Clerk will proceed to acquire the site. The site will accommodate approximately 90 temporary bungalows." As for the occupants, Mr. G. Burrows said the committee were having a special meeting 'for the purpose of going into the case of ex-Service men.' Then at the Council's meeting in April it was reported by the Committee that no objection had been raised by the Minister of Health to the Council's acquisition of the 11½ acre site, 'known as the Bradville Estate,' and that the purchase would now proceed; 'Authority was given for the seal of the Council to be affixed to the contract for sale for the portion of the Bradville Estate acquired by the Council for housing purposes.' In the agreement the only restriction was that the building of a hotel or refreshment house would not be allowed. The following year, in February 1946 it was announced that 12s a week was the recommended rent for the 90 pre fabs on the Bradville Estate, plus rates. A provisional list of 140 applicants had been made, with preference as far as possible given to members and ex members of the Forces. Of the 'Tarran' type, by May 1946 excepting the interior painting 14 of the pre fabricated houses had been completed, with a further 20 erected but awaiting internal fittings. The bases for all the houses were complete, and the contractors, Messrs. Gee, Walker and Slater Ltd., expected delivery of a further 37 houses that month. Then the balance of 19 during June. Despite the shortage of labour and fittings the contractors considered the site was remarkably well progressed, especially for a country site, and in further progress the roads on the site had all been made up. In layout the houses would form a rough square with a children's playground planned for the central ground. Completely detached from each other, and each featuring a large garden at the front and rear, the pre fabs consisted of two bedrooms, a sitting cum dining room, hall, kitchen, separate lavatory and bathroom. Every room was provided with a large cupboard space and wardrobes were built into the bedrooms. In the living room heating was supplied by a range, with hot air taken by ducts from the chimney to both bedrooms. Also to the towel rails in the bathroom and kitchen. Water was heated from the same source. As for the fittings these comprised a gas fridge, gas copper, gas cooker, sink and vegetable trays. Power points were provided for an electric kettle and iron. Adjoining the pre fab estate road construction was in progress between Althorpe Crescent and Stanton Avenue to accommodate the construction, at a cost of £1,300 each, of 30 permanent houses. All the properties would have living rooms on the sunny side, with the plans presently with the Ministry of Health. When the permanent houses and the pre fabs were complete over 1,000 people would be living 'over the hill' on the Bradville Estate, and in view of this a member suggested that a social centre might well be worth considering there. In May 1946 at the monthly meeting of Wolverton UDC the chairman of the Housing and Development Committee reported that having spent much time and care the committee had selected 86 married couples to be tenants for the Bradville Estate pre fabs. The allocations were;

Members of HM Forces;

Families with no children, 14; families with one child 38; families with two children, 15.

Overcrowding and cases of hardship;

Families with no children, 7; families with one child, 8; families with two children, 4.

Of the 86 nominated, 26 were from New Bradwell, 31 from Wolverton, 21 from Stony Stratford, and 8 from outside the Urban District (ie to cases of people living outside the district but who worked inside the district, at Wolverton, and had to travel a distance to and from work.)

Four pre fabs had been kept back, since it was felt that as the Estate would not be complete for several months a reserve was needed, for any cases of special hardship that might arise in the interim.

The successful applicants were then gradually moved in. However in October 1946 at the monthly meeting of Wolverton UDC a recommendation of the Housing and Development Committee was adopted whereby tenants on the Bradville Estate would be prohibited from keeping livestock or erecting buildings. This was because for the benefit of all the residents in the area provision was being made in the Bradville Field for the allocation of extra ground for gardens. Also for the keeping of livestock, and the committee felt that with the plots of ground for the houses being not very large they couldn't allow oddments of buildings to go up. In November 1946 on being appointed assistant surveyor to the council (from a position as engineering assistant to East Barnet Urban Council) 30 year old Ronald Tricker was offered a pre fab on the estate. With the pre fabs now developed attention could be given to other aspects on the Bradville Estate, and at their meeting in December 1946 the council adopted a Housing Committee recommendation to accept a quote of £168 16s from a neighbouring nurseryman. This was to supply and plant 50 standard trees, 100 flowering and evergreen shrubs, and approx 100ft of beech hedging. Also the committee recommended that several fruit trees should be planted in the grass verges of the estate on which the 90 pre fab bungalows had been erected. In other considerations, at the January meeting of the council in 1948 a discussion took place regarding the garages to be built on the Bradville Estate. Mr. F. Moore presented the report and stated that for the erection of the four garages on concrete bases, located on the previously approved site in Abbey Way on the Bradville Estate, the price of £270, as previously agreed by the Council, was now too low. Due to the increased cost of the concrete it would now be £347 and a proposition that the work should be done by direct labour was defeated by 8 votes to 6. Then in a further proposition the present tender was accepted. This was by 12 votes to 5 and an order for their immediate construction would be placed. The Committee also noted a future need for further garages. Two suitable sites were available in Bridle Crescent which together could accommodate a total of eight garages. The Surveyor reported having booked the bricklayer for 3 months ahead, and it was moved that a tender from Messrs. Betts and Faulkner for the work should be accepted. This was duly carried and by April 1948 at a unit cost of £82 the four garages were nearly complete. Inclusive of rates, taxes, and repairs, the Housing & Development Committee recommended a rent of 5s per week, with the garages let to Mr. F. Elson, 70, Bradvue Crescent, Mr. R. Tricker, 30, Bridle Crescent, Mr. R. Bardin, 13, Abbey Way, and Mr. J. Goodwin, 27, Abbey Way. In other matters the Surveyor reported his estimation of £8 each as the cost for the exterior painting of the pre fabs. If available extra painters would be employed to concentrate on the work, thus obviating any delay to that currently being done to the council's other houses. However due to the poor quality of the paint used on the pre fabs the council was making application to the Ministry of Works for a reimbursement of the cost, or for a grant. Despite the recent stipulation, contrary to their condition of tenancy two tenants of the pre fabs at Bridle Crescent were reported for keeping poultry in their gardens. As made previously clear the council had allocated provision in the nearby Bradville allotment field, and notice would be given for the offenders to remove the poultry from their gardens. In June 1948 as reported by the Housing and Planning Committee ten houses were now complete on the Althorpe Crescent Estate and were ready for occupation ; 4 were finished except for flooring, but work on the remaining 16 was slow.

In February 1947 Wolverton UDC had suggested to Bucks County Education Committee that the open space at Bradville would seem a suitable site on which to build a nursery school. This regarded both the large number of houses in the Bradville Estate area and the number of young children, and in response the Surveyor, Mr. Baker, had been tasked by the County Architect to send details of the available sewers. Also his observations regarding the road widths. The matter then lapsed until in August 1951 it was announced that an infants school for 120 children would be included in the school building programme for 1952/53. Bucks Education Committee had asked the council if they could buy the said piece of land and this was duly agreed, provided that the County Council would leave some ground for the children to play on. Also on the agenda of necessary facilities, in August 1956 the committee of Bradville Estate Social Hall Fund, founded in 1955, made a second attempt to hold their gala fete. Due to rain, earlier in the year their first effort had instead of the Bradwell Road Recreation Ground been held in the Bowyer Hall, and although at this second attempt rain again proved a problem it kept off just sufficient for the fancy dress parade to take place. In fact with the aid of tents the organisers were able to sport some sort of show. However since this had been performed at the previous occasion there was no opening ceremony. Nor crowning of the queen, Miss Barbara Johnson, who together with her attendants, Jeanne Bissell & Maureen Earl (who had taken the place of one of the original attendants, Sandra Knibbs, who was on holiday) took part in the procession on a decorated lorry. Also featured were sports, a comic football match between the ladies and men, and a comic pram race. Then in the evening the event concluded in the Labour Hall with a social and dance, to the music of Jack Durdin's trio. By now the pre fabs were well established as a welcome addition to the housing, although in August 1957 thirty six of the tenants lodged a joint complaint about the condition of their kitchen sinks. Following a subsequent inspection the Housing Committee reported that of 69 galvanised steel sinks 11 had seriously deteriorated, probably due to inattention. Yet it was not intended to replace any sink until it became defective or leaked. A regular feature of fund raising by the Bradville Estate Social Hall Fund was an annual Chrysanthemum and Dahlia Show. Also a Christmas bazaar, with that in 1959 held in the Bowyer Hall and opened by Nurse M. Draper. The Fund's committee had inquired about the possibility of erecting a pre fabricated building on the open space at Bridle Crescent but in March 1960 were informed by the Housing Committee of Wolverton UDC that "This would be completely out of touch not only with what there is now, but what there is likely to be." Additionally the Committee said that at that the time of developing the Bradville Housing Estate it was envisaged that this land would be used either for a community centre or would be kept as an open space. However it was now reserved in the town map as a place for a primary school and although the land had been sold to the County Council it was now understood that the Education Committee was debating whether to keep this school in the building programme. If the land was not required for that purpose then the Housing Committee deemed it should be re-acquired, and it was agreed that the County Council should be informed of this interest. Consequent to complaints from residents in Abbey Way, in April 1960 with regard to the condition of some of the municipal garages on the Bradville Estate the council considered replacing them with five of pre-cast concrete. As reported by the Housing Committee they had been erected about 12 years ago and from a construction of sheet metal were now hardly fit for purpose. Also facing demise was the prospect of a social hall for the Estate, for on Wednesday, May 4th 1960 at the annual general meeting of the Fund, held at their headquarters of the New Inn, it was asked by Mr. R. Clark, "Are the people of the Bradville Estate interested in having a social hall on their estate." A notice had been posted in the local press requesting 'All who are interested in the future of the above Fund please attend at 8pm.', but only 12 turned up. It was not possible to appoint a chairman and so an extra ordinary general meeting was held on May 26th. Mr. W.D. Labrum, treasurer, said they'd had a very quiet year and only £50 had been made. Indeed most of their ventures had lacked support and not least the fete, which despite perfect weather had not been a great success. The chairman of the fund, Mr. D. Keen, read a letter from Harold Faithfull, the president, who in apologising for not being present stated that £395 6s 7d had been raised. He was sure the time had now arrived to find a suitable site, and with the upkeep bound to be heavy suggested that once the centre was built they should ask the council to take over the funds. Towards this the chairman of the council, Mr. D.E. Morgan, had agreed to meet a deputation from the fund to discuss the possibility at a later date. However Mr. Keen reported that although Mr. G. Plastow, the Engineer Surveyor of the council, had been very co-operative no land was presently available for a hall. The committee had even approached several landowners but none were able to oblige. The Fund didn't want to see the enterprise flop but as pointed out by one member although the young wives had started this project only a few had attended the previous meetings. Mr. Keen said there could be only two alternatives. Either the money could be put into trust, or they could call an extraordinary general meeting. If it was put into a trust it might never be started again. During the past four years the committee had averaged £100 a year but during the last two years support had been dropping, and it seemed the people of the Estate were just not interested. In fact the piece of undeveloped land at Bridle Crescent of the Bradville Estate had lain idle since 1948, but having been sold for £1,300 some years ago by Wolverton UDC to Bucks County Council it was reported in July 1960 that the latter were now willing to sell to the former. Negotiations regarding the price were taking place and a meeting would be scheduled between the committee of the Bradville Estate Social Hall Fund, the New Bradwell councillors, and the chairman of the Council. However as they had previously stated the Housing Committee would not favour the erection of any pre fabricated building. Also they could not approve the proposal of the County Health Committee to build a pair of houses with district rooms and a garage for district nurses, this from being of the opinion that it would be a mistake to allow any such 'sporadic development.' Thus the site remained as an open space and was likely to remain so for another 10 to 15 years, as stated by the chairman of the Housing and Planning Committee at the meeting of Wolverton UDC in 1961 on Wednesday, December 27th. The land was 'zoned' in the town map for residential use and as owners of surrounding property the council was interested in buying the land from the County Council, which admitted they had no use for it. However they would only sell at the full development price and in view of this the chairman of the Committee said "We do feel there is no point in going ahead at the moment. The reason is quite obvious. If we don't intend to develop this for some time - we don't obviously because we have a lot on our plates with the Little Streets and it may be 10 to 15 years - it is no use buying that land at the market price and sterilising the money. Therefore we will leave the matter as it is."

A Coronation street party in 1953.

The Corner Pin development dates from the same period, eventually extending eastward along the Newport Road and joining the town in the first decade of the 20th century.

BUSINESS

A comprehensive story of the many trades and businesses would require a separate book or books. Therefore this section provides firstly an overview of the early years. For an in depth study a wealth of information can be obtained from the census records, trade directories, and local newspaper archives. Additionally some records of the Wolverton & Stantonbury Co-operative Industrial & Provident Society are held at the National Archives at Kew ref. FS 8/15/536.

THE BREAD AND FLOUR MILL COMPANY

In February 1857 a society was formed at New Bradwell to be called the New Bradwell Bread and Flour Company (limited). With the flour to be ground and dressed in their own mill the commercial intent was to supply the embryo neighbourhood with 'bread of a superior quality, without adulteration, on the best terms for cash.' As for potential investors, 'This society is incorporated under *The Joint Stock Company Act*, for limiting the liabilities of shareholders, by which act subscribers will not be liable beyond the amount of their shares; the capital is £1,000, in two thousand shares of 10s each, with power to increase the capital to £2,000.' This thereby provided a rival to G. Soffe who in April 1859 in calling attention to his genuine home baked bread, 'of the finest quality,' thanked his customers of Stantonbury and Wolverton Station for their support for the last 3 years. He hoped they would continue such favour, as no doubt did Mrs. Harrison, who could supply customers with new milk and cream twice a day from her dairy at Wolverton House.

Meanwhile progress was continuing with the New Bradwell Bread and Flour Company, the shareholders of which were informed at the fourth annual meeting at the mill on March 22nd 1862 that with Mr. McCrindle as the manager the machinery had been completed, and the mill had commenced operations at the beginning of the year. The contractors were Messrs. Death and Cox and by the efforts of several committee members the engine had been altered and re-cleaned to obtain a better supply of water. Additionally pleasing were the figures transacted in the baking department, equating to £2,445 3s 9d in 1858; £2,990 8s 8d in 1859; £3,001 6s 8d in 1860; and £3,775 17s 4d in 1861.

As for other traders in the town these now included J.F. Bailey, hatter and woollen draper at No. 1, Church Street; John Barwell, grocery & provision stores, drapery and clothing warehouse; and H. Kemp, plumber, glazier, painter, paper hanger, and furniture dealer.

In 1864 on the evening of Saturday, March 5th the members and friends of 'Wolverton and Stantonbury Bread and Flour Company' celebrated the union of the two societies with a tea in the schoolroom at New Bradwell. About 400 participated, and at a public meeting afterwards amongst the speakers on the platform was Mr. Pitman, of Manchester, who explained the principles of co-operation.

Of other occupations, in 1866 on the instructions of Mr. W. Pearce on Tuesday, May 15th an auction was conducted at 6pm by Joseph Redden at the Anchor Hotel, Newport Pagnell. This included a newly erected freehold house and premises at New Bradwell, which, 'with attractive corner shop and appurtenances', was in the occupation of John Sykes, tailor and postmaster. The rental was £20 pa, and also in 1866 on the instructions of the proprietor another auction was conducted by Mr. Redden at 6pm on Friday, August 17th. The venue was the New Inn, with Lot. 1 a freehold house and baker's shop with yard, buildings, etc., in School Street in the occupation at a rental of £20 of David Edwards.

In June 1867 the now titled Wolverton & Stantonbury Co-operative Society Ltd., of which Mr. J. Calder was the manager, advertised a good Cornish boiler for sale, 16ft by 4½ ft. Also announced was an extension of the machinery at their flour mills at Stantonbury, by which flour could now be supplied at 'the lowest market price for cash.' However in the following year there would be fewer customers when the railway company removed some hundreds of men from the works at Wolverton. In consequence trade in the district greatly lessened, and, convened by circular in 1869 on the afternoon of Saturday, March 20th, a special meeting of the shareholders of the Wolverton and Stantonbury Co-operative Industrial & Provident Society (Limited) was held at the society's mill. This was to consider the proposition; 'That the Wolverton and Stantonbury Co-operative Industrial and Provident Society (Limited) be wound up voluntarily.' With less than 40 shareholders attending the chair was taken by the chairman of the committee Mr.

Elliott. He then called on the secretary, William Booth, to read the minutes of the last committee meeting, at which an effort had been made to raise £200 by loans from the members of the committee. This was to meet the immediate claims of the corn creditors but having proved ineffective the secretary and several members of the committee felt they had no alternative but to come to the present meeting with the proposition. Should no circumstances arise between this meeting and a subsequent one to be called to confirm the resolution (if passed) it would be recommended that 'in an amicable voluntary manner' the Society should be wound up. In answer to questions from Mr. McCrindle, a former manager, the chairman said that not less 14 days and not more than 28 days must elapse before the next meeting, and in the meantime the business would continue. Seconded by Mr. Wray the resolution was then proposed by Mr. McCrindle and with a few abstentions the voting was 23 for and none against. Wednesday, April 7th was then decided as the date for the next meeting, to be held at 7.30pm at the mill where a liquidator would be appointed. This duly took place and with the chair taken by Mr. Elliott, chairman of the committee, the proposition was moved by Mr. Parker and seconded by Mr. Nelson. With 26 for and none against it was therefore carried unanimously.

Another meeting followed to appoint a liquidator who by recommendation would be George Bennett, auctioneer and estate agent of Buckingham and Stony Stratford. The proposal was put to him that the goods presently on hand should be sold at invoice prices at the Wolverton shop, with the Stantonbury shop closed to save expense. Additionally in the meantime Mr. Bryan, the manager, should bake the bread and rent the premises. Also if practicable that the mill should be let. Subsequently it was announced in August 1869 that the Wolverton & Stantonbury Co-operative Industrial and Provident Society Ltd. was in liquidation. In consequence at 2pm on Thursday, September 23rd - 'by order of the Mortgagees, under their power of sale, in one lot, and subject to such conditions as will then be read' - George Bennett would conduct an auction at the Victoria Hotel, Wolverton, of the steam flour mill, bakehouse, houses, shops etc. at Stantonbury.

Of alternative commercial opportunities a tobacco and cigar

business, 'capitally situated in the rising town of Stantonbury,' was advertised for let in May 1872 - 'Opposite the Post Office.' As for the fortunes of the baking business, in August 1874 on the instructions of 'the proprietor' an auction was conducted by George Bennett on Wednesday, August 26th at the Victoria Hotel, Wolverton, of 'a steam mill with a horizontal steam engine of 20hp by Handyside and Co., Derby, and a Cornish boiler that drives 3 pairs of stones - 3 for wheat, 1 for barley; The mill is admirably adapted for carrying on a large trade, having the advantages of railway and canal communication.' 'Adjoining the mill are two houses, shop, and bakehouse in which is fitted two large coal ovens and now in full trade. John Bryan occupies the houses, bakehouse, and shop at an annual rent of £38 and for several years has carried on the business of baking etc. on the premises. The mill is unoccupied. At the rear of the mill and houses is a large yard with stables, pigsties and premises, and adjoining is a piece of building land having sufficient frontage for the building of 2 houses.' In fact it seemed trade was picking up for in May 1877 tenders were invited by D. Edwards to erect a house, shop, bakehouse and outbuildings at Newport Street, Stantonbury. Applications were to be sent before June 1st and plans and specifications could be viewed at '106, Stantonbury.' Also, in February 1878 a 'strong, young, active man' was required by F. Moore, baker of School Street, Stantonbury, for his baking business - 'Must have knowledge of the trade.'

The former steam mill was on the right of this picture.

Possibly trading from his new premises, in 1879 on Wednesday, September 10th a charge of assault by David Edwards and his namesake son on Daniel Holloway was heard at Newport Pagnell Petty Sessions. Holloway said he was a grocer at Stantonbury and on August 28th had gone to Mr. Edward's shop about some sacks. However Edwards came out in a rage and Holloway said he'd explain if he'd allow him the time. It regarded a sack that his lad had taken away but Edwards and his son then called him and his wife liars. At this Holloway said he wouldn't take cheek from the boy, and resisted when Edwards told him to go out of the shop. According to a witness Edwards then struck him on the head, knocking his hat off. They both fell down the steps together and Edwards then struck him on the nose, making it bleed. Holloway was then charged with assaulting Edwards. However having listened to contradictory evidence the Bench dismissed both cases. Holloway had commenced his business in 1870 and in July 1884 he thanked his customers for their support, announcing that his son, J. Holloway, would now be taking over the trade of 'grocer, tea dealer, wine and provision merchant, greengrocer, coal dealer etc.'

In 1886 after 14 years in business also retiring from business was John Bates. This was due to ill health and on his instructions on Thursday, September 9th an auction was held at the Railway Tavern at 7pm by Messrs. Durham, Gotto, and Samuel of his freehold house, shop and premises. Also the goodwill of his trade as a grocer and general provision dealer. The adjoining cottage was rented by Mrs. Dickson at £5 4s pa, and had the advantage of a well on the premises. As for his former customers they could always patronise the seemingly revitalised 'Industrial & Provident Society', which in 1887 on the evening of Saturday, August 20th held their quarterly meeting in the Science and Art Institute at Wolverton. Here it was resolved to open the Stantonbury branch all day at the earliest opportunity, with it also announced that the new stores should be completed by October next.

Formerly of the water mill at Little Woolstone, in 1892 it was advertised that due to her retirement from business Mrs. S. Ready, of the Steam Flour Mill & Bakery, had instructed J.P. Goodwin to auction on the premises on Tuesday, March 22nd the baking equipment, utensils, three draught horses, and carts. Then because she was now leaving the neighbourhood all the household furniture at the Mill Cottage on Saturday, November 5th. (The story of Mrs. Sarah Ready and her family, and her new life in America, is told in the book in this series Woolstones & Willen.) Also that month on the evening of Tuesday 22nd the Industrial & Provident Society held an adjourned meeting at the Science & Art Institute at Wolverton. The object was to consider the question of the new stores at Bradwell, with the chairman saying the meeting would be aware that the society had purchased the property at Bradwell from Messrs. Lindow and Co. at Stantonbury. They had paid £500 and had asked a practical builder to provide the cost of building new stores and also of altering the present building. The cost of altering equated to £80 and for building a new stores £210. The probable cost of the buildings, fittings etc. would total about £800, and in view of this on the part of the members the committee thought it wise to build a new stores. The old shop could be let for various purposes at about £10pa but Mr. Aldred, in considering the financial position, asked if the society was in a position to build. In reply the secretary, Mr. Vickers, said that having investigated their resources the financial committee of the wholesale society were prepared to advance money on the property. As for the chairman, he said the place they already occupied had insufficient accommodation for the increased business they were doing - and indeed hoped to do. Consequent to

A BIG PUSH-OVER

Photo: Derek Snow, Newport Pagnell.

Miss Ann Rogers, star of "My Fair Lady" gives the pile of pennies at the Morning Star, New Bradwell, a final good luck hug before pushing them over last week. Mr. W. Howe, (left) the licensee, looks on.

The Morning Star (shown on p. 66) was one of the later public houses and occupied land on the meadow side of the Newport Road. In 1964 (above) a pile of pennies collected for charity got a ceremonial 'pushover'.

the discussions it was then moved, seconded, and carried that a new stores should be erected at Bradwell.

Indeed the project soon commenced and in 1893 on Saturday, March 25th a tea and public meeting was held by the 'Wolverton Co-operative Society' to celebrate the opening of a new branch shop at Stantonbury. About 120 sat down to tea and at the meeting afterwards Mr. C. Barley presided over a good attendance. Here the secretary, Mr. F. Vickers, read a statement showing the branch had first opened in October 1883 with £8 as the first week's takings. More lately the average week's trade for the quarter ending December 1892 was £42.

Then in 1894 at noon on Tuesday, July 3rd an auction would be conducted at Bradwell mill by Geo. Wigley of valuable machinery. Included would be an 18hp horizontal condensing engine by Handyside (Derby), a Lancashire 26hp boiler, and a massive grinding frame with 4 pairs of 4ft stones. Viewings could be arranged on application to Thomas Kibble, Thompson Street, Stantonbury. The end of the decade saw the sad loss of a link with Stantonbury's business past, when in 1899 on Monday, February 27th the death occurred at the age of 84 of Isaac Sykes. He was the father of the post master and for many years had been in business as a tailor at

Left: The windmill at the beginning of the 20th century, derelict but still with a sails framework.
Right: The restored windmill.

Stantonbury. When he had to relinquish this because of infirmity he then lived for several years in one of the Revis's Alms Houses, where he died.

BRADWELL WINDMILL

Today a prominent feature at New Bradwell is the restored windmill. Here are two accounts of its history, the first written by Sir Frank Markham in 1947, and a more recent account by Bryan Dunleavy in his book *Pure Republic* (2019).

"About 1750 Henry Wilmin owned a field of nearly 9 acres 'called or known by the name of the Yawles, bounded on the north-east by the road leading to Bradwell' and on the north west by what is now the canal. On his death in 1773 he left this property to his daughters Elizabeth Wilkinson and Mary Brooks and in 1788 the Bradwell enclosure Award confirmed their ownership. During the next 20 years the property changed hands several times. In 1800 the Grand Junction Canal was constructed which now became the north west boundary of the field and the Bradwell Road bridge was also built. About 1802 Samuel Holman became possessed of the southern strip of 1 acre and not only fenced it off but also laid plans for building a 'smock mill for thee grinding of corn.' In 1817 he mortgaged the 'lately erected smock mill' and the acre of land to William Curtis so the mill must have been erected between 1803 and 1816. The value of mill and land was £600. William Curtis died in 1826 and left his land and mill first to his wife and then to his 4 year old son William when he reached 21. In 1846 William the younger mortgaged the mill to John Lovell. He had married a year earlier Ann Basford and a third William Curtis was born on November 18th 1845. Like his father he became heir to the mill at 4 years of age. Meanwhile the mill was let to Mr Adams whose family continued as millers until 1864 when the great sails revolved for the last time. In 1867 the mill with its 'wheels, stones and machinery' were sold to John Abbott for £422 10s. Since then it has slowly become a ruin. The grandson of the last miller, Robert Adams, resides now at Stony Stratford.")

Bradwell Windmill (from *Pure Republic*)

The most prominent feature of New Bradwell at this time was the windmill, built by Samuel Holman in 1805 and operated by him until his death in 1825. Thereafter it was run by his widow and son. It was probably sold after this and the millers thereafter appear to be tenants.

Windmills were rare in the district. The river, relatively slow as it was, provided sufficient power for mills at Stratford, Wolverton and Haversham. In the 1841 census, William Carr is the miller. He appears to come from the long standing family of millers at Haversham Mill, sometimes known as Carr's Mill. He was recorded here with his wife Frances, both with given ages of 50. They had two sons, John, aged 14 and William 12, and employed a 20 year old William Lambert to assist with the working of the mill.

A few years later they moved to Castlethorpe Mill, where they are recorded for the next two censuses. I don't know much about mills, but I would imagine that a watermill (as Castlethorpe Mill was) would have been more productive than a windmill, due to a constant source of power.

The miller in 1851 was George James, born in Bradwell 33 years earlier. He has with him a 24 year old wife Mary and their 1 year old son Edwin. They employed a 13 year old female domestic servant Harriet Morris and John Colley, a 20 year old miller's assistant. But by the next census he had changed his trade to that of carpenter and the mill was in the hands of William James, 55, possibly an older brother.

The 1871 miller was Robert Saxby from Kent. He was 50 and with quite a large brood with him. There were nine children ranging in age from 1 to 22. Saxby was certainly a career miller. Starting in Kent, he moved to Weston Underwood for a few years prior to his move to Bradwell. After 1876 he moved with his large family to the Eling Tide Mill in Hampshire, and it was probably at this time that the Bradwell mill ceased to be a working mill. In 1881 it was occupied as a residence but not as a working mill.

The turnover would suggest that this was not an economic mill, except perhaps in its early days.

It was pretty much derelict for the first half of the 20th Century. The Wolverton Urban District Council acquired it for a mere £80 in 1949, which was possibly all it was worth. It was restored some years later.

St. James Street shops.

From the back of Spencer Street. The building with the tall chimney was a bakery.

BRADWELL AND NEW BRADWELL BUSINESSES

These pages from the trade directories list the many commercial enterprises from the beginning of the 20th century to the beginning of WW2. New Bradwell did not exist in 1854. The trade directory for that year shows only commercial activity at the wharf.

from the year 1577. The living is a vicarage, net yearly value £40, with residence, in the gift of the Lord Chancellor, and held since 1869 by the Rev. Kitelee Chandos-Baily B.A. of University College, Durham, who is also incumbent of Tattenhoe. Here is a small Wesleyan Methodist chapel and a Baptist chapel, built in 1856, with 250 sittings. There is a charity of about £13 17s. a year, left by the Rev. J. Hume for distribution to poor householders and for the education of six children; there are also 15 acres of land awarded to the poor in lieu of common rights when the parish was inclosed in 1788, the rent of which is given in coals. William Selby-Lowndes, jun. esq. is lord of the manor. Mrs. Jones and Robert Wylie esq. are the chief landowners. The soil is light clay; subsoil, clay and stone. The chief crops are wheat, oats, barley and beans. The area is 912 acres of land and 5 of water; assessable value, £10,745; the population, with New Bradwell, in 1911 was 3,938, excluding that place, 380.

The population of Bradwell ecclesiastical parish in 1911 was 420.

Post Office, Bradwell.—John Buckingham, sub-postmaster. Letters through Wolverton, Bucks, arrive at 7.20 a.m. & 12.15 & 6.35 p.m.; box cleared at 9.10 a.m. & 1 & 6.55 p.m.; sundays, 9.10 a.m. Stantonbury, 1 mile distant, is the nearest money order & telegraph office

Elementary School (infants), erected by the London & North Western Railway, & opened in 1891; transferred to County Council in 1903, for 40 children; Mrs. Ada Mills, mistress

NEW BRADWELL is a portion of this parish for civil purposes, but for ecclesiastical it is a separate vicarage annexed to Stantonbury; it is situated on the north-east side of the Wolverton railway works, and is principally inhabited by the men employed there. There is a station here on the branch of the London and North Western railway from Wolverton to Newport Pagnell, opened in 1867. New Bradwell is supplied with water and gas from works the property of the Railway Company. St. James' church, erected in 1860, for New Bradwell and Stantonbury, is a building of stone in the Geometric style, from designs by the late G. E. Street esq. R.A. consisting of chancel, nave of four bays, aisles, south chapel, south porch and an unfinished tower at the north-west angle, containing one bell: a north aisle was added

in 1890; there are sittings for about 500 persons. Owing to the "instrument" substituting the rights and privileges of St. Peter's to St. James's consecrated in 1850, being lost, or never made out, a special Act of Parliament had to be passed legalising 1,000 marriages on a fresh instrument title, the old church thus, on July 1st, 1909, becoming the chapel of a conventional district. The ancient church of St. Peter's, STANTONBURY, is situate close to the river Ouse and possesses many features of architectural interest, including a richly carved Norman arch between the nave and the chancel: a sanctus bell dated 1150, also a pedestal and arches separating the north aisle from the nave, chauntrey, also an altar and credence table of the time of King Stephen, were found in 1910: services are held here only during the summer months. The register dates from the year 1653. The living is a vicarage, annexed to that of Stantonbury, joint net yearly value £176. with residence and 2 acres of glebe, in the gift of Earl Spencer, and held since 1908 by the Rev. Allan Newman Guest M.A. of Trinity College, Dublin. The church and schools, with residences, were built principally by the shareholders of the London and North Western Railway Company, and opened in 1860. There is a Primitive Methodist chapel in Thompson street, built in 1865, costing £935, and affords 200 sittings; also a Baptist chapel in North street, and a Gospel hall in Caledonian road. There is a working Men's Social Club and Liberal and Radical Club, and the Bradwell and Wolverton Good Samaritan Society. The land is principally the property of Earl Spencer K.G. and the London and North Western Railway Company. The population of the ecclesiastical parish of Stantonbury in 1911 was 3,555.

Parish Clerk, Arthur Beach.

Post, M. O., T. & Telephonic Express Delivery Office, Stantonbury.—Charles Frederick Sykes, sub-postmaster. Letters through Wolverton, Bucks, arrive at 6.30 & 11.30 a.m. & 6 p.m.; dispatched at 9.30 a.m. & 12.25, 2.10 & 8 p.m.; sundays, 8 p.m

Wall Letter Boxes.—Newport road, cleared at 9.40 a.m. & 2.10 & 8.5 p.m.; sundays, 7.50 p.m.; & Bradwell road, cleared at 9.30 a.m. & 1.20 & 7.15 p.m.; sundays, 9.30 a.m

Elementary School (mixed), New Bradwell, built in 1859 & since enlarged, to accommodate 1,000 children; J. Irving Brooks, master; Miss Amy Williams, mistress; Miss Sarah Ann Heacock, infants' mistress

Railway Station, Bradwell, George Thomas Foxon, station master

BRADWELL.

PRIVATE RESIDENTS.

Bellairs-Harries Mrs. Bradwell house
Chandos-Baily Rev. Kitelee B.A. (vicar), Vicarage

COMMERCIAL.

Buckingham John, baker, Post office, Loughton road
Coe Elizabeth (Miss), grocer, 20 Vicarage road
Foulks James, shopkpr. 2 Vicarage rd
Sargeant Arthur, Bell P.H. Abbey rd
Stares John, farmer
Walters Henry A. W. beer retailer, Vicarage road
Wilson Edgar, Victoria P.H. Vicarage road
Wylie Charles, farmer, Stantonbury park (letters through Newport Pagnell)

NEW BRADWELL.

PRIVATE RESIDENTS.

Brooks J. Irving, 19 Queen Anne st
Budds William James, Stanton lodge, Bradwell road
Edward David, Glyn ho. Newport rd
Guest Rev. Allan Newman M.A. (vicar), The Vicarage, Bradwell rd
Miles Charles Henry, High street
Sansom Rev. Arthur Wm. (Baptist), 3 Newport road
Sutton John Charles J.P. The Mount, Bradwell road
Wilson Alfred William, Newport road
Wylie Alderman Robert, The Limes, Bradwell road

COMMERCIAL.

Bates Wm. grocer, 101 Newport road
Beach Arthur, general dealer & assistant overseer & clerk to Parish Council, parish clerk & insurance agent, 11 Queen Anne street
Bell Mark William, agent British Petroleum Co. 1 Newport road
Bellchambers Nathaniel Joseph, incandescent gas fittings, 103 Newport road
Blunt George, chimney sweep, 25 Newport road
Bradwell & Wolverton Good Samaritan Society (Sidney William Freeman, sec)
Brown Albert, shopkpr. 31 School st
Budds William James, surveyor & sanitary inspector for the Bradwell district of the Newport Pagnell Rural District Council, North st
Busby Harry, bill poster, 29 Newport road
Button George, butcher, 141 Newport road
Clark George, grocer, 20 High street
Compton Amy (Mrs.), shopkeeper, 48 High street
Cooper Jas. boot ma. 44 St. James' st
Curtis Caroline (Miss), shopkeeper, 3 Bradwell road
Davies William, house furnisher, 175 Newport road
Derricutt Fras. photogrphr.9 North st
Dormer Eleanor (Miss), dress maker. Caledonian road
Durham Fredk. grocer, 44 High st
Eales Emma (Mrs.), shopkeeper, 33 Queen Anne street
Elliott Annie (Mrs.), shopkeeper, 26 High street
Essam Thomas, boot & shoe maker, 34 St. James' street
Floyd Elizabeth (Mrs.), shopkeeper, 105 Newport road
Giltrow Thomas, Cuba hotel, 81 Newport road
Gurney Bros. monumental masons, Newport road
Harrup James, baker, 24 High street
Harvey Jn. Owen M.R.C.S., L.R.C.P. Lond. (surgery), 109 Newport road
Haseldine Heber, fishmonger, 4 St. Giles' street
Hepworth Joseph, shopkeeper, 25 Spencer street
Hewlett Joseph, shopkeeper, 139 Newport road
Hyde Frederick. shopkpr. 5 School st
Jacocks Frank, Railway tavern,Glyn st
Jesson Elizabeth (Mrs.), shopkeeper, 25 Queen Ann street
Kemp Henry & Sons, builders, 11 Newport road
Knight Frederick Arthur,boot maker, 7 Caledonian road
Liberal & Radical Club (T. H. Harris. sec.), 12 Newport road
Lines Henry William, hair dresser 181, & tobacconist 77, Newport rd
Lloyd Eliza (Mrs.), fancy goods dlr. 23 High street
London Central Meat Co. Limited, 32 High street
Masters Peter, baker, 4 Glyn street
Miles Charles Henry L.R.C.P.Lond. surgeon, & medical officer & public vaccinator No. 4 district, Newport Pagnell union, High street; & at 51 Stratford road, Wolverton
Moore & Pearce, bakers, 55 Spencer st

BUCKS. 4

76

James' street
Mynard Sidney Frederick, grocer, 175 Newport road
National Deposit Friendly Society (Fredk. Trood, sec.), 8 Newport rd
Neale Frank Edmund, news agent, 47 Newport rd. & printer, 2 Glyn st
Norman Arthur, greengrocer, 5 Caledonian road
Norman Dennis, shopkeeper, 83 Newport road
Nutt John Edward & Sons, wheelwrights, Newport road
Palmer Thos. butcher, 23 Newport st
Pearce William F. baker, see Moore & Pearce
Penny Edmund John M.D.Brux., M.R.C.S.Eng., L.S.A. (surgery), 191 Newport road
Puryer Alexander Charles, greengrocer, 27 Newport road
Pratt William Ernest, hair dresser, 30 High street

Robbins Kate (Miss), shopkeeper, 147 Newport road
Robinson Frederick, beer retailer, Newport road
Rolfe Caroline (Mrs.), midwife, 22 High street
Sayell David, fried fish dealer, 26 Spencer street
Scrivener Alice (Mrs.), confectioner, 56 Spencer street
Seabrook Frederick, undertaker, St. James' street
Sellick Edwin John, motor engineer, Newport road
Sharp Bros. drapers, 46 St. James' st
Souster Thomas, boot & shoe maker, 13 Queen Anne street
Squires Thomas, New inn, Bradwell rd
Stanton Frank M. baker, 173 Newport road
Stantonbury Assembly Hall (George Ashley, sec.), 131 Newport road

Dudley, sec.), St. James' street
Styles Percy, grocer, 52 High street
Sykes Charles Frederick, tailor, Post office, Glyn street
Tarry George, butcher, 46 High st
Tarry Sam, butcher, 17 St. Mary's st
Thomas William Hayman, County Arms P.H. 189 Newport road
Thompson Alfred Edward, plumber, 137 Newport road
Toogood Arthur, Foresters' Arms P.H. 21 Newport road
Tranfield & Co. builders, 17 Queen Anne street
Trood Walter, brewers' agent, 193 Newport road
Verrall Lionel Thomas, grocer, 9 Queen Anne street
Whitaker William, chemist, 32 St. James' street
Wolverton Industrial & Provident Society Limited (branch), 42 High st
Woodward Benj. boot ma. 50 High st

The Trade directory from 1939

BRADWELL, with NEW BRADWELL.

BRADWELL is a parish one mile south from the Wolverton station on the main line of the London, Midland and Scottish railway, 3¾ south-east from Stony Stratford and 4½ from Newport Pagnell, in the Buckingham division of the county, county court district of Bletchley and Leighton Buzzard, hundred, petty sessional division and rural district of Newport Pagnell, rural deanery of Wolverton, archdeaconry of Buckingham and diocese of Oxford. Gas and electricity are available. The church of St. Lawrence, given in 1275 to the priory of St. Mary at Tickford, is an ancient edifice of stone in the Early English and Decorated styles, consisting of small chancel, nave, south aisle, with an arcade of three bays, north porch and a western tower containing 4 bells, of which two were made by de Wymbris about 1300: in 1909 the bells were restored, and their number increased to six, the gift of Charles Daily esq. in memory of his father, but the upper part of the tower has been removed: remains of a 13th century inscription still appear on the chancel arch: the church was restored in 1868, and affords 170 sittings. The register dates from the year 1577. The living is a vicarage, net yearly value £320, with residence, in the gift of the Lord Chancellor, and held since 1927 by the Rev. Conway Davies M.A. of Selwyn College, Cambridge. There is a small Methodist chapel and a Baptist chapel, built in 1859, with 250 sittings. There is a charity of about £12 17s. a year, left by the Rev. J. Hume for distribution to poor householders and for the education of six children; there are also 15 acres of land awarded to the poor in lieu of common rights when the parish was inclosed in 1788, the rent of which is given in coals. Lt.-Col. W. Selby-Lowndes O.B.E., T.D., J.P. is lord of the manor, and Messrs.

Wylie Brothers are the chief landowners. The soil is light clay; subsoil, clay and stone. The chief crops are wheat, oats, barley and beans. The area is 677 acres of land and inland water; the population in 1931 was 421.

By the Bucks Review Order, 1934, New Bradwell was amalgamated with Wolverton to form the new parish of Wolverton, co-extensive with the urban district. Post Office, Bradwell. Letters through Bletchley. New Bradwell nearest M. O. & Wolverton nearest T. office

NEW BRADWELL is an ecclesiastical parish, through which the river Ouse flows, formed 31 March, 1919, and annexed to Stantonbury; for local government purposes it is attached to Wolverton, under Wolverton Urban District Council, of which it is a ward; it is situated on the north-east side of the Wolverton railway works, and is principally inhabited by the men employed there. There is a station here on the branch of the London, Midland and Scottish railway from Wolverton to Newport Pagnell, opened in 1867. New Bradwell is supplied with water and gas from works the property of the Railway Company. St. James' church, erected in 1860, for New Bradwell and Stantonbury, is a building of stone in the Geometric style, consisting of chancel, nave of four bays, aisles, south chapel, south porch and a tower at the north-west angle, containing one bell: a north aisle was added in 1868: there are sittings for about 300 persons. Owing to the "instrument" substituting the rights and privileges of St. Peter's to St. James's consecrated in 1850, being lost, or never made out, a special Act of Parliament had to be passed legalising 1,000 marriages on a fresh instrument title, the old church thus, on July 1st, 1909, becoming the chapel of a conventional district.

The ancient church of St. Peter's, STANTONBURY, is situate close to the river Ouse and possesses many features of architectural interest, including a richly carved Norman arch between the nave and the chancel: a sanctus bell, a pedestal and arches separating the north aisle from the nave, undated, and an altar and credence table of mediæval date, were found in 1910: services are held here only during the summer months. A new organ was installed in 1930. The register dates from the year 1653. The living is a vicarage, with that of Stantonbury annexed, joint net yearly value £300, with residence, in the gift of the Bishop of Oxford, and held since 1908 by the Rev. Allan Newman Guest M.A. of Trinity College, Dublin. The church and schools, with residences, were built principally by the shareholders of the London and North Western (now London, Midland and Scottish) Railway Company, and opened in 1860. There is a Methodist chapel in Thompson street, built in 1865, with 200 sittings; also a Baptist chapel

in North street, built in 1936, a Gospel hall in Caledonian road and a Salvation Army hall. There is a Working Men's Social Club and Liberal and Radical Club, and the Bradwell and Wolverton Good Samaritan Society. The manor of Stantonbury, originally called Stantonbury from the 14th century till the early part of the 17th century, is recorded in Domesday Book as belonging to Miles Crispin, whose subfeudatory here was Ralph. Ralph's descendants bore the name of Barre, and from them this manor obtained its appellative name of Barry in addition to Stanton, being held by them till the end of the 14th century. The manor of Stantonbury subsequently was held by the families of Vaux, Temple, Wittewrong, Spencer and now belongs to that of Wylie. The London, Midland and Scottish Railway Co. are the principal landowners. Post, M. O. & T. Office, New Bradwell. Letters through Bletchley

Railway Station

BRADWELL.

PRIVATE RESIDENTS.
(For T N's see general list of Private Residents at end of book.)
de Chair Maj. G. H. B., O.B.E., M.C. Bradwell house
Davies Rev. Conway M.A. (vicar), Vicarage

Barington May (Miss), draper, 25 Queen Anne st
Blunt George, chimney sweep, 25 Newport road
Bradwell Progressive Workmen's Club (Thos. H. Harris, sec.), 132 Newport rd. Wolverton 3128
Bradwell & Wolverton Good Samaritan Society (Albt. Edwd. Attar-

London Central Meat Co. Ltd. butchers, 22 High st
Martin Geo. confctnr.136 Newport rd
Martin W. (Mrs.), confctnr. 34 St. James' st
Max David Jn. M.B., Ch.B.Edin. physcn. & surgn. (attends 11 a.m. to 6 p.m. weekdays); surgery, 151 Newport rd

77

New Bradwell estate
Bell P.H. (Arth. Sargent), Abbey rd
Bird Thos. H. Mdr. Primrose rd. Wolverton 2124
Buckingham Arth. Wm. baker, Loughton rd
Davies Chas. Hy. chimney sweep, 54 Vicarage rd
°Foolks Edwin Geo. farmer, Manor farm
Hancock Alice Elsie (Mrs.), shopkpr. 20 Vicarage rd
Hancock Ernest, shopkpr
°King Harry, farmer, Glebe farm
Marchant Albt. poultry farmer, Meat ho
Old Bradwell Cricket Club (N. Chapman, sec.), 24 Abbey rd
Prince Albert P.H. (Jn. Whittaker), Vicarage rd
Stimson Roger, shopkpr. & post office, Primrose rd. Wolverton 3244
Turner Jn. Chas. nurseryman, 10 Vicarage rd. Wolverton 3100
Victoria P.H. (Jas. Smith), Vicarage rd
Wolverton Industrial & Provident Society Ltd. East view. Wolverton 2103
Wylie Bros. farmers

NEW BRADWELL.

PRIVATE RESIDENTS.

(For T N's see general list of Private Residents at end of book.)

Brown Albert J.F. Mabley villa, Newport road
Brownsill Jn. 11 Newport rd
Cotten Fredk. Wm. Wltr. The Mount, Bradwell rd
Guest Rev. Allan Newman M.A. (vicar), The Vicarage, Bradwell rd
Oldroyd Clifford Vipont, The Laurels, High street
Robinson Frederick, Glyn house,Newport road
Wylie John Alexander, The Limes, Bradwell road

COMMERCIAL.

Alcock Florence Sarah (Mrs.), hardware dlr. 26 St. James' st
Allen T. J. boot repr. 44 St. James' st
Asplin Herbt. J. butcher, 50 High st
Barber A. J. (Chemists) Ltd. chemists, 32 St. James' st
Barten Louisa (Mrs.), shopkpr. 24 High st

port rd
Busby Harry, bill poster. 29 Newport road
Carroll Harry Manning, wireless engnr. 175a, Newport rd. & 2 Wood st. Wolverton 3172
Chaplin Bertram Jn.drapr.28 High st
Clamp Wm. J. H. boot & shoe dlr. 97 Newport rd
Clark Clara (Mrs.), grocer,20 High st
Cook Regnld. Frank, shopkpr. 199 Newport rd
Costelow Bros. shopkprs. 33 Queen Anne st
County Arms P.H. (Jn. Geo. Clifford Elliot), 189 Newport rd
Cox Geo. Edwd. carpntr. 62 St. Giles' st
Craddock Fras. Chas. grocer, confectioner & fried fish dlr, Old Bradwell rd
Cuba Hotel (Arth. L. Freeman), 81 Newport rd
Davies Alice (Mrs.), shopkpr. 56 Spencer st
Derricutt Fras. haulage contrctr. 9 North st. Wolverton 2140
Dickens Fredk. Jn. shopkpr. 15 Queen Anne st
Durham Archbld. Jack, grocer, 44 High st
Elliott Hy. J. Gilbt. undertaker, 94 Newport rd. Wolverton 2175
Faithfull Bros. bakers, 4 Glyn st
Fildes Marjorie A. (Mrs.), M.B.,Ch.B. Manch. physcn. & surgn. 109 Newport rd
Forresters' Arms P.H. (Vincent West), 21 Newport rd
Foster Madge (Mrs.), confetnr. 26 High st
Fowkes Geo. boot repr. 9 North st
Gayner Sydney Geo. greengro. 46 High st
Goodman E. Bros. scrap metal mers. 73 East view, Newport rd
Gurney A. W. & Son, monumental masons, Newport rd. Wolverton 3140
Ingram Elsie (Miss), shopkpr. 135 Newport rd
Jones Frank, grocer, 1 Bradwell rd
Knight Fredk. Arth. boot repr. 13 Queen Anne st
Lane Thos. Hy. insur. agt. 68 Newport rd
Limes Hy. Wm. & Son, tobccnsts. 77 & 181 Newport rd
Lloyd Sarah Jane (Miss), fancy goods dlr. 25 High st

(Green), Newport rd
National Deposit Friendly Society (A. Young, local sec.), 2 St.Giles' st
New Bradwell Allotment Society Ltd. (Geo. Harry Cross, sec.), 5 Harwood st
New Inn (Thos. Squires), Bradwell rd
Oldroyd CliffordVipont M.R.C.S.Eng., L.R.C.P.Lond. physcn. & surgn. The Laurels, High st. Wolverton 3179
Osborne Florence Edith (Mrs.), news agent, 155 Newport road
Osborne Jas.Wltr. newsagt. 4a,Glyn st
Packer Albt. Edwd. haulage contrctr. 5 Wood st. & Glyn st
Palmer Thos. & Chas. butchers, 23 Newport rd. Wolverton 3165
Phillips Hy. T. shopkpr. 83 Newport rd
Pratt Wm. Ernest, hairdrssr. 6 Glyn st
Puryer Alice (Mrs.), confetnr. 27 Newport rd
Railway Tavern (Bernard Smeeton Garrett), Glyn st
Rainbow Eliza (Mrs.), confetnr. Newport rd
Read Eliz. Ann (Mrs.), fried fish dlr. 175 Newport rd
Riverside Tennis Club (Mrs. G. Seabrook, sec.), 24 Newport rd
Robinson Arth. registrar of births & deaths (attends mon. 12 noon to 1 p.m.), 11 Queen Anne st
Sayell Sarah (Mrs.), fried fish dlr. 26 Spencer st
Seabrook Ada (Mrs.). shopkpr. 30 St. James' st
Sellick W. G. & Son, motor engnrs. Newport rd. Wolverton 3117
Short Albt. Hy.fruitr.101 Newport rd
Simmonds E. (Miss), district nurse, 130 Newport rd
Stantonbury St. Peter's Football Club (Arth. Wood, hon. sec)
Stantonbury Social Workmen's Club (Bt. Cook, sec.), St. James' st. Wolverton 3141
Styles Fred, grocer & post office, 52 High st. Wolverton 2136
Tarry Sam & Sons, butchers, 27 St. Mary's st
Tattam Wilfred, grocer, 46 St.James' st
Taylor Thos. Fredk. watch mkr. 46a, High st
Turvey E. O. & Sons, builders & decorators, 29 Queen Anne st. Wolverton 3188

Turvey Lionel Geo. hairdrssr. 139 Newport rd
Verrall Victor Fredk. shopkpr. 9 Queen Anne st
Walters Harold Percy, carpntr. 17 Queen Anne st. & 44 St. Mary st

Warren A. & B. boot reprs. 2a, St. Giles' st
Wolverton Industrial & Provident Society Ltd. (branch), 32 to 40 High st. & 141 & 173 Newport rd

Wolverton Urban District Council Rates Office (attends tues. 2 to 4.30 p.m.; sat. 9.30 to 11.30 a.m.), 137 Newport rd
Woodward Benj. J.P. coal mer. Church st

BRADWELL ABBEY, formerly extra-parochial, is now a parish 2 miles south from Wolverton station, on the London, Midland and Scottish railway, 4 south-east from Stony Stratford and 5 from Newport Pagnell, in the Buckingham division of the county, county court district of Bletchley and Leighton Buzzard, hundred, petty sessional division and rural district of Newport Pagnell. Electricity is available.

About a quarter of a mile west from Bradwell stood the Benedictine priory of St. Mary, founded about 1155 by Maindelin, Baron of Wolverton, originally as a cell to the monastery of Suffield, the revenue of which in the 23rd of Henry VIII. was £33 11s. 2d.; the priory appears to have been partly rebuilt as a mansion, and is now a farmhouse; it was formerly moated and approached through an avenue of trees. Near the house is a small chapel now disused; it is about 19 feet long and 12 wide, with a south doorway of the Late Decorated period, good mullioned window at one end and similar windows on either side. Wolverton Industrial and Provident Society Ltd. are the principal landowners. The soil is cold clay; subsoil, stone and clay. The chief crops are wheat, barley and beans. The area is 447 acres; the population in 1931 was 18.

This parish is reputed to be extra-parochial for ecclesiastical purposes.

Letters through Bletchley. Bradwell nearest post office & New Bradwell nearest M. O. & T. office

Wolverton Industrial & Provident Society Ltd. Bradwell Abbey farm.

SELLICK'S GARAGE

Sellick's Garage on the Newport Road.

Born at Huntspill, Somerset, on August 4th 1879, Edwin John Sellick was the son of William Sellick, 'a striker at an engine works,' and his wife Emma. Both were born at Bridgewater and in 1881 with the family living at Huntspill their ages, as per the census, were respectively 25 and 26. In 1883 a daughter Emma was born but sadly she died that year. In 1884 on September 13th a son, William George, was born and in 1901 resident with his parents at Huntspill was in occupation as a fitter's apprentice. As for Edwin he was now employed as a steam engine fitter, boarding at 38, Albermarle Road, Taunton, with James Priest, a cabinet maker, and his family. In 1904 Edwin married Annie Pearce, born at Derby in 1878 on October 26th, and in 1911 they were resident in Spencer Street, Stantonbury, with Edwin in business as a motor cycle agent. Having obtained his first driving licence in 1902 he had owned a Triumph motor cycle and the business developed into the repair of motor cycles and bicycles. As for motor cars, his first had been a single cylinder Aster (apparently the only way it could get up Black Horse hill was in reverse!) and, being one of the original car owners in the district, in 1912 he bought a Standard Ten.

His brother William was also pursuing an engineering career and in 1908 when in occupation as an engine fitter he married Fanny Ethel Stevens at Huntspill parish church on August 4th. She was a farmer's daughter and had been born at Huntspill. In 1910 a son,

Raymond William Edwin Sellick was born on January 18th and in 1911 the family were living at Newcastle Cottage, Huntspill, with William in occupation as an engineer's fitter with the locomotive works of a railway company. Then in 1913 a daughter, Ruby Annie Sellick, was born on August 21st.

In 1915 William joined his brother Edwin in the business at New Bradwell but when called for war service he joined the RNVR in 1917 on June 25th. He was engaged as a motor mechanic in the London Motor Boat Section, associated with the vessel 'Hermione,' and during this time his wife was living at 9, Giles Street, Stantonbury. After demobilisation on February 26th 1920 he rejoined his brother in the New Bradwell business, which was advertised that year as being the sole district agent for Rudge-Whitworth motorcycles & cycles. Additionally for some years the brothers would have a contract with the Government for collecting the mail from Wolverton and delivering it by car to Newport Pagnell. Also they would operate a taxi and car hire service. In fact theirs was a car used at the first such wedding at Wolverton and the bride's mother was so worried that a policeman was placed on duty!

In other progress the Sellick's garage at New Bradwell was the forerunner of electricity in the district, having its own electric light plant long before the rest of the area. In 1926 it seems that Edwin joined a London firm as a consultant engineer and William, resident at 49, Newport Road, New Bradwell, took over the business, which in 1932 became agents for Morris and Singer cars. Yet despite having left the business Edwin appears to have retained links with the district, for in 1932 he was the outgoing Worshipful Master of the Wolverton Scientific Lodge of Masons.

In 1935 William's son, Ray William Edwin Sellick, joined the firm which thereon became W.G. Sellick & Son. Also that year Ray married Ethel Cownley of Wolverton. She was born in 1908 on August 27th at Great Harwood, Lancs., but in 1911 was resident at 21, Victoria Street, Wolverton, where her father was general manager of the Co-operative Society. In 1939 Ray and his wife were resident in Wolverton at 36, Western Road, his occupation being that of a garage proprietor and auto engineer. William and his wife were resident at 49, Newport Road, New Bradwell, and apart from being a garage proprietor he would be greatly involved with the New Bradwell Nursing Association. Also head ARP Warden, an entry from a school log book of July 22nd 1941 reading, 'Mr. Sellick, Chief Warden for New Bradwell, came and inspected every child's gas mask. Repairs were carried out by ARP members.' Meanwhile Edwin, in occupation as a consulting engineer, was living with his wife at Exeter but following his retirement in 1941 they returned to New Bradwell.

In 1946 the Sellick's acquired the engineering business and premises of the late Mr. C.H. Gabell at 27, Church Street, Wolverton, retaining Mr. J. Woodard as the resident mechanic. Then in 1958 came further expansion when the firm's garage was built at Wolverton in Stratford Road. However in 1968 the business was sold to a Hemel Hempstead firm on November 25th. Edwin died aged 93 in 1972. William died in 1974 at Northampton General Hospital on Wednesday, May 8th, and Ray died in 1991 on September 6th at 3, The Coppice, Dawlish.

Part of the garage preserved in the Milton Keynes Museum.

HARRY LINES

In 1940 on March 28th the death occurred of Harry Lines at the age of 85. For 55 years he had been a barber at New Bradwell, and in 1900 on July 14th when Day's Menagerie visited the town he went into the lion's cage for a wager and, in full view of the townspeople, shaved the keeper! He was presented with a certificate which he hung in his salon ever since.

Born at Leckhampstead he left farm work in his youth to seek work firstly in a shipyard at Barrow in Furness and then at the L&NWR railway works at Crewe. Subsequently at Wolverton Works as a striker but he then set up on his own account as a barber with the later assistance of his son. He continued in work until a week before he died. The business would then be carried on by his son whose siblings were four daughters and three sons, one, Harry, living in Australia. Apart from barbering in other activities Mr. Lines made two penny farthing bicycles, riding to London on one. However he returned by train! Also he repaired and recovered umbrellas, made walking sticks and also the scissors which he used in his business. He was buried in the grave of his wife who predeceased him by 22 years.

WILLIAM WHITAKER

Having been in business as a chemist at New Bradwell for 17 years, in 1941 William Whitaker died on Thursday, September 11th aged 75. A native of Lancashire he was educated at Manchester Grammar School and on passing the necessary exams practised first as a chemist at Accrington and then at Brierfield, in Lancs. Then to Redbourne in Hertfordshire and in 1912 to New Bradwell. He opened a shop in St. James Street but in 1929 acquired a practice at Hitchin, where he was joined in partnership by his younger son John Lightfoot Whitaker. He carried on working until he died, leaving a widow and two sons.

THE CUBA

Dating from around 1860, the Cuba is said to be the only pub in the country of that name. Of the early landlords the antics of those of 'Billy the Black' seem the most intriguing; not least from an episode involving the barmaid's bed! In 1875 the Cuba was purchased for £1,850 by Messrs. Allfrey & Lovell, as part of a package with other such premises. In 1882 Thomas Giltrow became the landlord and

The Cuba in better days - celebrating the diamond jubilee of Queen Victoria's reign.

the field directly opposite became commonly known as 'Giltrow's Field.' Here popular entertainments were staged but for larger events an open space at Corner Pin was used. This could accommodate travelling circuses such as that at which the barber Harry Lines, whose shop was next door but one to the Cuba, earned his certificate for entering the lion's cage and shaving the keeper! Thomas had a large family, to include a 2½ year old son Arthur who in 1886 on Monday, September 20th sadly drowned in the river. Leaving a widow, 8 sons and 5 daughters, Thomas died aged 78 in 1927 on Wednesday, January 19th, and that month the licence was transferred from Mrs. Giltrow to John Hyde, steward of Wolverton Workingmen's Club. In 1935 the licence was transferred from Sidney Russell (of marital tribulations) to William Goodman, from whom it was transferred in November 1938 to Arthur Litchfield Freeman. Then in later years Frank Richard Knight was the tenant in 1950. A new saloon bar was opened in March 1954 and in 1956 the pub hosted meetings of the New Bradwell Camera Club. That year in October the licence was transferred from Hubert Crowsley to James Hamilton, who arrived with his family from Coventry. A new lounge bar opened in 1957 on November 1st and it was by his wife that the Girl Guides were re-started at New Bradwell, with help in the organisation from her daughter Rita. Then in 1960 at the end of October James, his wife and 2 sons and 2 daughters left for a pub at Wellingborough. Presently the premises are forlorn and boarded up, being recently placed up for sale for offers of around £300,000.

A HALL FOR ALL REASONS.

The Assembly Hall, which became the Bowyer Hall, which became a fireplace showroom, which became Sid Telfers, which became DIY Dealz.

In the early development of New Bradwell a community centre in Newport Road was built known as the Assembly Hall. During the first decade of the 20th century this became the headquarters of the Liberal Party, indeed being variously known as the Liberal Hall and Liberal Assembly Hall. Then from a previous and unsuitable premises in 1912 the Salvation Army moved to the Hall, until in view of their increased membership a purpose built centre was

The former assembly hall on the Newport Road which has for many years been used for commercial purposes.

constructed in 1915.

Thereafter the Hall became favoured for holding various entertainments to include dances and concerts. Also for the meetings of various local societies, to include in 1924 the annual May Day rally under the auspices of the North Bucks Labour Women's Council, in 1930 the March meeting of the League of Nations, and in 1931 the Christmas party of the New Bradwell Baby Welfare Centre, for which the Hall seems to have been the venue. A bazaar had also been held at the Hall for the building fund of the Conservative Association, which hoped to have its own purpose built centre.

However in 1934 the Conservative MP for the Division, Captain Sir George Bowyer MC MP, who had held the position since December 14th 1918, purchased the Assembly Hall with the intention, after renovation and redecoration, for it to be tenanted by the Conservative Association. They would take care of the maintenance and administration, and in preparation new heating apparatus was installed and the lighting enhanced. Also the premises were completely re-decorated with the upper section of the interior walls painted cream and the lower portion royal blue. Similarly the roof was painted white and the gas pipes and girder supports picked out in blue. As for the exterior that part facing the road was painted cream with parts picked out in blue.

Thus bedecked with blue and white paper streamers and Union Jacks, on the evening of Friday, May 10th 1935 the official opening took place, with the premises now to be known as the Bowyer Hall. Apart from a use to further the Conservative cause it would be available for hire for other purposes, 'at reasonable cost.' In consequence in October 1937 the Stantonbury Mothers' Meeting changed their headquarters from the Social Club Concert Hall to the new premises, where the following year the Stantonbury Girls' Club began to hold their meetings. For many years with Bert Watson as pianist old time dancing classes had been taught at the Hall by Thomas Funge of Wolverton. At the age of 66 he sadly died in 1945 on Friday, October 12th but in 1947 the tradition would be revived, when from Thursday, November 20th classes would be held each alternate Thursday from 7.30pm until 10pm; 'Admission 9d.'

However the Hall was now under new ownership, for that year it had been sold by Lord Denham (Captain Bowyer having been made 1st Baron Denham) to the Conservative Association, and, with Monday meetings, was now the active headquarters of the New Bradwell branch of the Young Conservatives.

As for the other end of the spectrum, established in 1956 the Ivy Leaf Club would hold their get togethers at the Hall, and with a membership of around 130 many of the old age pensioners 'just live for Wednesday afternoons.' Nevertheless on the financial scene matters were looking bleak and the Hall was advertised to let on an annual tenancy - '1,200 feet floor space suitable for storage etc. Apply to the agent Conservative Club Bletchley.'

As a community amenity the hall hosted a range of activities. One illustration might be a dance school set up by a talented local dancer. Jennifer Brazier (at the time only 14 years old) hired the hall in 1958 to teach young children to dance. Beginning with a class of 12 children the dance school became popular. Jennifer took leave from the dance school for three seasons while she performed with the corps de ballet at Northampton's repertory theatre, but returned and later moved the school to Stony Stratford. She stopped teaching after 1971 to look after her own children.

Jennifer Brazier with a class at the Bowyer Hall.

Then in 1959 at a valuation court at Stony Stratford on Monday, January 16th statements that the Bowyer Hall was losing £100 a year were made. On the grounds that the property was uneconomical this regarded the objection of the Buckingham Conservative Association to the assessment of £80 gross, and in representing the Association Mr. W.S. Johnson said that for some time they had found the Hall costly to maintain. The expenditure greatly exceeded the income and even advertising the Hall to let in February and July of last year had produced no results; "I will say it costs us a considerable amount of money to keep the hall going. I do feel that this is the whole crux of the matter. We were prepared to let it, but could not." Despite being in agreement the Deputy Valuation Officer thought the figure they asked of £25 gross was too low. In 1956/57 there had been an agreement whereby the gross figure was reduced from £120 to £80, and he felt lowering the figure further would be too great a reduction. However Mr. Johnson replied that since they hadn't been able to let the Hall that was surely the basis of the assessment. In conclusion the chairman, Alderman L.O. Bull, ruled that the gross figure would be reduced to £40. Then in 1966 the problem was resolved when on the evening of Friday, June 3rd at the annual meeting of the Buckingham Conservative Association, held at Bletchley, Mr. Johnson, as treasurer, reported that the Bowyer Hall had been sold. Purchase had been intended by the trustees of the New Bradwell Methodist Church for youth work. However a higher offer was received and after his purchase Mr. C.P. Hiorns, of New Bradwell, who ran a building and decorating business, received planning permission to turn the hall into a large DIY and fireplace showroom. Indeed he had begun manufacturing fireplaces in his workshops, and with the intention to open shortly after Christmas said, "We hope to have the largest showroom for fireplaces in North Bucks. The building will have a complete new front, we are going to give it a proper 'face lift' and bring it up to date. It is something that is really required in the town. We will be giving the place a new slant again." In later years it became the DIY store of Sid Telfer and is presently DIY Dealz.

EDUCATION

A TIMELINE OF TEACHING

This meander through the years is in no way definitive. Just a compilation gleaned from various sources, and concentrating on the earlier years. No doubt present residents would be able to add their own recollections of school life in the more recent past and, if suitable for print, their comments on the teaching staff!

The schools were completed in 1860 and enlarged in 1892; 'Mr. Hull reported (January 14th) that he estimates cost of carrying out the extension necessary to meet the demands of the Educational Department at £850.' This was approved and ordered. Then in September 1903 they were taken over by Bucks County Council and again extended in 1906. In 1911 on the evening of Thursday, August 3rd a public protest meeting, regarding opposition by the ratepayers, was held in view of the proposal of the Education Authorities to spend some £6,000 in enlarging the Council Schools. The object of the meeting was to discuss the proposed alterations to the schools, and by a resolution to request the Education Authorities to build new boys schools instead. The meeting considered the sum would be a serious burden on the ratepayers and it was the general feeling in the parish that new buildings would be cheaper. Mr. Tranfield, a builder, thought the sum exorbitant, since the girls school of 1901 for 300 pupils had only cost £2,500. It was unanimously resolved to send a resolution. In consequence a new school for boys was built in Bounty Street in 1913. Of the original school in 1949 the girls' school became New Bradwell County Primary School which in 1950 was renamed New Bradwell County Junior School. The Bounty Street School became the New Bradwell County Secondary School, later renamed the New Bradwell Middle School, for boys and girls up to school leaving age. This remained the situation until 1975 when after the summer holidays in September the Bounty Street School became a Combined School. A new nursery unit was added the

The New Bradwell schools were designed by the distinguished architect, George Edmund Street (1824-1881). The buildings were completed by 1860.

The photograph below of the senior schoolboys was taken c. 1900.

following year. As was reported in the local press;

'New Bradwell's first school is to close. The 115 year old building has several times been described as a slum. The children aged up to 8 will transfer to New Bradwell Middle turning it into a combined school. Building work at Stanton High County County Middle School at the Primrose, Bradville, is nearing completion, and the education authority plan initially to establish a first school for children from the Stantonbury area in the same premises. The 5 to 8 year old children will share the same buildings but form a separate unit. Eventually a new first school will be built in the area for about 240 pupils who with children from Pepper Hill first school will feed the middle school. The St. James Street school was built in 1858 and last year parents protested angrily that their children should be taught in such a slum building when newcomers had the new Pepper Hill school for their children. Planning permission was sought by Bucks County Council to alter and extend the first school. Eventually the education authorities plumped for the alternative suggestion of absorbing the 200 pupils into the Bounty Street Middle School, which will lose many of its children to Stanton High Middle next term.'

1733

The Rev. J. Hume left a small bequest in 1733 for the education of 6 poor children belonging to the parish.

1858

With the increased population the need arose for sufficient religious and educational facilities, and in recognition the railway directors had agreed to set apart a generous sum towards providing a church, with accommodation for 800 persons, and school accommodation for the instruction of 100 boys and 100 girls, with dwellings for the masters and mistresses. Donations from the Church Building Society and also from individuals in the neighbourhood increased the fund, and with a plot of ground obtained at Stantonbury construction, to the designs of the architect, Mr. Street, began under the ministration and superintendence of the Rev. J. Lovekin, the chaplain of the company. Then in 1858 the foundation stones of the church and schools were laid on Whit Monday, May 24th 1858. Despite heavy showers in the morning hundreds of people came to witness the ceremony, at which that of the schools was laid by the Marchioness of Chandos, and that of the church by the Marquis, as chairman of the L&NWR.

1859

On Whit Monday after an address by Archdeacon Bickersteth, delivered to about 800 employees from Wolverton Works, the schools were pronounced open by the Marquis of Chandos. A tea was given to the children, after which Old English games were played. Apart from the Marquis and his wife several directors of the railway were also present during the day. As for the new edifice; 'The style is a most felicitous adaptation of the Early English, and the skill, taste, and boldness manifest everywhere bespeak the accomplished artist. Internally the arrangements are equally good and congruous. They accord with the exterior. There is no excess of ornament; on the contrary, everything is plain and simple; but the presence of a presiding good taste is felt throughout.' Grants would be paid yearly to the school by the Railway Company dependent upon performance. At that time school attendance was not compulsory and parents paid 1d a week per child which entitled them to the use of a lead pencil and a slate. Of the infants school Miss Emily Bailey was the headmistress and judging by entries from the log book she seemingly had a somewhat thankless task.

1860

The schools were completed on December 6th having places for 400 pupils.

1867

On February 11th Miss Bailey wrote, 'Received today from the National Depository, Westminster, this log book together with the following articles for school use:-

Admission Register, Ball Frame, Box of Letters, Six dozen Infant School Primers, Two Alphabet cards. Set of Scripure Prints with frames, Set of reading cards, Six dozen slates, Pencils, chalks and pens.'

On February 12th she wrote of having organised her school into three classes, 'having hereto worked with them grouped together, owing to not having working apparatus.'

On February 14th Miss Bailey wrote, 'The children having been so long neglected, I find it very difficult to keep such good order as I should like. Almost despair at times in teaching them their letters.' At this time whooping cough and measles were much prevalent.

On March 26th, 'Attendance very good this morning. 63 children present in time to be marked in the registers.'

By the inspector's report on July 14th, 'Miss Bailey has much work on her hands, the room is small and disadvantageous as an Infant's School. I hope some improvement will be made in this respect. Babies under three will not be allowed to attend the Infants' School.'

1868

By Miss Bailey's entry of June 29th it seems the children had found other pursuits; 'Sent to several of the parents to see why their children were sent to school late this afternoon. It appears they were sent from home in time, but after questioning them, I found they had been to the canal bathing.'

At this period school was not compulsory, as per the entry of November 27th; 'Selina (monitor), ends her duties today. Her mother is not sufficiently strong and cannot spare her any longer from home. Appointed Annie Walker to her place.' (On November 30th; 'Annie has commenced her work fairly, her only fault at present being so small for her age.')

1869

At the National School the headmaster of the Boys is George Henstock Howitt; of the Girls, Miss Ann Dunthorne; of the Infants, Miss Emily Bailey.

On February 4th Miss Bailey writes in the log book; 'Mary

Bennett was sent by her mother today to say she will not be able to come again. She is needed at home until the twin babies can walk.'

On June 21st Miss Bailey wrote; 'Sent home every child who had not brought its school money. I have received instructions from Mr. Cotter to allow no child to attend school without payment.'

1870

From the log book of the Infants' School;

January 20th

'Reproved first class children for being so fond of tale telling, one of another. Made them understand by simple illustrations and anecdotes, that it was wrong and God would not love them if they were not kind one to another.'

February 1st

'Impossible to carry on regular work, as it takes up all our time to keep anything like warmth either in ourselves or the poor children who do nothing but cry and complain of the cold. The room is more like a barn than anything else. Let the stove be ever so large, it never seems to warm the room. We might as well be without one.'

February 7th

'Cold still intense.'

February 8th

'School visited by the Rev. Cotter, who gave orders for the broken windows to be replaced.'

February 14th

'Expect to lose more children as the Company continue to remove men from here to Crewe each week.'

May 6th

'Only 4 children present at school at 2.00 O'clock. Waited some little time, but finding no new arrivals, closed the school for the afternoon. The absence of children is accounted for by a circus having arrived in the village during the morning.'

1871

From the Infants' School log book.

January 13th. 'All the elder children have been sent to the Girl's and Boy's School. The Infant Department is much smaller in consequence.'

1874

In July the teachers and pupils of Stantonbury Infants' School presented Miss Frances L. Eansor, their head monitoress, with a writing desk. She was leaving on Monday, June 22nd for an appointment as assistant mistress at the village of Pailton, in the Borough of Rugby. The vicar, the Rev. Cotter, made the presentation. Also given was a Bible with appropriate inscription plus a purse of 35s from the parishioners, this from being a member of the church choir.

1875

Summary of HM Governor's Inspector's report 1875.

'The Infant's School is only in a moderate state of efficiency. The principle schoolroom is too small for marching and has no gallery in it. Children failed to satisfy me in writing and arithmetic. A deduction of one tenth has been made from the grant in consequence of the faulty organisation and any appearance of irregularity in keeping the registers may entail the reduction of the above grant. The organisation of the school must improve greatly.'

1875

In 1875 on the evening of Monday, November 8th a concert was given at Stantonbury by the Stantonbury church choir and friends to commemorate the completion of the new wings of the schools.

1876

The head teachers are, George Howitt, Boys; Miss F.K. Wilkins, Girls; Miss A.E. Fielding, Infants.

1877

The head teachers are, George Howitt, Boys; Miss M. Dunmore, Girls; Miss Emily Pratt, Infants.

1882

In May 1882 at the annual inspection of the Stantonbury National Schools it was stated that H.M. Inspector, E.M. Kenny Herbert, wished it to be made known to the Rev. Cotter and the other managers that, pursuant to the Government's wish to judge the state of National education in Bucks, he had lately been asked to submit some of the worst and the best exam papers that he had obtained. All the best had been taken from the Stantonbury Boys' School, of which Mr. G.H. Howitt was the master.

1885

From the school log book.

> '1885 Jul. 31st The timetable was not followed on Friday as those who could be spared were making a banner for the procession which is to take place on Monday. The L&NW Railway Company desire all the children to be present at the opening of the park.' (This was Wolverton Park.)

1886

On the morning of Friday, October 1st Miss Scott was presented with a floral album and inkstand by the teachers and pupils. She was resigning from her post as assistant mistress in the Stantonbury Girls' School.

1887

The teaching staff are George Howitt, Henry Hippsley, John Hardcastle, masters; Misses Amy Williams & Kate Scales mistresses; Miss Ada Stephenson infants mistress.

Through the auspices of Miss Stephenson, head mistress of the Infants' School, the teachers of the Infants' and Girls' Schools presented Miss L.M. Scales, late teacher at the Infants' School, with a handsome set of wine decanters for port and sherry, with glasses to match. These were accompanied by a note; 'Stantonbury Infants' School, May 25th, 1887. The teachers of the Stantonbury Girls' and Infant Schools feel much pleasure in presenting the accompanying to Miss Scales as a token of their esteem, with the best wishes for her future welfare.' She was about to be married.

1889

At Chackmore School in October in place of Miss Howes, who after 11 years as mistress had resigned at Michaelmas, the managers appointed Miss Clara Eames. A certificated mistress, she came from the national school for girls at Stantonbury, where she had been assistant mistress.

1890

In October it was announced that as a result of the scholarship exam for entrance into training colleges, held last July in England and Wales, Charles Frederick Sykes of Stantonbury Schools had been placed in the first class. As such he was entitled to two years' training at St. Mark's College, Chelsea. He was the second teacher from the schools during the past year to obtain admission to the college, reflecting great credit on the headmaster, Mr. George Howitt.

1891

The teachers are, George Howitt master; Miss Amy Williams mistress; Miss Ada Stephenson infants mistress.

On Friday, January 30th Mr. Hardcastle, assistant master at the Stantonbury schools, who was leaving to take charge of the schools at Sawbridgeworth, Herts., was presented by the teaching staff with a travelling rug and pencil case.

In June Mr. Bateman, Assistant Master at the National Schools was presented by his fellow teachers with a dressing case and a silver mounted pipe on his leaving Stantonbury. Mr. Howitt, head master, made the presentation.

1892

In January the Education Department demanded the extension or enlargement of the school. The Company submitted an estimate of £850 for the work. Five tenders were opened and it was resolved to accept that of Messrs. Kemp and Sons of Stantonbury for £1,336 4s 4d. Further requirements of the Education Dept. increased the estimate of £850 to £1,350.

1893

On Thursday, March 23rd due to a measles outbreak the schools closed, within a month of exams.

On the evening of Saturday, November 11th a public meeting was held in the National Schoolroom to consider forming a Literary and Mutual Improvement Society. The Rev. A.C. Woodhouse was in the chair and said the object of the proposed society was to discuss literary and social subjects. Any subject that would tend to instruct and elevate its members should be open to discussion. The society should be non political and un-sectarian. Rev. Woodhouse was elected President, with a committee of Mrs. Woodhouse, Miss Williams, Miss Ada Williams, Mr. Howitt, Mr. Edgington, Mr. Ward and Mr. Ribchester.

In early December a public meeting was held in the National School to discuss the best means of conducting the 'Literary and Debating Society.' The Rev. A.C. Woodhouse presided. The rules were discussed with one amendment; 'That the age of membership be reduced from 16 to 14 years, as the object of the society is to encourage young people to inquire deeply into subjects that would tend to improve, mentally, and morally and so help them to better face the difficulties of life.' Mr. Ribchester was appointed secretary and it was decided that Mr. Woodhouse should formally open the society with a paper on Monday, December 11th. The secretary was asked to supply each member with a card of rules and conditions of membership.

On the evening of Monday, December 11th the first meeting of the Literary and Debating Society was held in the L&NWR schools. The president, the Rev. Woodhouse, gave the opening address on

'Our aim in forming the Society.'

1894

In October it was announced that Miss Heacock, head mistress for 5 or 6 years of the Oxford Lane (Great Marlow) Infant School, had obtained a similar position at the schools established and maintained by the Directors of L&NWR at Stantonbury. She would begin on October 15th.

1895

In September the L&NWR terminated their connection with the schools which reopened on October 1st under the direction of a school board comprised of the Rev. A.C. Woodhouse, Messrs. Ward & Wylie, and C.W. Powell (solicitor.)

On November 7th Miss Heacock wrote in the school log 'The cloakroom must be properly fitted with pegs and clothes horses, the children's jackets should not be admitted into any of the schoolrooms. A clock should be provided and the main entrance of the school should be paved. Wrote to the Board asking for 'Progress and Marks Books' on October 20th. Have not received them, and have come to the conclusion that they were not thought necessary for Infants' School use.'

1896

Mr. Stanley, assistant master at the Board Schools, Stantonbury, was presented at Easter with a dressing case from the staff and teachers. Then on Saturday, April 18th at a meeting of the choir the vicar presented him with a writing case on behalf of himself and the choir. Mr. Stanley was leaving to become headmaster to the Tingewick schools.

1897

In December additional gas lighting was put in the large room and one of the classrooms. 'The improvement is very great.'

1899

George Howitt master; Miss Amy Williams mistress; Miss Sarah Ann Heacock infants mistress.

1903

George Howitt master; Miss Amy Williams mistress; Miss Sarah Ann Heacock infants mistress.

On Thursday morning, September 17th at the meeting of Bucks County Education at County Hall, Aylesbury, the Elementary Sub Committee recommended that the number of managers for Bradwell Council School should be 9.

1906

From the school log book; 'May 8th. No children have been admitted under the age of 5 since last November, by order of the Education Committee.' 'May 11th. Order rescinded. 65 children have been admitted this week.'

1907

George Howitt master; Miss Amy Williams mistress; Miss Sarah Ann Heacock infants mistress.

In November six headmasters were invited to appear in view of the approaching retirement of the headmaster of Bradwell Council Boys' School. The managers were asked to consider the appointment of one of them to the post.

1908

On Tuesday, April 21st an inquest was conducted on a well dressed man who had mysteriously disappeared. A witness from Buckingham arrived and identified the deceased as John Pybourne, assistant schoolmaster at Stantonbury. It seemed he entered a Leicester hotel on the night of Friday, April 17th and drank some lemonade. He subsequently fell ill and when carried outside into the open air called out that he had been robbed of his purse. He then died almost immediately afterwards. However the purse containing £1 1s 8d was found under his body, a search of which revealed a number of bottles. These were found to have contained poisonous drugs, and at a post mortem it was discovered that he had been addicted to drug taking. Giving evidence, Priscilla Wheeler, wife of John Wheeler, a carriage builder of 155, Newport Road, Stantonbury, said the man had lodged with her for 4 years. He was assistant schoolmaster at Stantonbury Council Schools, and following influenza had complained of head pains a month ago. On the Tuesday he went to school as usual and after arriving home for tea went for a walk. When he didn't return she reported him missing to Wolverton police. She didn't know of any relatives, only that he came from Newcastle, but during his lodging he told her he was previously a chemist's assistant. Indeed whenever ill he would go to his box and mix his own medicines. A verdict of death due to heart failure was recorded.

1909

In June at the meeting of the Bucks County Education Committee, held at County Hall, Aylesbury, the Works Sub Committee of the Elementary Education Sub Committee reported that the Architect had submitted a scheme of enlargements and improvements at the Bradwell Council School.

In July on Thursday, 15th at Aylesbury the Elementary Education Sub Committee, Works Sub Committee, reported that the architect had discussed with the managers the scheme of enlargement and improvements of Bradwell Council School. The question was raised as to whether, in view of the proposed encroachment on the playground, it would not be desirable to provide for the boys by remodelling that department to form a two storey building. The scheme was sent to the Board of Education for their views. They replied that the proposed extensions did not encroach unduly on the playground, and suggested that a piece of the boys playground be reserved for infants. The Board further asked whether the proposed accommodation would suffice to meet the future needs of the locality.

1910

On Thursday, November 17th regarding the proposed reconstruction and enlargement of Bradwell Council School it was stated at a meeting of the Bucks County Education Committee, held at Aylesbury, that the committee had under consideration a resolution adopted by the Works Sub Committee at their meeting on November 3rd, 1910. This suggested that the proposed reconstruction and enlargement of Bradwell Council School should be postponed for six months, this being to ascertain whether a reduction in the child population might result due to the uncertainties of employment at Wolverton Works. The committee concurred with this and would recommend that the Board of Education should be informed accordingly. A detailed criticism of the building had been sent to the local authority in 1908, and they gave warning that if a definite undertaking was not given that the work would be carried out the Board would be obliged to make a serious reduction in the grant for the year. The secretary said it was quite clear that those alterations would take a year and if the children were not given a year's holiday the work would have to be done piecemeal. Mr. Wylie said the work was a large undertaking and what was to be done with the children during its progress he didn't know.

1911

J. Irving Brooks master; Miss Amy Williams mistress; Miss Sarah Ann Heacock infants mistress.

In March on Thursday 16th at a meeting of Bucks Education Committee, held at Aylesbury, it was stated that the Works Sub Committee had considered the resolution adopted by the Bradwell Parish Council on February 9th 1911 that a new school should be provided for the boys. It was estimated that a new school would cost about £5,500. However the scheme of enlargement and improvement of the existing Boys' Dept. would cost about £2,500 and Mr. E.M. Kenney Herbert was satisfied that this scheme would be satisfactory. After careful re-consideration the committee had instructed the Architect to proceed with the scheme already in hand for the reconstruction of the existing premises. This would provide accommodation for 376 boys, 304 girls, and 336 infants at about £5,000.

On the evening of Tuesday, July 11th, at the monthly meeting of the Stantonbury Council School managers a letter was read from the secretary of the County Education Committee. In this he pointed out that H.M. Inspector could not approve the appointment of Eva Garratt as a pupil teacher to the Newport Pagnell Council Schools. Therefore he asked the committee to arrange for her admission as soon as possible to Bradwell Council School. However the chairman, Ald. Robert Wylie, thought they should ask the teachers if they had room. The Rev. Guest said it was rather dictatorial; "You have to do this and you have to do that." It was resolved to ask the head teacher if she had room. The Rev. Guest had visited the school and found the order and respect excellent. A letter was read from the Bucks Education Committee informing the managers that the drawings for the alteration and enlargement of Bradwell school were practically complete and would be submitted to their sub committee on Thursday. However they were having trouble finding any reliable information about the run of the drainage, especially the surface water drains. The Rev. Guest said if the present plans were approved the view of the church would be hidden. When he met with Mr. Watkins on the subject he promised that the view would be protected as much as possible. The Rev Guest said the church was the only beautiful bit of architecture in 'that dull place.' The Rev. Leggatt proposed that the plans should be asked for and submitted to the local managers. This was carried.

At the meeting of the Bucks Education Committee at Aylesbury on Thursday, July 20th the Elementary Education Sub Committee, Works Sub Committee, had considered and approved the working drawings prepared by the Architect for the proposed remodelling and enlargement of Bradwell Council School; New buildings £2,850; structural alterations £2,500; Offices etc £200; Quantity surveyor's fees £130; Clerk of Works £150; furniture £170; total £6,000.' The Committee recommended that the County Council should be requested to approve a preliminary estimate of £6,000 in respect of this scheme.

1912

In June it was announced that the Board of Education had approved the site regarding Bradwell Council School and also subject to a few alterations the sketch plan of the proposed new school.

In June Majorie Giltrow, daughter of Mr. and Mrs. Giltrow of the Cuba Hotel, attained 8 years of perfect attendance at the Bradwell Council Schools.

In August Dr. Grindon wrote; "In New Bradwell school, of 46 girls only, two had anything approaching a reasonable amount of fat. The others gave me the impression of being too finely trained rather than starved. Some of them showing no physical defects had practically no subcutaneous fat. Forty nine boys gave me the impression of a very fine sturdy group, some of them really splendid children, physically, and it seems difficult to believe that they belonged to the same families as the girls."

1913

At the meeting of Bucks County Education Committee at County Hall, Aylesbury, on Thursday, February 20th, it was stated that for the proposed new council school the Local Government Board had sanctioned loans of £5,226 for the provision of the new school and £210 for furniture and fittings. The contractors, Messrs. G.H. Gibson and Sons, proposed to begin building operations on February 24th. Mr. Morris Brady was appointed clerk of the works at £3 a week.

In September the new council school for boys which was completed and furnished during the summer holidays was opened for use on Monday, September 8th.

1914

From the pupils attending the Bradwell Evening Schools, conducted by Mr. J. Brooks, ten boys sat for the Birmingham Technical Institute exam. Six passed with great credit, with one, Bernard Tapp of Old Bradwell, obtaining a first prize. At the monthly meeting of the Bradwell School Managers in July Alderman Wylie said to laughter "Oh, all good boys come from there. Does he work on my farm?" An excellent report of the state of the Bradwell Council Schools was received from Mr. E.C. Streatfield, HM Inspector, following his recent inspection. The girls department was conducted 'in the right spirit,' teaching was earnest, and physical training effective. The two younger classes were in the hands of capable teachers. In the infants department efficiency was well maintained under the guidance of the headmistress and as the matter was quite urgent it was hoped that the entire re-modelling and re-decorating of the infants' department would be put in hand at once. Four un-certificated teachers at the girls school who had performed over ten years service at the school wrote asking the managers to recommend a salary increase. Miss Williams, the head teacher, wrote to say that they had given valuable service, 'often under unfavourable conditions and at low salaries' and it was agreed to send the recommendation to Aylesbury. The Education Committee wrote saying that the committee had appointed Mr. W. Everall Baker as instructor to the Newport Pagnell and Bradwell woodwork centres and he would start in September.

In November the trustees of Bradwell Council School approved the plans of the proposed alterations to the school premises.

1915

In July in a written communication the Education Committee stated their appointment of Miss Bessie Punter as a trained certificated teacher in the Girls' School. Her remuneration would be £80pa.

1916

1916 March - The managers of Bradwell Council School have decided that the reporters shall not attend their meetings in future. A local newspaper responded 'Both Press and Public will be relieved.'!

In June the local Education Secretary wrote that the student teachers Sarah Mallard and Frances Whittaker were eligible to serve in Bradwell Girls' School. Mrs. Millard is an assistant teacher.

1917

In May at a meeting of Bucks County Council at the request of the Education Committee the Finance Committee recommended that Mr J. Brooks of Bradwell Boy's Council School should be granted an increase of salary to £205pa from £200 from April last.

In September it was stated that during the year the upper standards of Bradwell Council School had cultivated on the school gardens 50 poles by the boys and 40 by the girls. The land had been thoroughly dug in April and 20 bushels of seed potatoes resulted in the harvesting of 200 bushels of potatoes. Some were sold to defray expenses with the remainder divided amongst the workers on the plot at two bushels each.

1920

On account of her parents' illness Miss Heacock departed as headmistress of the Infants' School.

In August Minnie Brookes commenced her duties as Head of the Infants' Department.

1921

In April the staff of the Infants' Department are Minnie Brookes (head), Amy Harris, Eva Garratt, Alice Spriggs, Winifred Gamble, Grace Twistleton.

In June applications were invited for the post of School Correspondent for Bradwell Council School at £16pa.

1923

In September it was announced that Miss Williams, headmistress of the girls' department of Bradwell Council School, would retire on October 31st after 40 years of service. A fund for a testimonial was being raised by the managers and staff, with Mr. J. Brooks, headmaster, and Mr. F. Grant, school correspondent, as the joint honorary secretaries.

In succession to Miss Williams, on November 1st Miss Cary of Loughborough commenced her duties as headmistress of the Girls'

School.

December 21st; '27 girls are leaving school this afternoon being 14 years of age. Only 2 have succeeded in getting regular employment.'

1925

In October a fund was started at the Boys' School for a wireless set. A whist drive was arranged to help.

1928

J. Irving Brooks master; Miss Cary mistress; Miss Mary Brooke infants mistress.

Mr. H. Clayton-Jones left in April after 7 years on the teaching staff of New Bradwell Boys' School to become headmaster at Frankton School, Shropshire.

Miss Brookes resigned in December 1928 as head of the Infants' Department.

1929

On March 9th Miss Eckersley took over as head of the Infants Dept.

In August the staff are Miss Eckersley (head); Standard 1, Miss Berry; Class 1, Miss Spriggs; Class 2, Miss Rogers; Baby Class, Miss Garratt.

1930

When the Infants' School reopened after the Easter holidays Miss Spriggs, who had married during the holidays, returned as Mrs. Hancock.

In August Miss Eckersley terminated her duties as head of the Infants' Department.

September 1st; 'I, Phyllis Penn, commence my duties this morning as Head of the school.' (The Infants' School.)

1931

February

'The proposed alteration in the existing educational system at the Wolverton and Bradwell Council Schools has caused a great deal of discussion among parents in this neighbourhood and a demand for an early and an official explanation was made at a specially convened meeting in the Technical College Wolverton. A few weeks ago the Bucks Education Committee called a meeting of the New Bradwell and Wolverton School Managers when the proposals were laid before them. It was a private meeting but it was subsequently learned that the scheme entailed the building of a new school estimated to cost about £4,400 and an extension to the present buildings at a cost of £1,400. The proposals also include plans for the education of senior girls from the age of 11 to 15 at Wolverton School, and the senior boys at Bradwell. This means many of those now attending in their own town will have to make a daily journey of about 2 miles to and from school. It was decided to form a Parents' Association with Mr. A. Jones as chairman and Mr. R. Orchard as secretary and to send a resolution asking for an early meeting to the committee.'

1932

On Saturday, July 2nd members of the New Bradwell Council Schools Meccano Club held their summer outing to Wickstead Park, Kettering. Thanks were expressed to the organiser Mr. Harding, an assistant master at the schools.

At the New Bradwell Bathing Station, on the evening of Friday, July 29th Cliff Harding, sports master, an assistant master at New Bradwell Council Schools, was in the deepest part of river when he was seized with cramp. A man fishing nearby waded in and dragged him to the bank. He was taken to the house of a friend where Dr. Atkinson applied artificial respiration.

With Miss Cary responsible for the arrangements, on the afternoon of Friday, October 14th a jumble sale was held by the teachers and pupils of New Bradwell Council Schools to help raise funds to provide a gramophone for educational purposes.

1934

Some 40 Guides and Brownies were enrolled in the early weeks of the year. The Guides meet every each Tuesday evening at New Bradwell Council Schools.

1935

In January for having been over 7 years 'never absent, never late,' Charles Walker and Jack Williams were presented with watches.

On the afternoon of Friday, September 27th the schoolchildren presented Miss Eva Garratt with an electric toaster and polishing cloths. She was about to be married, and having been associated with the New Bradwell Schools since 1911 had taught in the infants' class for many years. In married life she would live at Newport Pagnell.

1936

On Thursday, May 21st at a meeting of Bucks County Education Committee at Aylesbury the Elementary Education Sub Committee reported that the conveyance of the premises of the Bradwell Council School had been completed after several years 'of difficult and complicated negotiations.' Subject to pressure of work in the County Architect's Department the committee hoped that the necessary alterations to the premises would be carried out during the summer holidays.

On August 31st the Infants Department was transferred to the new premises. Only the Hall and the babies room remained as before.

1938

In January a master at New Bradwell Council Schools, Jack Pimbley of 32, King Edward Street, hoped to get enough clubs interested for a revival of the North Bucks Cricket League.

At the end of the Easter term Miss Cary relinquished her position as headmistress of New Bradwell Girls' Council School. She would be leaving for a similar appointment at the Thomas Grey Junior Girls' School at Slough. Janet Hasler became the acting head.

Having been an assistant teacher at New Bradwell Girls' School for 7 years, Dorothy Mary Gower married Charles Beckett, only son of parents of 48, Windsor Street, Wolverton, at St. Mary's, Bletchley, on Saturday, September 10th. She was the only daughter of parents at Bletchley, and the newly weds would live in Gloucester Road, Wolverton.

In October it was reported that Bucks County Education Authority had decided that the reorganisation of the New Bradwell Council Girls' School would be effected at the beginning of the next educational year. The county architect had been authorised to make any structural alterations that might be necessary.

1939

On May 31st Miss Phyllis E. Penn, headmistress of New Bradwell Council Infants School since 1930, terminated her duties, having been appointed headmistress of Aylesbury Queen's Park Council Infants' School.

On June 1st Mary Thomas began as temporary headmistress.

1940

On June 1st Mr. J.C. Harding, of 23, Green Lane, Wolverton, began a teaching appointment at the Home Office Approved School, Mobberley Boys' School, Knutsford, Cheshire. He had been an assistant teacher at New Bradwell Council School for 8½ years and had been appointed deputy head. On Friday, May 31st at an assembly in the hall he was presented by the boys and staff with an 8 day clock. He was chairman of the North Bucks Schools Athletic Association, secretary of Bucks County Schools Athletic Association, and honorary secretary of North Bucks Schools Football Association.

1940

In March Mr. J. Brooks retired after 32½ years as headmaster of the Boys' School. Mr. Maynard, senior assistant at the Manor Park Senior School, Slough, would take over as headmaster on April 1st.

1941

On joining the RAF, in February a teacher at New Bradwell Boys' Council School, Mr. J. Pimbley, was presented with a fountain pen and electric razor by Mr. B. Salmon on behalf of the staff and pupils.

In May, Bucks County Council established a nursery school at New Bradwell for children aged 3-5, for evacuees and residents. The accommodation was the Baptist Schoolroom which opened with 27 children. Attached to the New Bradwell Infants' School it came under the jurisdiction of Miss Thomas, headmistress. Miss Bird, senior teacher, was in charge of the new school with the assistance of two juniors. 'An observer on visiting found the children sitting at brightly coloured tables, amusing themselves at games, some of which have been provided for them, and others which children brought themselves. In the corner of the room is a sandpit in a galvanised surround and at this some children were playing and making sand heaps. The youngsters appeared to be very happy. They are provided with rusks and milk during the morning prepared in the kitchen adjoining the hall. The teacher said "It is not just minding them for mother but teaching them to help themselves." In the afternoon they rest on canvas beds which are folded up when not in use. A blanket is provided and each bed is numbered so each child has their own bed. Each child has a toothbrush, comb, flannel, and towel and a special room is provided for washing purposes.'

In August applications were invited for the post of temporary full time caretaker at New Bradwell Council School. Remuneration would be £12 10s per month plus a temporary war bonus of 15s per month.

On Saturday, October 25th the wedding took place at the parish church of Hanslope of Lilian Mary Willingham, a teacher at New Bradwell Council School, and Ronald Tomes, of Ridge Barn Farm, Cuddington, near Aylesbury. She was the daughter of Mr. & Mrs. Herbert Willingham of 2, Barnwell Buildings, Hanslope, and having begun a teaching career at an early age had held appointments at Ashton and Woodford Halse. A year ago she was appointed as assistant at New Bradwell Infants' School, where for the rest of the war she would teach during the week, living at the home of the groom at weekends. A lieutenant in the Hanslope Girl Guides, and having been involved with the movement in the village for 15 years, a guard of honour was formed at the ceremony by the Guides, Rangers and Brownies. Of the wedding gifts the staff of the Infants' School presented her with a frameless mirror, and from the children a set of scales and a cushion. Stratford upon Avon would be the destination for the honeymoon.

1942

At St. Georges' Church, Wolverton, the wedding took place on Saturday, November 14th of Enid Coles, a teacher at New Bradwell Girls' School, and Russell Gerrish. She was the eldest daughter of parents of 61, Stacey Avenue, and the groom, a member of the US Civilian Technical Corps, attached to the Air Ministry, was the son of Mr. and Mrs. Charles Gerrish of Potsdam, New York. He wore his uniform at the ceremony. Of the wedding presents the staff and pupils of the school gave a pewter biscuit barrel.

In 1942 on the afternoon of Friday, July 24th at a leaving gathering in the school hall of the Boys' Council School Mr. A.E. Green was presented with a cruet set. In the early part of the war he had come to New Bradwell with Leopold School, Willesden, London, and with some of the boys having already returned he had now been recalled. In outside activities he had been a playing member of the New Bradwell and Wolverton Town cricket teams and a Flight Officer in the Air Training Corps. At New Bradwell under his guidance the boys had contributed some 'decoration work' on the 'blitz' walls, and in his leaving remarks he said "I have been teaching for twenty years, and I have not had better work from any school than that from you boys this year."

1946

In February applications were invited for the post of caretaker at the New Bradwell Council Schools.

Miss Elsie Miller died on Saturday, June 15th at 74, Newport Road, New Bradwell. She had been headmistress at New Bradwell School for less than two years.

In June the death occurred of John Irving Brooks, a headmaster of New Bradwell Council School for over 30 years. He retired in March 1940 and moved to Swansea.

In September 'another disgruntled parent' complained that their son fell over in the playground and due to the re-tarring completely ruined his suit. The parent said the tarring should have been done long before the children went back to school. Not in the last week of the holidays.

At St. George's Church, Wolverton, on Saturday, September 28th the marriage took place of Beryl Iris Stevens, the only daughter of parents of 69, Bradwell Road, New Bradwell, and Albert Donald Drinkwater, the only son of parents of 107, Anson Road, Wolverton. Since its formation she had been an officer in the New Bradwell Company of the St. John Ambulance Nursing Cadets, and members in uniform formed a guard of honour at the ceremony. The bride had been a teacher at New Bradwell Junior School for the past 3 years whilst the groom, recently demobbed from the RAF, was on the staff of Lloyds Bank, Ryde, Isle of Wight, where the newly weds would live. A reception for 35 guests was held in Bowyer Hall, New Bradwell, with the honeymoon to be spent in London. Of the wedding gifts the staff and pupils of the New Bradwell School presented a china tea set and a silver jam dish.

In October it was announced that Mr. J. Pimbley BA of 20, Newport Road, New Bradwell, had been appointed to a post at the Ministry of Defence. He would start immediately but continue to live in New Bradwell for the present. He had been a teacher at the New Bradwell school since 1933 but resigned on joining the RAF. He served from 1941 to 1946, being commissioned after three years in the ranks, and was engaged on important intelligence work at Air Ministry HQ. His education had been at New Bradwell Council School, Wolverton Grammar School, and at the College of St. Mark and St. John, Chelsea. For several seasons he had been captain and secretary of New Bradwell Cricket Club.

1947

In October the first annual general meeting of the New Bradwell

Council Schools Parent Teachers Association was held in the Boys School. With Mr. F. Tompkins as president it was formed 18 months ago with the meetings well attended and several social occasions held.

1949

In July the necessary building work in connection with the reorganisation of the New Bradwell Schools commenced. The arrangements approved were Infants' Department 135 children with a staff of headmistress, 3 assistant teachers, and nursery staff; Junior Department 186 children, with a head, and 5 assistant teachers; Senior Department 198 children with a head and 6 assistant teachers.

In August Miss Hollis, headmistress of the New Bradwell Infants' School, left for a similar position at Chingford. Sarah Mallard, head of the Girls' Department, terminated her engagement as headmistress.

With the New Bradwell Schools being reorganised, when the new term opened in September new 'heads' appeared in two departments. The former Boys' School was now the Secondary Modern School with Mr. C.W. Lynes as headmaster; the former Girls' Department was now the County Primary School with Mr. B.J. Salmon, the former Boys' head as headmaster. Both schools now had mixed pupils.

In August a revived magazine of the New Bradwell Boys' School titled 'Teamwork' was being printed throughout the school by the boys of classes 1 & 2. The press was purchased and equipped by the school, and the front piece of the illustrated magazine was a crest in yellow and black, similar to that of the Barry or Stanton family. The editor was Mr. .J Gibson with Mr. K. Hooton in charge of production, and Mr. A.J. Corby tending the printing.

1950

Returning from a visit to his mother at Huddersfield, in June in a motor cycle accident near Chesterfield twenty nine year old Douglas Pinckard, was killed. Married, he lived at Stewkley. He had been a teacher at the primary school at New Bradwell, to which he had been transferred from the Boys' School at the reorganisation a few months ago. During the war he was stationed at Wing, being decorated for bravery whilst serving in the RAF by the King at Buckingham Palace.

In October, Mr. and Mrs. Fred Trodd of 36, Towcester Road, Old Stratford, celebrated 50 years of marriage. They moved to Old Stratford 14 years ago having previously lived at Deanshanger and New Bradwell, where Mrs. Lilly Trodd (nee Satchell) had taught in the Girls' School from 1901 to 1922. She was born in 1868 on July 12th and Fred in 1874 on January 16th. Originally a butcher on his own account he had been employed as a storeman at Wolverton Works for 30 years. Lilly was a native of Lincoln, where the couple had married. (Fred died in January 1952 and Mrs. Trodd then went to live with her niece, Mrs. Audrey Chapman, at 'Woodcroft', 25, Cosgrove Road, Old Stratford. She died aged 84 in 1953 on June 25th, with the funeral held at Cosgrove.)

1951

In March, Bucks Education Committee were unable to approve a resolution of the Divisional Executive, namely that the present rest centre at New Bradwell County Secondary School should be converted to use as a dining room, with a new canteen kitchen provided. The Executive Officer, Mr. N. Hawes, reported that a letter from Mr. D. Cooke, the Chief Education Officer, stated that it would not be possible to provide a kitchen for £1,000 for the number of meals. Presently at two sittings 220 meals were being served. It might be possible to convert the hut into a classroom or they could ask the architect to investigate converting it as a kitchen.

New Bradwell County Junior School have a new badge for their Festival of Britain Exhibition. This is adapted from the arms of the Vaux family, who were lords of the manor of Stantonbury.

Having been a member of staff at New Bradwell County Secondary School since April 1947, Jack Gibson left on November 30th to join the Royal Navy for air duties with commissioned rank.

During the war he had been an observer in naval aircraft and was now returning for similar duties. Resident in High Street, Haversham, he was formerly clerk to Haversham parish council.

At the end of term in July presentations were made by Miss Phillips, the headmistress, to Miss Heather Mary Belgrove, nursery class teacher of New Bradwell Infants' class. She was the only daughter of Mr. & Mrs. W. Belgrove, of The Olde Wharfe, Bugbrooke, Northants., and at the church of St. Michael and All Angels at Bugbrooke would marry Mr. Ernest Evans, of Wallasey, Cheshire, on July 28th. He was employed by the Vacuum Oil Company at Birkenhead, and after a honeymoon at Betys Coed the couple would take up residence at Wallasey. When the accommodation was in the Baptist Church schoolroom she began as nursery class teacher at New Bradwell in August 1943, and the following year moved with the children to the present building after Easter. She then left in 1946 to teach at a Northampton school, returning to New Bradwell after two years.

In September it was resolved to cut down the number of hours of the canteen staff.

Towards gaining additional support, in October the Parent Teacher Association conducted a house to house canvass for members. This was decided at the annual meeting at the school, when in presiding Mr. F.H. Tompkins made an appeal for more members. He said all the efforts for the Association were for benefit of the children attending the schools. This enabled the provision of things the Education Authorities couldn't supply and during the past year grants to the schools had amounted to £42.

1952

On the evenings of Friday, March 28th and Monday, March 31st in the large hall concerts were given to open the new stage at New Bradwell County Secondary School. The programme included plays performed and written by the pupils.

In the Infants' School on the afternoon of Tuesday, April 1st the headmistress, Miss Phillips, presented Mrs. Mills, of King Edward Street, with a grey handbag. She was retiring as nursery school caretaker after 8 years, and the gift was from the children, the teaching staffs and friends.

1953

In 1953 at the end of the Easter term New Bradwell County Secondary School bade farewell to Mrs. J. Gibson. She had been at the school for 5 years and was presented with a tea service. With classes commenced for girls it was due to her enthusiasm that lacemaking had been revived, having in February 1949 written to the local press appealing to readers for bobbins, pillows and brass pins; "If anyone can help they will help to keep a fine tradition of our County alive and give creative satisfaction to the children. I should be glad to arrange for the collection of any such articles that may be offered." In fact there would be a good response, to include bobbins from 85 year old Mrs. Wilding of Rushden. She was still making lace and her mother had exhibited lace at the 1851 Crystal Palace Exhibition. As for the schoolgirls at New Bradwell, as perhaps the only such exponents in the country they would achieve national prominence, with photographs taken by a London agency for publication in worldwide journals.

At the end of August among the resignations of teachers were those of Miss K.S. Cope and Miss D.W. Shakeshaft from New Bradwell County Secondary School, Miss D. Smith (who had charge of the nursery class), and Miss Y.M.J. Hobbs from the New Bradwell Infants' School, and Miss E. Bird from the junior school. New appointments effective from September 1st would be Mrs. B.E. Bell, Mrs. E.M. Tilley, Miss J.M. Clarke, Miss D.J. Mills and Miss G. Thorpe.

In November improvements to the lavatory and sanitary accommodation at the New Bradwell Schools were included in the County minor works programme.

1954

In July the North Bucks Divisional Executive agreed to a recommendation that from the coming autumn term children from

Old Bradwell County Infants School would be transferred at the age of 7 to New Bradwell County Junior School. Previously they stayed at Old Bradwell until the age of 8.

1956

On Saturday, December 15th at St. Paul's Church, Daybrook, Nottingham, Miss Mary Cawthorne, only daughter of Mr. and Mrs. T. Cawthorne of 31, Marina Drive, Wolverton, married Robert Brown, a structural engineer from Brixton. Since April she had been a teacher at New Bradwell County Secondary School, and in London as her new home would continue her profession as a domestic science teacher.

In October tenders were invited by Bucks County Council for the building of a new staff room at New Bradwell County Junior School.

1958

William Henry Orvik Sansom, a 19 year old teacher at New Bradwell Secondary Modern School, was killed on Saturday, July 26th when his motor scooter was in collision with a van driven by Maurice Smith of Sunny View Farm, Castlethorpe. He had been teaching at New Bradwell for almost a year, prior to taking up a scheduled place at Keble College Oxford, in 1959. The younger son of Mr. and Mrs. Arnold Sansom of 114, London Road, Stony Stratford, he had been visiting friends in Hanslope. At the time of his death his mother was on a Continental tour and was informed of the news whilst at the home of a sister in Denmark.

In April at the end of term at New Bradwell County Secondary School the headmaster, Mr. W. Walter, presented his deputy, Mr. K. Hooton, with a brief case from the staff and members of the school. At the beginning of next term he would take up the post of deputy head at Newport Pagnell under Mr. C.W. Lynes. During WW2 Mr. Hooton served in the RAF in various theatres as a Flt. Lt. navigator. After demobilisation he went to college and then began teaching at New Bradwell Secondary Modern School in 1948. Married with two daughters his home was at Haversham.

In July it was reported that the deputy head of the junior school, Mr. Ron Stephens, would be going on a 12 month course to Cambridge. Resident in Wolverton, before coming to New Bradwell he held a teaching appointment in Australia. He had been at New Bradwell since 1954 and intended to return to the school. Keen on sports, music, and local history he was presently compiling a history of Old Bradwell.

On Friday, July 22nd, having been teaching in North Bucks for nearly 18 years Mrs. M.A. McNeill retired from New Bradwell County Junior School where, teaching all subjects, she had commenced at its opening in September 1949. Prior to that she had been on the North Bucks relief service and taught for a while at Stony Stratford primary school. In retirement she would continue to live at Cranfield, where her husband was employed, but ultimately she hoped to return to her native Scotland, where before coming to North Bucks she had taught for 19 years. On her last afternoon at New Bradwell she was presented with a chromium tea set.

In October it was reported that 37 year old Mr. Harold Ernest Manistre, deputy head of Cranford Park Junior School, Hayes, Middlesex, had been appointed head of New Bradwell County Junior School. Resident in Lakes Lane, Newport Pagnell, with his wife Daphne, who he married in 1949, he would begin on January 1st in succession to Mr. B.J. Salmon.

In December a farewell presentation was made to Mr. B.J. Salmon, headmaster of New Bradwell County Junior School. As read the entry in the school log book on December 21st; 'This afternoon the children assembled in the Church Hall at 3.00pm, to make a presentation to Mr. B.J. Salmon, Head of this school, who is retiring at the end of the year. Mrs. Johnson presented him with a transistor radio, Philip Roberts wished him well, and Sheena French presented his wife with a bouquet.'

1966

On April 4th the schoolchildren were taken to a reserved site at Corner Pin to watch the Royal party go past, it having been the occasion of the Royal visit to North Bucks.

1967

The school and parents attended a presentation to Mr. Mower, the caretaker for many years, who was retiring. George Baldwin would be the new caretaker.

1970

In March Mr. Manistre left the school to begin duties at Newport Pagnell. Mr. Walter would take over as temporary headmaster. On September 3rd Mr. B.M. Siddons began duties as headmaster of the New Bradwell Middle School.

1975

On July 18th New Bradwell Middle School closed down at 3.30pm. It reopened as a Combined School on September 2nd. 'The 9 year olds and over were admitted, and the younger children had to stay at home for 2 more days, as the alterations were not complete.'

1985

In 1985 Mr. B. Siddons retired as headmaster, to be succeeded by John White.

1996

In February at the age of seventeen Anthony Manchester was voted onto the board of New Bradwell School. He had the backing of parents and was thought to be Britain's youngest school governor.

HEAD TEACHERS

Head teachers are often long remembered by their past pupils (and staff!) In this section in random order are recalled some of those who held such positions at New Bradwell.

GEORGE HENSTOCK HOWITT

'Tall, well built, with a commanding figure and dignified bearing.' A well remembered headmaster, 'with his unique personality, strict disciplinarian, yet kindness itself.'

George Henstock Howitt was born at Sneinton, Notts., on February 4th 1843 to (as stated in the census) his American born father, William, and mother Ann (nee Henstock), born in 1821 at Cotgrave, Northants. In 1851 George was living with his parents and siblings at St. Pancras where his father, aged 30, was headmaster at Camden Town National School. Then in 1861 George was a pupil at Peterborough Training College which, built between 1856 and 1864 by Sir George Gilbert Scott, in the red brick Gothic style, was a training college for schoolmasters in the dioceses of Peterborough, Ely and Lincoln. (It closed as such in 1914.)

In August 1863 George came to Stantonbury when appointed headmaster of the school, which opened on the 31st of that month. At that time there were some 50 pupils and many of the subsequent entries in the log book lament their poor attendance, and the difficulty in getting them to work and behave. In consequence the headmaster had to seemingly enforce harsh measures, albeit with it noted in the report of HM Inspector in May 1864 that 'he appears to use the cane a bit too much and should find other ways to enforce discipline.' Nevertheless in May 1865 it was stated that being the 'Master, probationer' he would shortly receive his certificate, and in May 1866 he is said to be a certificated master of 'the 3rd division of the 2nd degree.' In the log book in November of that year George wrote that the school was closed as "I was obliged to be away." In fact he was temporarily staying at his parent's address in Hamilton Street, St. Pancras, for on November 22nd he married Sarah Ann Hipwell. Born at Kettering she was resident in Hamilton Street, the daughter of Richard Hipwell, an inn keeper. (Ann, George's mother, died in September 1868 at 21, Hamilton Street.)

At Stantonbury, George and his wife took up residence at the school house and in 1867 and 1868 he is stated as being 'a certificated master of the 3rd division of the 2nd degree.' Then in May 1869 certificated of the 2nd degree; in May 1870 as 2nd division 3rd degree, and in May 1871 as 'first class.' As for family matters in 1873 on February 23rd a son, Arthur George Hipwell Howitt, was born.[12] In 1891 George and his wife were living at the school house but now with the addition of Sarah's unmarried brother, Alfred Hipwell, who, living on his own means, had been born at Brixworth, Northants. With an enthusiasm for music George would delight in teaching pupils part songs, of which the Inspectors at their annual examinations would speak highly in their official reports.

Apart from his school responsibilities for many years George would also be choirmaster and organist at St. James' Church at Stantonbury, firstly under the Rev. Cotter and then the Rev. A.C. Woodhouse. Indeed in 1901 on Wednesday, January 2nd in appreciation of his 35 years as choirmaster he was presented by the Rev. Woodhouse with an oak mounted barometer by Negretti and Zambra. Subscribed for by the parishioners this bore the inscription; 'Presented to Mr. Howitt by the members of the choir and other friends in the congregation of the Church of St. James, Stantonbury, Bucks, as a parting gift in remembrance of his 35 years work as Choirmaster, Dec. 1900.' The occasion was a social held in the Board Schools, with a programme of songs and selections on various instruments.

As for educational achievements, during his time as headmaster of the school he would be specially mentioned in the Government Blue Book as one of the 5 best schools in England.

After such a distinguished career, having resigned as head of the Stantonbury and Bradwell Combined Council Schools he was the subject on Wednesday, July 29th 1908 of an appreciation at a gathering in the school yard. Here as the work of Mr. E. Hayle, of Stony Stratford, Alderman. R. Wylie presented him with an illuminated address on vellum of over 100 subscribers. Also a rosewood 8-day clock (supplied by Messrs. Barratt of Northampton), and a purse of gold, towards which the managers, teachers, old boys and friends had all contributed. Mr. W. Ward, school manager, presided over a large attendance and among those present were Mr. C.F. Sykes and Miss Heacock. During his school career George had worked under 3 forms of Government - Voluntary, School Board, and the Council system - and in his reply he said that on coming to Stantonbury in August 1863 he had been greatly impressed by the appearance of the children. Compared with those he had left in the slums they looked 'so wonderfully clean.' As he returned to his seat the Bradwell Band struck up 'For he's a jolly good fellow.' Resident at 52, Stratford Road, in retirement he remained active by becoming a member of the Potterspury Board of Guardians and a member of Wolverton Rural District Council. However having been unwell for some time in 1916 he was taken ill on the night of Thursday, November 16th and, with Dr. C.H. Miles in attendance, he died at his home on Friday, November 17th. The funeral was held on the Tuesday afternoon at St. George's Parish Church. He left a widow and a schoolmaster son Arthur George Hipwell Howitt, to whom with effects of £3,360 5s 2d probate was granted. His widow and brother in law continued to live at 52, Stratford Road, with the death of the latter occurring in January 1924, and the former in January 1928.

THE WILLIAMS SISTERS - & THEIR BROTHER

Thomas Williams was born at Shrewsbury in 1813, and when resident in Bond Street, Dudley, on October 6th 1840 at the parish church he married Mary Ann Briggs, of Stafford Street, Dudley. A coach maker by trade, he was the son of John Williams, a labourer. Mary was the daughter of William Briggs, an excise officer. In 1842 at Dudley a son, John, was born, and in 1844 at Stourbridge a daughter, Ann Elizabeth. In 1844 Mary died and in 1851 as a widower Thomas, now employed as a coach trimmer, was living at 10, Austin Street, Birkenhead, with son John, daughter Ann Elizabeth, and his unmarried sister in law Elizabeth Jane Briggs. Born at Cambridge she was aged 27 and engaged as his housekeeper.

However on June 29th in 1856 Thomas and Elizabeth were married at the parish church 'in the parish of Liverpool,' and in 1858 at Birkenhead a son, Heber Martin Williams, was born. He was baptised at the church of St. Mary on May 16th.[13] Then at Birkenhead a daughter, Amy, was born in 1860, baptised at the church of St. John on September 8th. With Thomas in railway employment as a coach trimmer he was presumably working away when in 1861 at the time of the census Elizabeth was resident at Austin Street, Birkenhead, with unmarried Ann, who was now a pupil teacher, son Heber, and daughter Amy, age 9 months, born at Birkenhead.

In 1864 on December 6th a daughter, Ada, was born at Birmingham, with the family now living in Rocky Lane. Later they moved to New Bradwell and in 1871 were resident at 38, High Street, comprised of Thomas, continuing in occupation as a coach trimmer, Elizabeth Jane, Amy, and Ada. However Heber was living at Brook House, Cheadle, with the family of Anne Elizabeth, his father's daughter by his first marriage. She was married to a schoolmaster and two children would be born of the union.

In 1872 Elizabeth died on October 5th and as a widower in 1881 Thomas (who was now a foreman coach trimmer at Wolverton Works) was living at 38, High Street, New Bradwell, with Heber, who was a clerk at the railway works, being also a lieutenant in the 1st Bucks Rifle Volunteer Corps, and Ada, a pupil teacher. As for Amy, she was living at Broadwater, Sussex, at a lodging house in Belle Vue in occupation as a teacher in a Government elementary school. This was probably the National Free School for Girls (also known as Christ Church National School) which opened in 1817. (The building today is flats.)[14]

Then in 1883 when lodging at 28, High Street, with Henry Hillier and his wife, she was an elementary school teacher at New Bradwell. In 1885 Thomas died on July 6th at 38, High Street, New Bradwell, with probate granted to his married son Heber, of 10, Morland Terrace, Wolverton. At New Bradwell both Amy and Ada involved themselves in community life and in 1893 on the evening of Saturday, November 11th attended a public meeting, held in the National Schoolroom. This was to consider forming a Literary and Mutual Improvement Society, and as chairman the Rev. A.C. Woodhouse said the object was to discuss literary and social topics. Any subject which would tend 'to instruct and elevate' its members should be open to discussion, with the society to be non political and un-sectarian. Amy and Ada were elected to the committee and both being single were living in 1901 as elementary schoolteachers at 36, Thompson Street, New Bradwell.

In 1908 on Tuesday, August 4th Ada, 'senior certificated assistant girls' mistress at Stantonbury Council School,' died after a long illness at the age of 43. The funeral was held on the Friday afternoon with amongst the mourners her siblings Amy, headmistress of the Girls' Department of the Council School, and Heber, of Wolverton.

In 1911 Amy was living at 17, Harwood Street, Stantonbury, and in 1923 her retirement was announced as headmistress on October 31st. This was after some 40 years of service and a fund was opened for a testimonial, with Mr. J. Brooks, headmaster, and Mr. F. Grant, school correspondent, as the joint honorary secretaries. Her successor would be Miss A.H. Cary of Loughborough, to begin her duties on November 1st.

In retirement Miss Williams lived in Harwood Street, New Bradwell, where in 1934 on the morning of Saturday, October 13th she stumbled, or fainted, and fell onto a gas fire in her bedroom. With her clothing set alight she suffered severe burns to her chest and face, and was found by Miss Meacham, who assisted with the housework. Sadly Miss Williams succumbed to the injuries and died that year on November 16th. Attended by a large gathering the funeral was conducted by the Rev. Newman Guest, with interment in the grave of her sister in the churchyard of St. James. Probate was granted to Dorothy May MacKellar, wife of William Matheson MacKellar.

CHARLES WILLIAM LYNES

Born in 1912 on April 15th, Charles William Lynes, whose mother Edith (nee Butler) was from 1917 until June 1944 infants teacher at Gawcott School, was early educated at St. John's Royal Latin School, Buckingham. Then at Goldsmiths' College, University London, where, from being keen on sports, he played cricket and football. His first teaching appointment was at a 'Home Office Approved School', Redhouse Farm School, Buxton Lamas, Norfolk.[15]

From there in 1935 he came to a teaching appointment at Newport Pagnell, where in 1938 he married Miss Doris Kathleen Stapleton. She was born in 1916 on February 3rd and they would subsequently have a son. At the outbreak of WW2 as an assistant schoolmaster, being also an ARP Warden, Charles was living with his wife at 81, Lakes Lane. During the war he served for 5 years in the RAF as an instructor and after the war commanded the local company of the Home Guard for a while.

As second master at Newport Pagnell Secondary Modern School he was treasurer of the parent Teachers' Association but in 1949 was promoted to headmaster at New Bradwell Secondary Modern School. Formerly the Boys' School this came into being at the beginning of the September term in 1949 and now took both genders from the ages of 11 to 15. Mr. Lynes was keen on youth work and in 1950 under his leadership a 'tanner a task' scheme was inaugurated from September 25th to October 2nd. The idea had been a success in other districts, and with the object to augment the school's stage fund a successful concert last May had started the idea. However monies were still needed and each pupil was asked to perform tasks as requested by friends, relatives, neighbours etc. These were then entered on a card carried by each worker. In other involvements that year he invited the parents of pupils to visit the school on the evening of October 11th. This was to view a display covering the school's curriculum and introducing a programme of singing by the school choir, items by the school dance team, a PT display, and some short boxing bouts, he hoped they would gain a greater understanding of the work of the school. Indeed it was the aim of the school to prepare the children for life after their schooldays. In referring to the school uniform, an example of which was displayed on a tailor's dummy, he asked the parents to help make it universal throughout the school. Not only would it promote a smart appearance but also encourage the wearers to take a pride in their appearance, and engender a team ethos. He thanked the PTA for supplying and serving the refreshments, and for an hour the visitors were able to freely wander about the rooms and discuss with the pupils examples of their work. Exhibits included a display of Bucks pillow lace work, needlework, knitting and embroidery. As for the boys a model stage was shown.

This was complete with miniature furniture and interior lighting, it being the school's intention to raise money to build a stage in the hall under the supervision of the woodwork master. Also on view was a large display of garden produce from the school's own gardens. As part of the 14s to 15s school year, towards introducing pupils to the jobs available in adult life visits were organised to local factories such as Aquascutum in Bletchley, and the printing and railway works at Wolverton. Additionally excursions were made to the House of Commons, and for hearing first hand about different employments talks were given in the school by various exponents to include police officers and nurses.

Mr. Lynes remained at New Bradwell until the end of 1959, having been promoted to headmaster of Newport Pagnell County Secondary School. In consequence on the afternoon of Friday, December 18th at the end of term assembly he was presented on behalf of the staff, associates, and past and present pupils with a matching pen set by Mr. W.J. Green, chairman of the governors. In reply Mr. Lynes thanked all the contributors and said the canteen staff and his clerical assistant had given him an addressing stamp and stationery. He would commence his duties in January 1960. As for other activities, in June 1961 he stood as an Independent candidate in the by election at Newport Pagnell, occasioned by the death of Mr. H. Mason. He duly won although only 926 out of a total electorate of 3,370 had voted. His wife died in 2001 and Charles died in 2003.

SARAH ANN HEACOCK

Sarah Ann Heacock was born at Spark Brook, Aston, Birmingham, in 1860 on August 25th, and in 1861 was living at 15, Lawrence Street, Birmingham, with her parents, Robert, aged 30, a gunsmith, his wife Sarah, age 22, born at Winchester, and sister Eliza Alice age 1, born at Birmingham. As an assistant schoolmistress in 1881 Sarah was lodging at 142, Radcliffe Road, Tonge with the Haulgh, Lancashire, with Henry Lawson, a machine setter, and his wife. Around 1889 she became schoolmistress at Oxford Lane (later Oxford Road) Infant School, Great Marlow, and 'generally always achieved the highest grant.' Then as headmistress in 1894 she obtained a similar post at Stantonbury, and in the schoolroom at the Great Marlow school on Friday, October 12th was presented with a testimonial in the form of a fitted ladies dressing case and framed photos of scenes of local interest. In the presence of the clergy and subscribers the vicar made the presentation.

At Stantonbury she became headmistress in 1894 on October 15th and would soon be recognised for her abilities, as evidenced by an extract from an inspection report; 'Miss Heacock has reorganised this school and improved its condition wonderfully during the time she has had charge of it. It is definitely going to thrive under her and become a first class infant school.' Indeed she swiftly made many improvements; '1895 Nov. 7th. The cloakroom must be properly fitted with pegs and clothes horses, the children's jackets should not be admitted into any of the schoolrooms. A clock should be provided and the main entrance of the school should be paved. Wrote to the Board asking for 'Progress and Marks Books' on October 20th. Have not received them, and have come to the conclusion that they were not thought necessary for Infants' School use.' Her mode of discipline continued and in 1897 'Miss Heacock's work shows her to be a first rate Infant Mistress. Her school is in admirable order.'

For many years her residence would be 19, Harwood Street, New Bradwell, and in other activities she was a member of the Stantonbury Hospital Saturday Committee. She remained as headmistress until her marriage in 1917 to a widower, Alfred Nathaniel Nicholson. Born in Norfolk he had moved to Newport Pagnell in 1875 as clerk to Messrs. Powell and Newman, an old established firm of solicitors. When this passed to the late Mr. Charles W. Powell he then became confidential clerk. Having a wide knowledge of the law, and having acted for some years as Mr. Powell's deputy at the Petty Sessions, when his employer died in February 1914 he was unanimously elected clerk to the Newport Pagnell and Fenny Stratford Benches of Magistrates. He was also clerk to the Income Tax Commissioners, among other public offices, and since early 1914 had been clerk to the Justices for the Newport Pagnell and Fenny Stratford Petty Sessional Divisions. His marriage to his wife Maria Goodman produced 5 sons and 5 daughters and following her death in 1915 he married Sarah Heacock one Monday in October 1917, with the Rev.

Newman Guest officiating.

They then lived at Newport Pagnell at 'The Uplands,' Wolverton Road, with Sarah continuing as schoolmistress under her previous name. She closed her duties as headmistress in 1920 on May 20th. This was probably due to her husband's failing health, for in 1921 just before Easter he was removed to Northampton Hospital on March 31st. There he underwent two operations but complications developed and he died two weeks later at the hospital on the afternoon of Saturday, May 21st. He was 67. Subsequently Sarah lived alone at The Uplands but later moved to Letchworth. At the start of WW2 she was living as a retired schoolmistress at 15, Broadwater Avenue, Letchworth, where she died in 1945 on September 10th. As for her past connections with North Bucks, in 1946 on Wednesday, April 10th Mr. P.C. Gambell, on the instructions of her executors, auctioned the detached residence known as 'Uplands', 84, Wolverton Road, Newport Pagnell, let to Mr. A.C. Holmes at £75pa.

ELSIE MILLER

A native of Barrow in Furness, Elsie Miller was born in 1902 on June 21st. Firstly at Smethwick she began her teaching career in 1923 and at the outbreak of WW2 was living as a schoolmistress in Hendon at 105, Hale Drive, resident with Annie Miller, a widow, born in 1872 on January 27th. After the outbreak of war she continued teaching in London, where she was also a warden, and often under the obvious difficulties had to teach in houses. Having been headmistress at New Bradwell for less than 2 years, in 1946 she died on Saturday, June 15th at 74, Newport Road, New Bradwell. This was the home of her sister Annie Elizabeth, born in 1895 on June 9th, and her husband Edward Brown. Born in 1902 on January 13th he was employed at Wolverton Works and the couple had married in 1928 at Barrow in Furness. Elsie's home at New Bradwell had been 147, Old Bradwell Road, but 7 weeks before her death she had been taken ill, and spent 5 weeks as a patient at St. Mary's Hospital, Paddington. The funeral took place on the Tuesday afternoon, and included amongst the mourners were Miss Mallard, Girls' headmistress, Miss Stevens and Mrs. Evans, of New Bradwell Infants School, Mr. G.T. Maynard, headmaster of the Boys' School, and the school managers.

AILEEN HELEN CARY

Succeeding Miss Williams, in 1923 on Thursday, November 1st Miss Aileen Helen Cary, of Loughborough, commenced her duties as headmistress at the Girls' School at New Bradwell where, allegedly possessed of a 'fierce disposition', she would certainly make an impression on the pupils; "If we were naughty in some way, like talking etc., we had to stand outside the classroom and pray the Governess, Miss Cary, would not see us because she punished us, sometimes with a whacking. I enjoyed my schooldays ..."!

During her time at New Bradwell, resident at 36, King Edward Street, New Bradwell, she became involved with the New Bradwell District Nursing Association, being present at the first meeting in 1927 on March 18th. Here she was appointed secretary, compiling all the minutes, and signed as secretary at her last meeting in 1938 on January 11th. Excepting a period of hospital treatment in 1934 this was after continuous service, and with a letter of thanks to be sent it would be noted that - 'a sample to be displayed' - she had selected china and cutlery as a present, for which £6 6s had been collected. In other activities she would be president of the Girl Guides, and assistant secretary of the County Library. In 1938 she was appointed for a similar school position at Thomas Gray Junior Girls' Council School, Slough, and relinquished her position at New Bradwell at the end of the Easter term. On behalf of all the children she was presented by the school captain with a bedside electric standard lamp. Then in a further presentation one evening at the school the Girl Guides met and on their behalf Miss Betty Boddy presented her with silver fruit spoons and servers. The gift from the Nursing Association would be china and cutlery, conveyed to her by Miss Penn, head mistress of the Infants' School and a member of the Association Committee. At Slough Miss Cary would take up residence with another schoolteacher at 4, Adelphi Gardens, with this still her address when in 1970 she died on November 21st, leaving £12,022.

FRANCES BEATRICE HOLLIS

Frances Hollis and mother.

At St. Saviour's Church, Islington, in 1910 on July 16th the marriage was conducted of Clarence Montague Hollis, a jeweller's assistant, aged 27, and Beatrice Sarah Gray, also aged 27, born at Bishopsgate, London. The following year they were living at 47, Ockendon Road, Islington, and in 1913 on April 23rd a daughter, Frances Beatrice Hollis, was born. In 1918 the family were resident at 43, Church Road, Southgate N9 and then in 1933 at 124, Wellington Road, Enfield, in which year Frances began teaching. This was at a London Junior School, where at Enfield she switched to teaching infants.

In 1939 she was living with other teachers at Wroe Dairy Farm, Marshland, Wisbech, the home of James Pacey & his wife, and in 1946 became headmistress at New Bradwell Infants' School. There she remained until August 1949, when gaining a similar position at Chingford, Essex. In consequence at New Bradwell Infants' School on the morning of Friday, August 12th 1949 the staff and children assembled in the hall to present her with parting gifts. Mrs. Evans, the deputy head, opened the proceedings, and three scholars each handed Miss Hollis a £1 note as the surplus cash from the collection. Two other children handed her a leather blouse case and two others a bedside electric reading lamp. Saying she had been very happy at New Bradwell she gave brooches to her staff, a brooch and bangles to the nursery staff, ear rings and a brooch to the lady caretakers, and a biro pen to the male caretaker. On Friday, August 19th she then left for her new position where she would help to start Longshaw Junior School.

In 1954 she came as headmistress to Churchfields Infants School, South Woodford, in the borough of Redbridge, where in later years she was remembered by a past pupil as allegedly 'A bit of a dragon but with a good heart.' However when she retired in July 1973 she said of the contemporary conditions; "Teaching now is a lot more relaxed, schools are more friendly and there are more good relationships between parents, children and staff." After a 'well deserved' rest touring Germany and Italy she then intended to do voluntary work, "especially teaching in a school for the mentally handicapped." She died in 1991 on October 27th at 12, Snakes Lane, Woodford Green.

Frances Hollis in later life. Her mother is on her left.

PHYLLIS EDITH PENN

Born at Bedford on November 10th 1898, Phyllis Edith Penn was baptised on December 13th, and in 1901 was living at 91, Victoria Road, Bedford, with her siblings and her parents George Henry Penn, a gymnastic instructor, and her mother Edith. Phyllis attended the Girls' Modern School, Bedford, and in 1911 was living at 85, Victoria Road, Bedford, with her parents (her father still a gymnastic instructor but now an 'Army pensioner'), her mother, and her unmarried sister Mabel, a student, aged 29. Her mother died in 1922 and with their widower father Phyllis and Mabel continued to live at the same address. After several appointments as an assistant mistress in Bucks, in 1930 Phyllis was appointed as headmistress of New Bradwell Council Infants' School, and as such was living in 1939 with her schoolmistress sister Mabel (born in 1881 on August 16th) at the same Bedford address. However in February that year she was appointed as headmistress of Aylesbury Queen's Park Council Infants' School, this being in succession to Miss G.A. Jones, who had resigned as headmistress after 32 years. The school closed in February 1976 and in 1987 on August 14th Phyllis died at the Mid Bucks Medical Centre & Residential Home, Wendover Road, Wendover, Aylesbury.

SARAH MALLARD

Sarah Mallard was born at Kilsby, Northants., on September 1st 1898. Her father, John, was a signalman on the railway, and in 1911 Sarah was living with her siblings and parents, John and Lucy Jane (nee Howick), at 69, Bridge Street, Stantonbury. In June 1916 the local Education Secretary wrote that as a student teacher Sarah was eligible to serve in New Bradwell Girls' School. Indeed in 1938 on June 7th she became headmistress and continued to live with her parents, who by 1939 had moved to 37, Windsor Street, Wolverton. It was there in August 1940 that the tragic news was received that Sarah's younger brother, Sergeant Observer John William Mallard, had been killed while serving in the RAF, to which he had been apprenticed in 1929. He was buried with full military honours in the churchyard of St. Nicholas, Cottesmore, his parents and sisters, Sarah, and Mrs. Medcalf, of Bletchley, being present. Sarah terminated her engagement as headmistress of the Girls' Department in 1949 on August 12th but continued to live locally. When resident in Bettina Grove, Bletchley, she died in 1985 on November 26th.

(On the night of August 3rd 1940 Fairey Battle L5433 of 103 Squadron took off on a Night Flying Cross Country Exercise from RAF Newton in Nottinghamshire. The aircraft was noted to climb, then stall and hit trees on the approach to RAF Cottesmore, having mistaken it for Newton. The pilot, Sgt. Gerald C. Brams RAFVR, from Cricklewood, was killed, with his funeral taking place at Hendon Cemetery and crematorium. Sgt. Mallard, the observer, suffered injuries from which he died on August 5th. He was 27 and married to Nora Elizabeth Mallard of Nottingham. The wireless operator/air gunner was a Sgt. Davies, who was slightly injured. Both Sgt. Brams and Sgt. Mallard were listed as 'Experienced pre-war airmen who had served with distinction during the Battle of France.' In fact Sgt. Mallard had been with 103 Squadron from the start of the war, serving up to the evacuation. The Fairey Battle of the crash had been delivered to 103 Squadron in 1940 on July 6th, in which month on the 21st it saw action bombing the chemical works at Rotterdam.)

JOHN IRVING BROOKS

John Irving Brooks was born in 1879 on August 2nd at Hope, Flintshire, where in 1881, together with his sister, he was living with - both born at Bersham, Denbighshire - his father, in occupation as a schoolmaster, and his mother, Martha. In 1891 with his sister, and now also a brother, he was living with his parents at Rose Cottage, Penyffordd, in the parish of Hope, where his father was an elementary school teacher. Then by 1901 his father was head teacher at the Board School, where John was an assistant teacher.

In 1903 at Hawarden, Flintshire, John married Mary Ellen Bellis, born at Hope on May 4th 1877, and in 1904 on May 17th a son, also named John Irving Brooks, was born at Long Crendon, Bucks.

In 1908 John and family came to Stantonbury where, with John as headmaster of the Council School, in 1911 they were living, 'successive from 45, Thompson Street,' at 'Grindleford,' 19, Queen Anne Street. In June 1913 at the monthly meeting of the Bradwell School Managers as headmaster of the Boys' School Mr. Brooks wrote regarding the new school and the suggested staff. He said there would be 4 rooms for 38 boys each, and 5 rooms for 36 boys each. Presently the staff included 5 certificated and 2 uncertificated teachers. Therefore to avoid overcrowding he suggested that the managers should advertise for 2 uncertificated teachers, namely a man and a lady teacher for the lower class. There were now 352 boys on the school books and with Alderman Wylie saying the schools would be ready by the end of August it was agreed to advertise for the 2 teachers requested. At Stantonbury he also conducted the Bradwell Evening Schools, and in July 1914 it was announced that of the ten 'lads' who sat for the exam of the Birmingham Technical

Institute six had passed with great credit. Indeed Bernard Tapp, of Old Bradwell, had obtained a first prize.

In May 1917 at a meeting of Bucks County Council the Finance Committee, at the request of the Education Committee, were recommended that from April last John's salary should be increased from £200 to £205pa.

Apart from school activities, in June 1937 he was included in the nominations for the vacancy in the New Bradwell Ward. Also, with the tensions of a probable war, he became an ARP Warden and at the outbreak of WW2 was resident at 19, Queen Anne Street, with his wife and also Stanley Cooper, born in 1903 on May 5th, a married (and probably evacuated) school teacher. In March 1940 John retired after 32½ years as headmaster. Known to many as 'Boss Brooks,' from his enforcement of discipline, he was held in regard and respect by those that he taught, and with a number of old boys having organised a fund, on Tuesday, March 19th, at a gathering of nearly 200 he was presented with parting gifts in the concert room of the Progressive Club. Mr. J. Pimbley BA, an old boy, and now a member of staff, had been the chairman of a committee making the arrangements, by which Mr. Brooks received a mahogany bureau and his wife a cut glass flower vase. With Master Cecil Clayton making the presentation, the staff of the boys, girls and infants schools presented a timepiece and a date indicator, whilst his wife was handed a bouquet of narcissi and daffodils on behalf of the Leopold Road school evacuees. The new headmaster at New Bradwell Boys' Council School would be Mr. Maynard, senior assistant at the Manor Park Senior School Slough, to begin his duties on April 1st. In retirement John lived at Swansea but in 1946 on June 25th he died on a visit to his son at 132, Connaught Road, Luton.[16]

GEORGE THOMAS JOHNSON MAYNARD

Baptised at the church of St. Saviour's, Bath, George Thomas Johnson Maynard was born in 1908 on January 10th. In 1911 with a brother and two sisters he was living at 4, Highbury Terrace, Bath, with his parents (William, in occupation as a cabinet maker, and his wife Annie), his paternal grandmother, and an uncle. In 1929 he began as a teacher at Slough although it was at Bath at St. Andrew's Church that in 1934 on August 3rd he married Gwendolen Lucy Hill. Born in 1908 on October 13th she was the only daughter of Mr. & Mrs. Louis Albert Hill of Slough, but formerly of Bath. In 1939 George and his wife were resident at Alvista Avenue, Slough. George was senior assistant at the Manor Park Senior School, Slough, and also a sergeant in the Bucks Special Constabulary. As for Gwen she had long been involved with the plays of the Slough Amateur Dramatic Society, and in their 1940 production of 'The Housemaster' she took the role of 'Cris.'

That year with George appointed as headmaster of New Bradwell Boys' Council School he was presented on leaving his position at Slough with a fountain pen. Also a fruit bowl, made by the boys in the school wood turnery. At New Bradwell he began his duties on April 1st yet still retained a family connection with Slough, where his father in law was headmaster at Thomas Gray Boys' School.

In early 1941 George formed a Youth Centre for those aged 14 to 20. The officers elected were president, Mr. A. Brown JP; chairman Mr. G.T Maynard; secretary Mr. S. Mynard; treasurer Mr. G. Sprittles, with an acting committee. For the funding it was decided to charge 6d for membership and a weekly sub of 2d. Indoor and outdoor sports would be arranged, with meetings held on Tuesdays and Thursdays. Then in 1946 in succession to his father in law he was appointed as headmaster at Thomas Gray School at Slough. In consequence at New Bradwell at the close of term on Wednesday, December 18th he was the subject of a presentation before a large gathering of pupils, staff, managers and parents. Mr. F.H. Tompkins, chairman of the managers, presided being supported by the other managers and Mr. G. Turnbull, the School Correspondent. Of the teaching staff Mr. B.J. Salmons commenced the proceedings by conducting the children in singing several carols. After announcing the holidays he then welcomed the managers, parents and all present, saying the occasion was to bid farewell to Mr. Maynard on his last day at the school. He paid tribute to Mr. Maynard's service and also that of Mrs. Maynard, for having helped out during the times of staff shortage. On behalf of the assembly the chairman then presented an embossed coal box and companion set in brass, and

Mr. Salmons gave a cheque as the remainder of the money. As the work of the boys, also presented was a book containing lino cuts and bearing the signatures of the staff, managers and almost all the pupils. In recounting his time at the school, in reply Mr. Maynard reminisced that he had cycled from Haversham to New Bradwell School on 2,500 occasions. Also he mentioned the wartime experience, when sometimes there had been as many as 80 pupils in a class due to the evacuees. Also the fire drills, when every boy had to be out of the classroom into a secure place within 15 seconds. (As for the boys, during the austerity of the wartime years they thought he must be very wealthy, as he wore a different suit every day!) Of 119, Marlborough Road, Slough, in 1982 on December 4th he died suddenly at The Princess Christian Nursing Home. The funeral was held on December 10th at 3pm at Slough Crematorium, with 'No flowers, no mourning.' His widow died at Slough in 1999.

Bradwell Bos Choir 1931. Standing in the middle row are John Salmon (Choirmaster) and Irving Brooks (Headmaster).

BADEN JOHN SALMON

Baden John Salmon was born on 12th August 1900 at Marshfield, Gloucestershire and baptised on 16th September. In 1901, together with his siblings - all born at Marshfield - he was living in Hay Street, Marshfield with his father Worthy Salmon, aged 36, a grocer's porter, born at Marshfield, and his mother Alice Amy, also born in the same village. They had married in 1891 and in 1911

John Salmon in his den.

the family comprised Worthy and Alice and their children: Baden John, Bernard, Bruce, Abbey and Amy. At Marshfield the family residence was 'The Chains' at 20, Hay Street. This later became the Chain House Café which, run by Mrs. Green and Mrs. Moules, was still in existence in the early years after WW2.

In 1921 John was attending Bristol University for teacher training and that year became assistant master at New Bradwell Boys' School. On Saturday, 28th July 1928 Baden (now only known as John) married Miss Gladys Mary Speaks, born on 2nd August 1902. She was the second daughter of Mrs. Speaks and the late Mr. C. Speaks of 37, Victoria Street, Wolverton, and up to the time of her marriage, had been employed in London with Dickins & Jones. The honeymoon was spent in Torquay. With his place taken at New Bradwell Boys' School by Mr. J. E. H. Warren of Olney, in January 1932 John was appointed headmaster of

Tingewick Council School. There he remained for nearly 5 years until in October 1936 Miss L.D. Moslin, senior mistress of Buckingham Senior School, was appointed as headmistress. Mr. Salmon was then placed on the unattached staff, but in December 1937 returned to New Bradwell to assist Mr. J. I. Brooks.

In 1938 a son, John Richard Salmon, was born. John senior was recorded as 'an elementary schoolmaster' at the outbreak of WW2. He was resident with his wife at 61, Gloucester Road, Wolverton. He became headmaster of New Bradwell Boys' Council School and in 1947 on 18th November gave an account of a headmaster's work and duties at the fortnightly meeting of the 'New Bradwell Men's Fireside.'

In 1949 the New Bradwell schools were re-organised and when the new term opened in September the former Boys' School was now the Secondary Modern School, with the Girls' School becoming the County Primary School. Both schools had mixed pupils and the respective heads, having been appointed only a week before, were Mr. C. W. Lynes and (former head of the Boys' School) John Salmon.

Then in other appointments, at the annual ceremony of installation, held at the Craufurd Arms Hotel on Monday, 16th January 1950, he was installed as Worshipful Master of the Scientific Lodge of Freemasons, Wolverton. Also that year, under his supervision, the pupils produced their own school magazine 'Team Work.' Mr. Salmon sent a copy to the manufacturers of the printing equipment who, suitably impressed with the quality, displayed it on their Adana printing stand at the Ideal Home Exhibition at Olympia.

In other school matters, in October the following year, he was elected chairman at the annual meeting of the New Bradwell Parent Teachers' Association. This was held at the County Secondary School, where it was decided to seek additional support by conducting a house to house canvass for members. In presiding, Mr. F. H. Tompkins said that all the efforts for the Association were for the benefit of children attending the schools and enabled them to provide the school with items that the Education Authority couldn't supply. Indeed, during the past year, grants to the schools had amounted to £42.

John retired in 1960 and on Wednesday, 21st December over 200 children of the New Bradwell County Junior School assembled at 3pm in St. James Church Hall to say farewell. His association with education in the county had spanned some 40 years and on behalf of the staff he was presented with a transistor radio by Mrs. L. M. Johnson, one of the managers. Philip Roberts wished him well and Sheena French presented Mrs. Salmon with a bouquet. John died on 17th May 1964 at Charing Cross Hospital, Westminster, having developed pneumonia following a diagnosis and surgery for carcinoma of the stomach. At this time, his son John Richard was pursuing his medical studies at Charing Cross. His widow Gladys died on 9th January 1974.

HENRY MANISTRE

In succession to Mr. B.J. Salmon, Henry Manistre, aged 37, from a position as deputy head of Cranford Park Junior School, Hayes, Middlesex, was appointed as the headmaster of New Bradwell County Junior School. He would live at Lakes Lane, Newport Pagnell, and begin his duties on January 1st 1961.

June 1961 - B.J.Salmon (retired Headmaster) presenting Cup to captains of the winning "House - Raymond Wood & Sally Palmer - at the Annual Sports of New Bradwell Count Junior School. Mr Manistre, Headmaster since 1st January 1961 standing in group."

HEALTH AND WELFARE

DR. JOHN LOVE

John Marion Lewis Love was born in 1901 on September 16th, one of the children of 45 year old Gilbert Love, a medical practitioner, born in County Tyrone, and his 40 year old wife Wilhelmina, born in the city of Cork. With his siblings, parents, a sister in law and a niece he was resident at Great Budworth, Cheshire, and in 1921 on April 6th commenced medical studies at Queen's University, Belfast. It seems he subsequently held appointments at the North Riding Infirmary Middlesbrough, and as resident Medical Officer at the Royal Victoria and West Hants. Hospital, Bournemouth. In 1933 at the parish church Finchley on August 12th he married Norah Clarke aged 22 of Finchley, where in 1938 they were living at 13, Claremont Park. Then in 1939 with John as a medical practitioner they were resident at 60, Ravenscourt Road, Hammersmith. With the outbreak of war he joined the RAMC and from being a lieutenant in 1940 was a captain in 1942, resident at 60, Ravenscourt Road.

It would be in 1945 in a hotel bar that in a chance conversation with Dr. Patrick Joseph Delahunty, a fellow Irishman, he accepted the offer of a partnership in a medical partnership at Wolverton.[17] In 1946 he married Phyllis Ann Garrod and would practise at New Bradwell for almost 26 years, being in other activities president of the New Bradwell branch of the British Legion from 1950, and associated with the cricket club and other organisations. For 23 years he was a member of Wolverton Urban Council and chairman 1961-63. He retired in 1971 but suffered from ill health and died at his home 8, Beech Avenue, Olney, in 1974 on April 30th. He left a widow and a son, Michael. The funeral was held at St. James', New Bradwell, on Friday, May 3rd.

MARTIN MILES

Martin Miles was born at Stoke Hammond, the son of a farmer, and his medical career is best stated verbatim - in the usual abbreviated form - in the entries in the Medical Directories;

1870

'MILES, Martin, Wolverton and Stantonbury, Bucks -MD Metrop. Coll. N. York, 1858; L.F.P.S. Glasg. and L.M. 1865; (Char. Cross); Mem. N. York Med. Soc.; Surg. Carriage Departm. L. and N.W. Railw., and Friend-in-Need, Nat. Union, Provin., Briton, and Empire Assur. Cos., I.O. Odd Fells, Victoria and Unit. Kingd. Benef. Socs.'

1875

'MILES, MARTIN, Wolverton and Stantonbury, Bucks - L.R.C.P.Edin. and L.M. 1873; L.F.P.S. Glasg. and L.M. 1865; (Char. Cross); Mem. N. York Med. Soc.; Surg. Carriage Departm. L and N.W. Railw., and Friend-in-Need, Nat. Union, Provin., and other Assur. Cos., I.O. Odd Fells. Victoria, Unit. Patriots, and other Benef. Socs.'

By 1881 he was resident with his family at 39, High Street, New Bradwell, as a medical practitioner, whilst on the wider scene he was extolling the virtues of SCOTT'S EMULSION OF PURE COD LIVER OIL WITH HYPOPHOSPHITES is far superior to plain Cod Liver oil, and, as the following shows, is easily digested:- I have prescribed 'Scott's Emulsion' and taken it myself. It is palatable, efficient, and can be tolerated by almost anyone, especially where cod liver oil itself cannot be borne. From any chemist at 2s 6d and 4s 6d.' He died in 1885 on the afternoon of Thursday, December 10th when whilst visiting a neighbour in a professional capacity he suffered an apoplectic fit and died within about 20minutes. He had practised in the neighbourhood for over 20 years.

CHARLES HENRY MILES

The grandson of the late Martin Miles of Tyrrels Manor, Stoke Hammond, landowner and lord of the manor, Charles Henry Miles was born at Fenny Stratford in 1859 on January 8th to Martin Miles, born at Stoke Hammond, and his wife Eliza, born at Buckingham. In 1861 he was living in Cross Street (now Aylesbury Street), Fenny Stratford, with his father, who was in occupation as a chemist and druggist, his mother and siblings. Then in 1871 the family were resident in the High Street, New Bradwell, where his father was now a surgeon. Charles attended the local school but in 1874 at the County Court on Friday, July 10th an action was

Top: Dr. Charles Miles with his wife Harriet (nee Cotter)
Bottom: Dr. Miles at a hospital fete in 1925.

brought by himself as a minor, and by his 'next friend' (actually his father, Martin Miles) against the headmaster of the boys' school, George Howitt. The action claimed that on May 19th 1873 the headmaster had beaten him 'immoderate and excessive,' whereby he was 'greatly injured and damaged.' £50 was claimed but witnesses for the defence stated that Miles had been generally very cheeky and badly behaved. So much so that the headmaster removed him from the premises, during which the alleged injuries occurred. Charles stated that the master had seized him by the throat with his left hand and thrashed him with a cane. Also that he was knocked down and struck in the chest, whereupon he went home and complained to his parents. He had suffered greatly ever since, with an inability to swallow and a general weakness, conditions which a surgeon of Stony Stratford, Frederick Dufty, corroborated. Several pupils of the school were called and also confirmed the evidence. However the defence claimed that the accusations were greatly exaggerated. Also they brought attention to the amount of time that had elapsed before the proceedings were commenced. Regarding the supposed exaggeration the judge agreed, saying the master was only doing his duty. He then gave judgment for the defendant with costs, at which 'The verdict was received with applause by the Court, which was at once suppressed.' It seems that possibly as a result of this incident Charles was also educated at Trinity College, Stony Stratford. Then in further progress at Waterloo College, London, University College, London, and the Hospital and University of London Middlesex Hospital. An expert horseman, in his early life he was a member of the Royal Bucks Hussars for seven years, and being a prize shot and swordsman gained a silver cup for best shot in 1881 and a silver cup for swordsmanship in 1882. The latter was repeated in 1883 when he was also medallist of the London Exhibition of rifle shooting. As for his medical career, in 1884 he passed the preliminary examination of the Royal College of Physicians for the diploma of LRCP London. This had been held during the week beginning January 28th at the College, Pall Mall, and then in 1886 on July 12th, when of the University College Hospital, London, he passed the Second Professional Examination for the qualification in medicines, surgery and midwifery of the Royal College of Physicians of London and the Royal College of Surgeons of England. In 1887 on June 20th he passed the final exam, qualifying for the Diploma LRCP Lond. Also that year he was granted a certificate to practice as a licentiate of the Society of Apothecaries, receiving the Diploma LSA Lond. In 1888 he was admitted Licentiate of the Royal College of Physicians and then took over the medical practice at Stantonbury of his late father. He had died in 1885 and for the interim the practice while Charles was at college had been conducted by Dr. J. Anderson. In 1888 at the meeting of the Newport Pagnell Board of Guardians he was appointed as medical officer for Stantonbury and in 1891 was resident at New Bradwell at 'The Laurels' in the High Street, New Bradwell. This was his address when in 1892 on April 23rd at St. Stephen's Church, Paddington, he married Alice Harriett Cotter, the only daughter of the late Reverend Cotter of Stantonbury. In addition to his extensive medical practice he was also the founder and proprietor of the North Bucks Private Hospital and School of Midwifery at 51, Stratford Road, Wolverton.

However he would be in need of medical attention in 1915 having sustained injuries in a serious accident on Thursday, April 22nd. When returning in the afternoon in his brougham from Old Bradwell, on nearing the white gate leading to a field which he owned on the Old Bradwell side he met Mrs. Maycock of Loughton, who was driving towards home. For some reason the horse turned to the opposite side of the road and running sharply up the bank and down into the ditch bolted towards Old Bradwell. The traces broke, the coachman was thrown into the ditch, and with the brougham overturned and smashed the doctor was unable to crawl out. When the brougham overturned a thick plate glass had penetrated behind his left ear dividing the scalp down to the bone for about 7 inches. Fortunately the Rev. K.T. Bailey had chanced by and with another person's assistance took Charles home in his carriage. A local doctor attended the injuries and fortunately Charles began to progress satisfactorily. For many years he was lecturer on ambulance and nursing under Bucks County Council whilst in other pursuits he was an author and president of the Bradwell United Silver Band. He would also own a great deal of property in the neighbourhood, and as an advocate of healthy living and accommodation built 'West

The front entrance of the house at 51, Stratford Road, Wolverton, which still bears the 'private hospital' inscription on the window light. It was set up by Dr. Miles of New Bradwell.

View,' as a row of houses on garden city lines in an elevated position in Bradwell.

In 1927 his wife died at Dorchester on November 27th and it was around this time that his health began to fail. Much of the property was auctioned when his frailties began to take a serious turn some 3 months before his death. This occurred at The Laurels on the evening of Saturday, June 7th 1930 and on the Wednesday the well attended funeral was held at New Bradwell.

THE NEW BRADWELL GOOD SAMARITAN SOCIETY

The New Bradwell Good Samaritan Society was established in 1872 at the New Inn on Monday, December 9th by Andrew Williamson, Stephen Blunt, Robert Sutton and Dan Millward. Each gave a small contribution towards the initial expenses, such as the cost of stationery etc., and the vicar, the Rev. C.P. Cotter, was prevailed upon to preach a sermon on the parable of the Good Samaritan. For a penny a week members of the society and their families would then be covered for the cost of treatment at Northampton Infirmary, either as in or out patients. In 1873 the first anniversary was celebrated on Tuesday, December 9th with a supper served by Mr. Dan Millward of the New Inn. The Rev. Cotter, president of the Society, was called to the chair, with Mr. Robert Wylie of Lime Cottage as vice chairman. Congratulating the members on the success of the society the Reverend then called upon the secretary, Mr. Williamson, to read the report. About £11 had been realised for the hospital. Nine guineas had been paid and the society had received six in and 12 out patients letters. Various toasts were proposed and a vote of thanks was given to the Rev. Cotter.

At the annual dinner in 1874, held at the New Inn on the evening of Wednesday, December 9th, some 70 were present for a fare served by Mr. Millward. The room had been decorated by Mrs. and Miss Cotter and after the dinner the meeting was held with the vicar, the Rev. Cotter, in the chair. Sir Ludlow Cotter proposed the toast of the evening after which the vicar called upon Mr. Williamson, the secretary, for a statement of the work of the Society. He duly read the report, which showed the Society had begun in 1872 with 4 members. At the last annual dinner there were 20 members but now there were 186. Since the Society commenced they had paid £35 3s 6d to Northampton Infirmary and there had been 24 in patients letters and 48 for out patients. The income for 1874 by the members contributions of 1d per week and donations from friends amounted to £31 11s 4d, and after paying the Infirmary and meeting some incidental expenses a balance of £3 9s 6d was now held by the treasurer. The annual dinners were a regular feature and now termed the Stantonbury and Wolverton Good Samaritan Society in 1891, at the occasion held at the Railway Tavern, the sum of £3 was presented by the committee of the Stantonbury Floral and Horticultural Society. This was through its dissolution from circumstances beyond their control, and also that year having taken a great interest in the society for many years Mr. Robert Wylie was unanimously elected president.

In March 1894 the Society decided to give an additional 10 guineas to the Northampton Infirmary and so obtain for the use in Stantonbury and Wolverton bed rests, bed pans, ice cups, air cushions, inhaler, bath etc. Throughout the years the society provided a much needed service for its members. Also much needed income for the hospital, at the Governors' meeting of which in January 1934 the secretary, Mr. A.E. Atterbury, presented 100 guineas on behalf of the society. Then in November 1944 the society announced the appointment of Mr. R.G. Alderson of 12, Bedford Street, Wolverton, as secretary in place of the late Mr. A.E. Atterbury. Mr. M. Bird of 42, Queen Anne Street, New Bradwell, was elected assistant secretary, and Mr. Daniells of 16, High Street, New Bradwell, as outside collector, in succession to the late Mr. T. Kightley. With the advent of a national service for health, in 1948 at the 75th meeting of the Society, held on the evening of Tuesday, March 16th in the Boys' School, the chairman, Mr. F.H. Tompkins, said this would probably be the last but one general meeting of the Society in its present form. This was due to the beginning of the National Health Service that year on July 5th when the Society would not be called upon for vouchers for hospital treatment. However he hoped the society would carry on in a modified form. Indeed it did and for an annual subscription sick room requirements could be borrowed by members of the society, which was finally dissolved in 1987.

HOSPITAL FUND

For the support of Northampton Hospital, in 1904 the Stantonbury Hospital Fund was founded. Held in the Newport Road Recreation Ground the main event was a fete which took place annually. The following is a just a selection of those which took place until the beginning of WW2.

1907

On Saturday, August 31st, lent by the parish council the recreation ground was the centre of attraction. Lead by the Salvation Army brass band at 2.30pm a procession toured the principal streets. Collections were taken along the way and afterwards the Wolverton and District St. John Ambulance Corps gave an ambulance display. Mr. F. Fisher's String Band played musical selections at intervals and a concert was later given by the united choirs of the Free Church Sunday Schools. A popular attraction was Thurston's switchbacks loaned to the committee by the proprietor, who also gave generously to the fund.

1916

On Saturday, July 1st rain completely washed out the outdoor attractions at the annual Hospital Fete. The deluge began just after the opening ceremony and in places the recreation ground was a quagmire. No sports could be held and dancing to music by the Bradwell United Band took place at the Assembly Hall. With Alderman Wylie presiding for the opening, on the platform were the Mayor and Mayoress of Northampton, Mrs. J. Strachan & Mr. Walker of Wolverton, Mr. F.H. Parkes (the honorary secretary), Mr. J. Knapp JP of Linford Hall, Miss Williams, Miss Heacock and Mr. J.I. Brooks. Also the chairman of the local Hospital Saturday Committee Mr. F.H. Tompkins. Due to the weather the street carnival was abandoned and the open air concerts by the Stantonbury Girls' Club were instead held to a packed attendance in the Social Clubroom.

1924

In June at the opening ceremony of the Stantonbury fete some 4,500 people were present in the recreation ground. As chairman

Whit Monday was a traditional day for celebration. The day also became an opportunity to raise money for charity, in this case the Northampton Hospital Fund.

The top photo from 1910 shows a coal cart decorated with flowers for the parade.

The second photo, (p. 148) taken c. 1920 shows some of the participants in a New Bradwell fete to raise money for the Hospital Fund. .

of the committee Mr. F.H. Tompkins said that last year at a cost to the Hospital of about £125 Bradwell had sent 10 inpatients and 86 outpatients. However the town had donated £210 plus a subscription of £10 10s. Prior to the fete 'bevies' of young ladies had sold scarlet pimpernel flags, and in the morning a fancy dress parade took place of comic and fancy characters. Also a decorated street organ toured the town and neighbourhood, and on a visit to the town also assisting in the fund raising was the Lewisham Salvation Army male voice choir. Various sideshows and competitions proved an attraction of the day, and in the afternoon and evening the main feature was the presentation of a pageant entitled 'Midsummer Revels,' performed by the Stantonbury Girls' Club. Under the direction of Mrs. Abbey and Mr. D. Norman. 230 girls took part, 'and the spectacular effect was quite bewitching and entrancing. Witches and fairies, with attendant spirits, gaily disported in diaphanous robes and garments on the greensward, and for the nonce mundane things were forgotten by delighted spectators.' The Bradwell United Band provided the accompanying music and a dance was held in the Assembly Hall.

1927

On Monday, June 6th the Mayor and Mayoress of Northampton were some 20 minutes late in arriving at the Stantonbury Hospital Fete. Scheduled for 2.30pm the opening was performed by the Mayoress, and in explaining the delay the Mayor said that due to a busy morning they didn't finish until 1.30. Then when about to set off his car wouldn't start.

1930

The annual fete of the Stantonbury Hospital Fund took place on Whit Monday in the recreation ground. Some 1,500 people attended and in the afternoon the chairman of the Fund, Mr. F.H. Tompkins, said in introducing Dr. Eric Shaw, of Northampton General Hospital, that last year New Bradwell had sent 240 patients to the hospital costing about £430. Then in opening the fete Dr. Shaw spoke of the need for an increased income due to the increased facilities now offered by the hospital. Featuring 250 performers the afternoon variety carnival was under the direction of Dennis Norman and not, as in previous years, the entire work of the Stantonbury

Girls' Club. An appeal had been made to local organisations to each present a scene, with that of the Bradwell Girl Guides being 'A Detective Story.' This dealt with the theft of a lady's handbag by a youth who was then tracked down by the Girl Guides - 'who dealt with him rather severely'! As for the New Bradwell Branch of the Junior Imperial and Constitutional League they presented 'A Masque of Empire,' whilst prehistoric football was the contribution by St. Peter's Football Club. A repeat performance of the carnival was given in the evening which ended with a dance in the Assembly Hall.

1931

On Whit Monday a feature of the Stantonbury Hospital Fete was 'The Pageant of the Years,' which, with some 120 performers in period costume, had been written and arranged by Eric Bellchambers of New Bradwell. In fact this was the first time that a historical pageant had been attempted, and comprised various scenes. In brilliant sunshine the fete was opened by Charles Wylie and during the morning a fancy dress parade had taken place in the town.

1938

This being the Silver Jubilee of the Fund, on Whit Monday a procession in the morning was lead by the Bradwell United Silver Prize Band and the retiring Carnival King and Queen, followed by two decorated lorries and the individual entrants for the fancy dress parade. The fete was opened by Mrs. K. Knapp of Denham, Bucks., and in the evening a ladies football match took place between the New Bradwell and Bozeat teams. The day then concluded with a dance held at the County Arms.

1939

The fete on Whit Monday attracted 2,000 people. There were the usual sideshows and attractions and 200 performers took part in a picturesque pageant. The fete opened with the crowning of the Carnival Queen, Miss Linden, and amongst the events was included a comic football match.

NEW BRADWELL & DISTRICT NURSING ASSOCIATION

In 1874 the Wolverton and Stantonbury Sick Benefit Society was founded, and in 1875 with a dinner for some 50 persons the members celebrated their first anniversary on Saturday, July 31st in the club room at the Radcliffe Arms, Wolverton. In the chair was the president, Mr. Roberts, who said they had started with 50 members and now had 182; "We have had 188; but 20 left and a good job too, for they were no good to the society, and 14 fresh ones joined. We have had a hard pull through the winter. We have paid a considerable sum away, and we still have a good balance in hand." (£82).

Then in 1877 on Saturday, January 20th the first meeting of the Society since its registration under the Friendly Societies Act was held at its registered club house the Radcliffe Arms, Wolverton. Further details are scarce but more certain is the story of the New Bradwell & District Nursing Association founded in 1926. That year a meeting was held in the Infants' School on the evening of Wednesday, April 21st with Mrs. Penny of Wolverton presiding. With a good attendance Dr. S. Holden, Medical Officer of Health for Bucks, spoke of the need for a nurse in the district and ideally two, one for sick nursing and one for midwifery. Old age pensioners would receive the service of a nurse free as would those in receipt of parish relief. Miss Cary, the honorary secretary, then submitted the rules which were agreed to. In May 1927 the Association finished its first year with a balance in hand of £63 5s 5d and 451 subscribers. In 1928 at the Girls' School on the evening of Tuesday, May 15th Mr. J.C. Sutton JP presided at the annual general meeting, being supported by Miss Cary. The balance sheet showed an income of £302 18s 1½d and a balance in hand had increased from £63 5s 5½d to £96 12s 5d. In her report as secretary Miss Cary gave the number of subscribers, excluding old age pensioners and those in receipt of outdoor relief. During the year the nurse had dealt with 511 cases involving 4,233 visits. The chairman commented on the excellent report and although 27 new members had been welcomed during the year he still thought the number insufficient for a place the size of New Bradwell and appealed for the workers to encourage new members to join, the subscription only being less than 2d a week. All the officers were re-elected.

With a small attendance in 1929 on the evening of Monday, May 13th the third annual general meeting of the Association was held in the schools. Mrs. Grant presided and Mrs. S.G. Clarke presented the financial statement for the past year. This showed a total income of £227 7s 11½d to which had to be added a balance in hand of £96 13s 5d brought forward from the previous year. Donations amounted to £16 4s; members subscriptions £125 9s 11d; and County Council grants totalled £59 9s. Expenditure for the year was £192 7s 6d leaving a balance in hand of £131 12s 10½d. The president then read a report from the Rev. F.H. Rollinson who having audited the books stated they were so well kept that his task had been a pleasure. In her third annual report Miss Cary as the honorary secretary said that 414 cases had been nursed during the year. The nurse had made 3,363 visits, of which 1,652 had been for general nursing. 240 children had attended the minor ailments clinic and of other statistics the Association now had 503 members, an increase of 25 on the previous year. This excluded old age pensioners and those receiving outdoor relief, who were attended free. The following officers were then reappointed - Mrs. Grant, president; Miss Cary, honorary secretary; Mrs. S.G. Clarke, honorary treasurer; Mesdames Billingham, Brooks, Beach, Peddar, and Scott, committee. Miss Eckersley was co-opted to the committee. The president then outlined the proposals of the committee regarding alterations of the rules. These affected the fees for the attendance of the nurse to non subscribers. Also the fees for midwifery and maternity cases. Afterwards the president expressed thanks to Mr. Scott for the concert he organised for the Association's funds, and to all those who had given prizes for the whist drives and competitions held for the benefit of the Association. However the memberships subscriptions would not provide for the nurse's salary and there were many things they had to pay for to keep the Association going. Thanks were expressed to the collectors and officers for their work during the year.

In 1929 at the meeting of the Wolverton Urban Council in May the Highways Committee reported that they considered that if the request from the New Bradwell and District Nursing Association to allow a street lamp to remain alight all night outside the nurse's residence was granted a precedent would be created, which the

Council would not be prepared to concede to generally. Col. Hawkins pointed out that the nurses were employed by voluntary associations and were an enormous help to the whole community. He moved that the matter be referred back for reconsideration and this was seconded and carried by 9 votes to 5.

In 1932 there was a small attendance on the evening of Tuesday, May 10th at the annual general meeting of the New Bradwell and District Nursing Association held at the Girls' School. In presiding Mr. J.I. Brooks said a membership of just over 400 out of a population of nearly 4,000 was not very encouraging. Miss Cary, the honorary secretary, read a letter of appreciation from residents of the parish for the work of Nurse Roberts. Mr. S.G. Clarke as the honorary treasurer presented the financial statement for the last year showing an increased balance of £5 4s 9d. Donations were £14 3s 6d and members subscriptions £115 16s 9d. County grants for midwifery, health visiting, nursing OAPs, and school work totalled £66 16s. Miss Cary presented the annual report which showed the membership not including OAPs and those receiving outdoor relief was 405, a decrease of 30 on the previous year. The nurse had attended 551 cases, 10 less than previous year. 23 cases were sent to the nurse by the local doctors. The attendance of children at the Minor Ailments Clinic was 883 and 15 OAPs had been attended by the nurse. 14 ladies acted as collectors each month. Mr. Brooks referred to the loss of the president Mr. J.C. Sutton who had died.

In 1933 the annual general meeting was held in the Girls' School on the evening of Tuesday, May 9th. Mr. J.I. Brooks presided over a small attendance supported by Miss Cary, the honorary secretary, and among others Dr. Keane and Dr. P.B. Atkinson. The financial statement read by Mrs. S.G. Clarke showed a useful balance in hand despite the reduced grant of £20 from Bucks County Council. The decrease had been made up for by the efforts of the Committee which had organised entertainments which raised £19 5s 10½d. In her report of the past year Miss Cary gave the membership at 387 excluding OAPs and people receiving outdoor relief. The membership showed a decrease of 18. The nurse had attended 574 cases, 23 more than last year, and included 28 cases which were sent to the nurse by the local doctors and 18 cases conducted without a doctor in attendance. The attendance of schoolchildren at the Minor Ailments Clinic during the year was 915 and 15 OAPs had attended. Mr. Brooks as the auditor spoke of the excellent condition of the books kept by the treasurer. Dr. Atkinson praised the work of Nurse Roberts, saying she had visited as many homes as in some places which had two nurses. The officers elected for the ensuing year were Mr. J.I. Brooks president; Miss Cary honorary secretary; Mrs. S. Clarke honorary treasurer; Mrs. F. Grant chairman; Mesdames P.B. Atkinson, A. Beach, F. Billingham, S. Peddar and Miss Penn as committee.

In 1934 at the meeting of the association Miss Cary was absent in London for hospital treatment. In 1935 at the annual general meeting at the Girls' School on the evening of Tuesday, May 21st, it was stated that this was the first time they'd had to touch their bank balance. They needed more members and in view of the town's apparent apathy in May 1937 the association posted an 'S.O.S. Message' in the local press asking 'Does New Bradwell really want a resident nurse.' It seemed the answer was yes, for at the annual meeting in the Girls School on the evening of Tuesday, May 25th there was a good attendance to discuss the matter. Mr. J.I. Brooks, the president, was in the chair supported by Miss Cary the honorary secretary. Dr. Marjorie Fildes was also present and it was explained that the reason for such a notice being issued by the committee was because the Association in future had to include Old Bradwell in its working area. Also provide for the upkeep of a car for the nurse. This additional district is the result of a new Midwifery Act under which the County Council are to amalgamate areas. Mr. Brooks was pleased with the attendance but wished it had been more. More members were needed to meet the additional expenditure. There were over 1,000 houses in New Bradwell but only 400 members. If they required a resident nurse the extra expenditure was for an increase of £30 in her salary and the upkeep of a car. Also there was the question if only one nurse could do it. He thought their membership should not be less than 600. Miss Cary said the County Council would provide the car but the Association would have to pay for its maintenance. She intimated that their nurse was retiring at the end of May and the members had subscribed £7 10s 0d as a gift of appreciation. Mrs. Coleman suggested that the town be again canvassed by the collectors and it was agreed it should be done. Answering a question Mr. Brooks said he understood if there was no Association the County would provide a nurse to visit the town but only for midwifery cases. Voice "That is no good here!" On the proposition of Mrs. Leather seconded by Mrs. Rawbone it was decided to continue the Association. Mrs. Brownsell said each street should have a collector but Miss Cary said she had found difficulty in getting collectors. Mrs. Coleman volunteered to take on any street and accepted the collection of Bridge Street. Mrs. Conway-Davis of Old Bradwell said they would carry out their own collecting at Old Bradwell. The election of officers was made with Dr. Marjorie Fildes to be chairman succeeding Dr. Madge Atkinson who had left the neighbourhood. The 11th report of the Association showed 412 members not including OAPS and those receiving outdoor relief. The nurse had attended 592 cases. Thanks were given to the 16 ladies who acted as collectors. In June 1937 the association appointed Nurse Jennings who was a Queen's Nurse to fill the vacancy caused by the departure by Nurse Roberts who had been given a gift of money. Dr. Marjorie Fildes had taken over the presidency.

In 1940 at the annual meeting in May Mr. J.I. Brooks resigned as president due to leaving the district on retirement. Mr. W.G. Sellick was elected president. Mr. S.B. Shepherd was elected honorary treasurer and Mr. E. Brown subscription secretary. Mr. Turnbull reported that Nurse Simmonds had made 5,136 visits. The membership was 605, an increase of 18 on last year. The balance on the accounts was £324 16s, an increase of £84 7s 7d over 1939. Members subscriptions totalled £171 18s 6d. In August 1940 the temporary address of Nurse Simmonds was c/o Mr. Shepherd, chemist, 42, St. James Street and in October the new permanent address was 100, Newport Road. In 1941 in May at the annual general meeting it was decided to invest a further £75 in National Savings certificates as a contribution to War Weapons Week. The total investments in War savings was now £300. Nurse Simmonds said she had prepared 1,102 children for diphtheria immunisation.

In 1942 at the annual general meeting of the association on Thursday, May 28th Mr. W. Sellick presided. Only 12 persons were present. The reduction of the balance in hand - £394 18s 10½d to £272 7s 8d - was mainly due to the purchase of a car for the use of the nurses (£168) and a typewriter (£14). The secretary said that during the year it had been necessary for a new home to be found for the nurse. Owing to no suitable accommodation being available this proved difficult for a time but the tenancy of a small house, No. 2, Wood Street, New Bradwell, was fortunately obtained and the committee decided to rent the house for Nurse Simmonds who was willing to provide her own furniture and effects. This arrangement had proved satisfactory and the committee felt justified in continuing it. Due to the growth of the work in the district and the difficulty of reaching the New Estate and Old Bradwell, especially in bad weather, the committee felt it necessary that a car should be provided for the nurse. The County authorities were approached with a view to obtaining a purchase grant and an upkeep grant but the application was turned down. As a compromise they suggested that additional work should be undertaken by the Association when the question of car grants would be considered at some future date. The committee decided to buy a car which was now being used by the nurse. During the period Nurse Simmonds was in hospital it was not possible to arrange a whole time nurse and so in accordance with arrangements made with the County Superintendent the work was divided between three nurses whose duties were mornings, afternoons, and nights respectively. The membership was now 668, an increase of 56. Put on record was appreciation of the work of Nurse Simmonds whose salary had been increased according to scale by £12 a year as war bonus. All the officers were re-elected.

In 1943 the annual general meeting of the association was held on May 13th in the Girls' School. Mr. G. Turnbull, honorary secretary, said "Owing to wartime difficulties, we were asked by the County Authorities to include Great Linford in our district; this was fully discussed by the committee, and only agreed to as a wartime measure, and this was only possible owing to the fact that we had already purchased a car. In consequence, Nurse Simmonds has had one of the busiest years on record, as the figures of her report show, and her work continues to give satisfaction. Early in the year the nurse had a period of illness, and Nurse King, of Stony Stratford, acted as a relief satisfactorily." The membership was now 733 to include 43 new members from Great Linford. In 1943 on Saturday, September 19th the association held a flag day and raised £18 1s.

At the 18th annual general meeting in May 1944 Mr. G. Turnbull, honorary secretary, said the inclusion of Great Linford Nursing Association had increased the work of the nurse. In November 1944 two elderly ladies, Mrs. Osborne and Mrs. Petty, of Newport Road, made articles by 'make and mend' and by selling them made £2 10s for the association. In 1945 at the annual general meeting at the Girls' School on Monday, May 14th the secretary, Mr. G. Turnbull, said they wished to build up a large balance to buy a house for the nurse. The idea of the house was to have an assistant nurse. She didn't want one at the moment but she was not able to have her days off. A relief nurse had been sent when the nurse had time off. In 1948 at a meeting on Tuesday, June 29th at the Girls' School practical suggestions were made regarding the disposal of the £300 balance of the New Bradwell & District Nursing Society. This was in view of the organisation being taken over under the New National Health Service, and presiding at this final public meeting was Mr. W.G. Sellick supported by Mr. G. Turnbull, the general secretary. Also present was his wife, as the honorary treasurer, and Mrs. H. Cross, subscription secretary. Mr. Sellick said they were proud of the fact that the Association had made good progress during its 22 years existence and regretted this was the last meeting under the present constitution. Those attending were entitled to say how the balance of £303 should be spent. Their ambition had been to build up their balance to buy a house for the Association for the benefit of the nurse, Nurse Simmonds. She had been with them for 10 years and although very practical in her work her duties had increased considerably and it was found necessary to engage another nurse. Thus Nurse Thompson had been with them for 8 months. He thanked all the collectors for their service over the years and to the various officers. Honorariums were voted as in previous years to the secretary of £15 15s and subscription secretary of £2 2s. The nurses had covered New Bradwell, Old Bradwell and Great Linford and the president said there was the question of the future of the nurse's car. After a lengthy discussion it was decided to hand it over to the Government, for the future use of their nurse, but it was pointed by the treasurer, who quoted from official correspondence, that associations could not have any say in the manner in which articles handed over should be dealt with. The president then asked for suggestions on the disposal of the £303 and Dr. Love, the resident doctor, thought it a shame that any nurse should be allowed to live in a house that did not have a bath. Therefore he felt money should be set aside to improve her living conditions. Also he suggested an oxygen tent and a Dunlop pillow mattress, saying a man with a fractured spine had to come out of hospital due to a shortage of beds and lie "on one of those things I hate - a feathered mattress - which most people, I believe, like round here." (laughter.) The Rev. Ray Smith said the reason the bath was not provided was because of the uncertainty of the tenancy of the house. If there had been a more certain tenancy no doubt they would have acted differently. It was decided to set aside a sum for house improvements, and also for the suggestions made by Dr. Love. It was also agreed that of the remaining money certain sums should be devoted to the Stony Stratford Physiotherapy Clinic, the New Bradwell Nursing Cadets, and the Bradwell and Wolverton Good Samaritan Society. Mr. F.J. Billingham was elected the new chairman and the Charity Trustees would be chosen to supervise the business following July 5th.

In April 1950 the final meeting of the Association took place. Mr. F.J. Billingham presided supported by Mr. G. Turnbull, honorary secretary, with the object to allocate the small remaining balance. After all the expenses had been paid since the Government take over it was agreed amongst others to allocate Nurse Simmond's residence, 2, Wood Street, New Bradwell, the provision of a bath and geyser, and internal decorations £54 15s 3d. ; equipment given for the use of Dr. M. Fildes and Dr. J.M. Love £19 0s 6d; New Bradwell and Wolverton Good Samaritan Society £27 16s 3d;. New Bradwell St. John's Cadets £15.

RELIGION

BAPTIST CHURCH

As recalled in later life by William Sturgess, the Baptist church had been started in Bradwell by his mother in June 1855, when permission was granted for the use of two rooms on the second floor at 78, Middle Street (later named Spencer Street), New Bradwell. Here a Sunday School was conducted with a later use for evening services. The house, where he was born, was the home of his parents (his father also named William Sturgess). Young William would become so attached to the Baptist cause that having during his earlier years conducted an infants' class at the house in 70 years he would never miss a Sunday School anniversary. The two rooms were later made into one, with a pulpit erected and forms placed for the congregation.

Then in 1856 a special church meeting was held at Stony Stratford to discuss building a chapel at Bradwell. In consequence in order to proceed with the plans trustees were appointed in January 1857; namely Ebenezer Forster, Baptist Minister, Stony Stratford; Richard Barter, grocer, Stony Stratford; Lewis Osborne, draper, Stony Stratford; Frederick Woollard, leather seller, Stony Stratford; Edward Hayes, boat builder, Stony Stratford; John Robinson, painter, Bradwell; Alec McGrindle, book keeper, Bradwell; James Nettleton, fitter, Bradwell; Isaac Ward, carpenter, Bradwell; Francis Harris, timekeeper, Wolverton; David Price, brass finisher, Wolverton; and William Charnock, fitter, Old Bradwell. During the month it was agreed to purchase a piece of land for £36 from Brother John Walker of Loughton, who in all weathers would ride his pony along the road from Loughton through Old Bradwell and into Bradwell to attend the Sunday evening service at the Chapel. In April 1857 the contract for building the chapel was awarded to John Pickering, a builder of Newport Pagnell, and construction began at the corner of North Street and Bradwell Road. A decision was made to build a vestry adjacent to the chapel and also a schoolroom, at an estimated cost of £64 10s. As for the former premises at 78, Middle Street, these would be used as a Boys' Day School. The girls were allowed to use

The second Baptist Chapel, opened in 1936 at the corner of Bridge Street and the Bradwell Road.

the vestry of the new chapel, and it seems that the schoolmaster was a Mr. Robinson. Indeed it was the Rev. J.C. Robinson who would be the first minister.

The Baptist Church was opened in 1857 on September 26th being officially enrolled as the Bradwell Branch of the Stony Stratford Church in 1858 on February 8th. However it would be some years before a house was acquired as a Manse to accommodate the ministers.

In September 1862 a Mr. Brooks is noted as superintendent of 'Stantonbury Baptist Sabbath School' but in 1863 on Sunday, January 25th the Rev. Robinson preached his farewell services, having resigned on appointment as minister to the chapel at Brington, Northants. In the evening the chapel was crowded and on the Monday evening a tea was held in the chapel for some 200. Afterwards a public meeting took place and presiding in the chair the Rev. E.L. Forster, the Baptist minister of Stony Stratford, spoke regarding Mr. Robinson's departure, and called upon Mr. McCrindle to present him with a testimonial. Also presented was a purse of 10 guineas from the members of the New Bradwell Baptist connection. Others spoke in tribute to the Reverend's service, and on the Tuesday evening the young ladies of the Bible class presented him with a richly chased silver pencil case.

In 1863 on Sunday, December 27th an excellent sermon was preached at the Baptist Chapel by Mr. John Minett. He was a student from Mr. Spurgeon's Tabernacle, and several members of the congregation were moved to remark that they hadn't listened to such a sermon for a very long time. Indeed so much so that in October 1864 he accepted the pastorate of the Chapel.

In 1867 on Sunday, August 25th the annual meetings in connection with the Buckingham Branch of the London Sunday School Union commenced. At 2pm on the Monday afternoon Mr. Charnock, of Stantonbury, presided over a conference, and during the sessions it was announced that Stantonbury Baptist School had been admitted to the benefits of the Union.

In 1868 on Sunday, June 14th the anniversary of the Stantonbury Baptist Sunday School was held. A well observed sermon was preached in the morning by Mr. Bass, of Olney, who during the afternoon addressed the children and parents. Then such was the attendance in the evening that many people had to stand. On the Monday the chapel was filled by teachers and friends who had gathered for their anniversary tea drinking. Sadly after a long illness the pastor, the Rev. John Minett died aged 28 on November 28th.

He was succeeded by the Rev. Josiah Hart and in February 1869 the New Bradwell Baptist Chapel was registered for marriages, with that of Emmor Augustus Balls and Miss Eliza Walker being the first. This was conducted on Whit Monday, May 17th, and to mark the occasion the couple were presented with a Bible inscribed on the first page with suitable words written in different coloured inks.

Towards clearing the debt on the building, in 1874 on March 30th and 31st a bazaar was held in the chapel. On Good Friday a well attended public tea was provided, and in the evening the bazaar was continued for the sale of those items unsold during the two days. An overall sum of £37 was made. During February 1875 the chapel was closed for necessary repairs and at the re-opening on Sunday, March 14th two sermons were preached by the Rev. J. Allen of Olney. On the Monday a public tea was given at which the pastor, the Rev. Josiah Hart, said that for the five Sundays of closure the Rev. Cotter had allowed them to worship in his schoolroom. A collection was then taken to defray the expenses of the chapel renovation.

In April 1877 Mr. David Bottrill Gardner, of Bristol College, accepted a unanimous invitation to the pastorate of the Baptist Chapel, and as a token of esteem in 1878 with the Rev. Cotter presiding he was presented on Monday, May 20th with a purse of gold by members of the Baptist Chapel and friends.

In 1879 on Sunday, October 5th the Rev. John Mathews began his ministry of the chapel. Born at Oxford, he came from West Haddon where on September 27th prior to his departure he had been presented by the Misses Nelli Manton and Florence Underwood with a testimonial in the shape of a electroplated teapot, purchased by the members of the Band of Hope. At New Bradwell in the morning his opening discourse was on 'Church Prosperity.' Then in the evening on 'Religious Revivals,' and on the Monday for some 90 persons a public tea was provided.

In June 1880 tenders were invited to erect a new school and classrooms, plus alterations of the Baptist chapel. Plans and specifications could be viewed at Mr. T. Cherry's, Buckingham Street, Wolverton. Also that month on Saturday 19th the annual treat to the scholars of the Baptist Chapel Sunday School was held. Some 200 children assembled at the chapel and then travelled to Loughton in conveyances, the first of which sported a large banner inscribed 'Stantonbury Baptist Sunday School, formed 1855.' Sports were indulged in a field at Loughton followed by a tea. Then sports and pastimes, before a return was made in the evening.

Whilst of adequate accommodation the New Bradwell chapel had rather uncomfortable benches and a large pulpit. In consequence such tribulations were attended and following other necessary alterations in 1881 on the afternoon of Tuesday, September 27th services in connection with the re-opening were commenced. A sermon was preached by the Rev. Dawson Burns MA, of London, and the congregation could now listen from comfortable seats, with the benches and the pulpit having been replaced by a long platform. Having a rostrum in the centre this was entirely the voluntary work

164

of the friends and members of the congregation, many of whom had worked in the evenings and on Saturday afternoons. At a cost of £21, raised by voluntary contributions and collections, the most important change was the addition at the back of the chapel of another schoolroom. Of dark red brick this was 36ft square and 22ft high, whilst as for the old schoolroom, 'which at the best wore a very depressing aspect,' this would now be used as a classroom. The entrance in the old school room had opened onto the public road, and thus the noise created on Sunday afternoons by idle louts outside the door disturbed the teaching. The new entrance now obviated this, through running up the side of the chapel direct into the new schoolroom, with a gate to close the end of the porch. The overall cost of the alterations and additions had been about £270, and after the preaching a public tea was held in the new school room, followed by a public meeting.

Due to declining health in 1895 in January the Reverend Mathews closed his 15 years pastorate at the Baptist chapel, having been a Baptist minister for 53 years. In 1897 to be near his employment at Wolverton Works, William Sturgess moved to Wolverton and so ended the role of 78, Middle Street, as the meeting place for the Sunday School and Good Templars.

In 1899 a former pastor of the chapel, David Bottrill Gardner, applied on Wednesday, May 10th at Northampton County Court for his discharge from bankruptcy. As an accountant he was formerly of 33, East Park Parade, Northampton, and the Official Receiver reported that the receiving order had been made on February 22nd 1897. He had formerly been the Baptist minister at Stantonbury but when his health broke down he moved to Australia and entered the pastorate of St. Kilda Church on January 1st 1883, conducting his first service on Thursday, January 4th. While in New South Wales he paid his creditors 10s in the pound, being then employed as cashier to the Government Exhibition at Melbourne. After 12 years in Australia he returned to England and in June 1890 entered the service of Messrs. Brice and Co., at a time prior to the firm becoming a limited liability company. He began with a salary of 35s a week and when the firm was turned into a limited liability company he became secretary. His salary increased, and just before the bankruptcy was

£500pa. From the total liability only £30 was due to creditors which were unconnected with his position with regard to Brice and Co. Ltd. Therefore as regards his private affairs he was perfectly solvent. In fact when asked about the cause of his insolvency he said "I am not insolvent. I am forced into the Bankruptcy Court to protect myself against claims arising out of transactions entered into by me on behalf of Messrs. Brice and Co. Ltd." In the final conclusion the Judge granted the discharge, albeit suspended for two years as the shortest time possible.

In 1900 the anniversary and re-opening services of the Baptist Chapel were held on Saturday, Sunday, and Tuesday, November 10th, 11th, and 13th. These commenced with a tea for some 125 on the Saturday afternoon. The tables had been arranged by three ladies of the congregation and in the evening the choir performed a concert under choirmaster Mr. Dormer. On Sunday morning and evening the usual services were conducted by the pastor, the Rev. Herbert Francis Chipperfield. He was born at Bushy, Herts., and before coming to Stantonbury had been a member of Mount Pleasant Church, Northampton. Then on Tuesday evening a public meeting was held in the chapel. The total proceeds of £11 were applied for the Renovation Fund.

In 1904 on the afternoon of Wednesday, November 23rd a two day bazaar was opened in aid of the organ fund. This was held in the chapel with the intention to commemorate the 7th anniversary of the settlement of the pastor, the Rev. Chipperfield, and the jubilee of the Sunday School, by the purchase of a two manual pipe organ for the church. The present American organ in the chapel would then be transferred to the schoolroom. An appeal had been made to the local population although for the past two years there had been no full time employment at Wolverton Works, and 500 had recently been discharged. The opening ceremony was performed by the Rev. Philip H. Smith, pastor of College Street Church, Northampton, who was also president of the Northampton Association of Baptist Churches, to which Stantonbury was affiliated. The Rev. Chipperfield presided over the large attendance and of several entertainments later in the day the competitions of hat trimming and button sewing had been organised by Mrs. Thomas and Miss Cowley. Additionally two

Rev. Leggatt and his wife

concerts were performed in the chapel by some 40 scholars of the Sunday School, and on the Thursday the bazaar was opened by Mr. R. Wylie. In appreciation of his 8 years' ministry, in 1905 in October the Rev. Chipperfield was presented with a marble clock and purse of gold.

In 1907 on Wednesday, July 10th the official recognition services of the Glasgow born Rev. James Leggatt, of Wolvey, Warks., the new pastor of the church, were held. However during most of the day the rain fell in torrents and some people had to stay away. At a service in the afternoon the special preacher, Mr. H. Davis of Fuller Church, Kettering, said that he had met Mr. Leggatt some six years before at Kettering. A tea then followed and with Mr. J. Siddons, president of the Northants. Baptist Association, in the chair, at a crowded meeting in the evening the church secretary, Arthur Warton, said the church had been without a pastor for a year and seven months. During this time Mr. Leggatt had been one of the interim preachers and such was the impression he made that he was afforded a unanimous invitation, which he accepted. He had been at Stantonbury since the first Sunday in May and the congregation had now been increased by 6 new members.

Having realised the need to extend their church and schools, in 1908 on Wednesday, February 12th the Baptists began a three day bazaar towards raising the estimated cost of £400. This was held in the schoolroom where the Rev. Leggatt said the Baptist Church had been founded as a branch of the Stony Stratford church in 1856, when the present building was erected. Then in 1882 the school was added at a cost of £300. The Rev. Leggatt remained as pastor until 1913 when he accepted a call from the Queensland Baptist Union in Australia. Prior to his departure he and his wife attended a farewell gathering in the Baptist Chapel on the evening of Tuesday, February 25th and during the event it was stated that whilst he had been at Stantonbury the chapel debt had been paid, and they now had a balance of £180 towards their extensive improvement and renovation scheme. Inscribed "As a token of esteem from Baptist friends at Stantonbury, Feb., 1913" he was presented with a gold watch, and on behalf of the Sunday School and Band of Hope Mrs. Leggatt received a silver tea pot and umbrella.

In 1913 on Sunday, September 14th the new Baptist minister, the Rev. Arthur W. Sansom, began his ministry. A native of Launton, near Bicester, his unanimous invitation had been consequent to having occupied the pulpit on two occasions. In fact he had received an invite from a larger church but preferred that of Stantonbury. Formerly the organising secretary of the Oxfordshire Band of Hope and Temperance Union, he completed his preaching engagements at Oxford on Sunday 7th, and on the same afternoon presided at a large meeting of the Wesley Hall Brotherhood, at which he was presented with 'a useful gift.'

The inconvenience of the church lacking a Manse to accommodate their ministers was remedied around 1918 by the purchase of 35, Queen Anne Street, New Bradwell, on the corner of Queen Anne Street and King Edward Street, for £355. This was thereby the residence of the Rev. Edmond Frederick Forsdike, and his wife Kate, when he became the new minister in January 1920. Born in London, on leaving school he was engaged for several years in business in the City and became a local preacher in London and the Home Counties. Being of the Baptist faith he then studied for three years under the supervision of the Rev. J.W. Ewing MA, DD, who became the General Superintendent of the London Area under the Ministerial Settlement and Sustentation Scheme of the Baptist Union. In 1909 he entered Spurgeon's College and on the completion of his college course in 1914 accepted the pastorate of the Baptist Church in Blunham, Bedfordshire. Then in 1918 he took up an invitation from the YMCA to work with the BEF in France, going in 1919 with the Army of Occupation to Germany, being stationed north of Cologne and near the neutral zone. In France and Germany he had worked with their canteens and recreation huts and returned to England at the end of that year, then beginning his duties at New Bradwell in 1920 on January 11th.

As a result of their two day sale of work, in 1923 in the last week of November the Baptist Church members raised over £120 for their

Manse fund. The deficit was now £138 but by 1924 the Manse had been paid for. That year important decisions were taken as to whether to improve the church or to erect a new building. In consequence in 1925 the proposed scheme to build a new church on a new site was discussed at the annual social of the Baptist church, held in the schoolroom on Wednesday, January 21st. With the pastor, the Rev. E.F. Forsdike, presiding it was thought that this should be a long term consideration due to the cost. The amount was estimated at £3,600, of which the church intended to raise a minimum of £2,500. As presently the site of some 12 allotments the favoured plot was on the corner of Bradwell Road and Bridge Street, and towards the building funds on Wednesday, December 2nd 1925 a two day sale of work was opened. Mr. A.R. Cleaver, of Northampton, presided and lengthy details of the scheme were given by Mr. A. Brown JP, the church secretary. The original plan had been to rebuild three quarters of the buildings but after a costing and report from an expert it was deemed better to have a new structure. However this would not be within the pastorate of the Rev. Forsdike, for in 1927 he accepted that of West Street Baptist Church, Dunstable, vacant since the departure of the Rev. Elias George some two years ago. On Sunday, March 27th 1927 he conducted his farewell services at New Bradwell and on the Saturday at the end of a concert was presented by the church secretary, Albert Brown, with a gold watch. His wife received a silver plated cake stand, and each of their three children a small gift. Additionally on behalf of the New Bradwell Branch of the British Legion Mr. P. Styles presented the Reverend with an ever sharp pencil. Then in May members from the New Bradwell church attended the Reverend's induction service at Dunstable.

In succession to the Rev. Forsdike, in 1927 on Sunday, October 2nd the Rev. Frederick H. Rollinson began his ministry at New Bradwell. A northerner, born in Middlesborough, he became a preacher in his teens and gained admission to Rawdon College, affiliated to the University of Leeds. Whilst there he spent his weekends preaching in every class of church 'as far north as Newcastle and south as Leicester,' with his first ministry in the Leeds district at Horsforth from 1922 to 1925. In the autumn of 1925 he then moved to the church at 'Weston-by-Weedon' where he ended his ministry on

Tuesday, September 20th. In preparation for his arrival the members had cleaned the church at New Bradwell and re-coloured the walls etc., and on Saturday, October 1st at a welcome tea in the schoolroom Albert Brown, the church secretary, introduced him and his wife to many of the members. Fortunately a new gas heater installed in the large vestry made it more suitable for mid week meetings, and a new pulpit had been provided for the chapel. In 1930 on the afternoon of December, Friday 12th the second day of a sale of work in the schoolroom took place. This was opened by Mr. W. Cleaver of College Street Baptist Church, Northampton, and during the proceedings Mr. A. Brown mentioned how they appreciated the help from those connected with the Northants. Baptist Association. Since last December the New Church Fund had risen by £103 and this was their second effort of the year. Indeed since 1924 they had added £300 to their New Church Building Fund which presently stood at £1,080.

In 1932 at the church meeting on Wednesday, January 20th the Rev. Rollinson announced his acceptance of an invitation to become minister of New Street, Chipping Norton. Thus at New Bradwell he concluded his ministry on Sunday, March 6th 1932, having on the previous evening been presented at a social in the church schoolroom with a gold watch. In succession, having first occupied the pulpit on November 27th the previous year, the Rev. Edward J.E. Briggs began his ministry in 1933 on January 1st. He was duly ordained on Thursday, January 12th and to attend the service his mother had travelled from Winchester, where his father was deacon of a Baptist church. Born in 1905 on June 11th at Winchester, the new minister had attended the city's Peter Symonds School until the summer of 1923, then leaving to spend three years with a firm of booksellers at Rugby. During that time he became a member of the local Baptist Church, the City Road Church, and due to the inspired influence of the Rev. J.H. Lees began to visit small village churches as a local preacher. Then in 1926 he applied for entrance to Regent's Park College, London and having passed the preliminary exam gained a degree of Divinity at London University. He was then granted a further course of two years for post graduate work at the Oxford branch of Regent's Park College, next securing a place in the Second

Class of the Honours School of Theology in Oxford University, gaining a BA. However his tenure at New Bradwell proved somewhat brief for in 1934 at a special church meeting on Monday, November 19th he announced having accepted an appointment as minister at Dewsbury. In relating the circumstances he asked to be released on January 14th 1935 and this was unanimously agreed.

Under his chairmanship a Building Committee had been formed and it was decided to purchase a plot of land at the end of Bridge Street for the future development of the church. For this purpose plans were being formulated and with the cost of erecting and furnishing estimated at around £2,500 the fund now stood at £1,600. The requirement had arisen through the increased population and the need for repairs, and it had been the first intention to purchase the neighbouring house. However when negotiations made little progress investigations regarding the present site took place, at which the owner of the house then offered the property for sale! Yet such an enlargement was deemed inadequate and during the rebuilding there would be no alternative place for worship. It was therefore decided that the section of allotment ground to the east side of Bridge Street, New Bradwell, would be the most suitable location. This was not least from having a good hard road along its full length on the north side, being conveniently placed for public services. The land was owned by the LMS Railway Co. and the dealings which commenced at the end of 1933 culminated with the company agreeing to sell the extent for £250 in March 1934. The area comprised 1,936 sq yds and firstly the church would be built and then the schools. With the land thus secured it left the church with £1,500 towards the building costs. A start was anticipated for 1935. In the second week of January 1935 the 26th anniversary of the Womens' Own was held in the church schoolroom. Also during the week, prior to his departure for Dewsbury the Rev. Briggs was presented with a cheque by the members of the church. The presentation was made by Mr. A. Brown and additionally the Young People's Class presented him with a wallet, and the Good Templars Lodge a silver pencil. Then in a brief return to New Bradwell on Easter Monday 1935 he married Miss Daisy Essam, only daughter of Mrs. and the late Mr. T. Essam of Church Street, Wolverton. Decorated with flowers by the ladies of the church the Baptist Chapel was crowded, and of the more than 100 presents the members of the church had given a suitably inscribed 8 day clock. After a honeymoon at Great Ormsby the couple would make their home at Dewsbury.

Following a unanimous invitation, in 1935 on Sunday, April 28th the Rev. Robert Williams of Ardington, near Cirencester, began as pastor in succession to the Rev. Briggs. He was born in 1904 on February 6th at Wingate, in the county of Durham, and on leaving school became a miner. Having been taught in its Sunday School he became associated with the Methodist Church and from later being a Sunday school teacher was nominated at the age of 17 to be Sunday School superintendent. He also represented the Sunday School at the quarterly meetings of the local Methodist Church. With considerations to enter the ministry he was accepted in 1927, with his first appointment being for a year at Bellingham, in Northumberland. Then a Theological College at Manchester in 1928. On finishing his training in 1930 he went as minister to Arlington, Gloucs., where he remained for 4½ years. As for other matters he was soon to be married. In May 1935 plans for the new Baptist Church had been approved by the Council, and so as to enable Bridge Street to conform to the by law width of 36 feet were subject to the owners of the site yielding a strip of 2 foot on the north side of the plot. Also the Highways Committee had decided that negotiations should be opened with the Trustees to yield an additional strip of 2 foot along the same side. In exchange the council would provide a slab footpath to continue in line with the remainder of Bridge Street. No objections were raised by the Trustees. That year at a bazaar held in the church schoolroom on Wednesday, November 20th Mr. A. Brown explained how it had been decided to erect a church of over £3,300. He said the land had been purchased a year ago and a building committee set up, on which the Northants. Baptist Association was represented. A figure of £2,600 was envisaged for a church to seat 250, and with plans and specifications prepared by an architect negotiations duly commenced. Then when the first tenders came in the lowest was £3,675, which the trustees and members felt they couldn't entertain. Not least since the total would be £4,000. The architect, Mr. Lawson Carter FICA, of Northampton, then made revisions and a second tender came in at £3,030, meaning a total of over £3,300. This was agreed and with the contract awarded to Messrs. C.E. Ivens of Litchborough, work would begin immediately. Towards the necessary amount £1,695 had been raised, and a loan from the Baptist building fund would be needed.

Then in July 1936 it was announced that the new church would be officially opened for divine worship on Saturday, September 12th. As a body the Wolverton Urban District Council would attend and also at the first service on Sunday morning, September 13th, for in extending this welcome the church secretary pointed out that the opening of a new church was one in which a local authority should be interested. Such occasions were infrequent and therefore they wished the morning service on the following day to take the form of a civic service. Following much progress by the builders in 1936 on Saturday, March 28th the stone laying of the new church took place. After divine service in the present church, at which the Rev. D.J. Hiley Hon. CF of London, gave an inspiring address, the congregation made their way to the site of the new building where, with crowds lining the main roadway, a large number of people had gathered. Friends from other Baptist and Non Conformist churches were present and with the singing led by the choir the proceedings began with the appropriate hymn 'The Church's one foundation.' Afterwards prayer was offered by the Rev. L. Curwood, the Baptist Church Minister of Stony Stratford, and as a former minister the chairman of the gathering was the Rev. F. Rollinson, of Chipping Norton, who spoke of his pleasure at being present. Now at Minchenhampton, as another former minister the Rev. E.F. Forsdike had sent a congratulatory letter. In fact in 1925 he had started the shilling fund which raised £220, of which £130 had been donated by four families. The church secretary, Mr. A. Brown, said the tender for the new church from the builder, plus the necessary alterations to accommodate the organ, and other expenses attached to a new building, meant that the cost now totalled almost £3,500. The New Church Building Fund had finished up last year with £1,817, and from the outset the money had been invested in the Northampton Town and County Building Society. With the interest, and the income due from a couple of sundry efforts, the fund now stood at £1,892, leaving a deficit of £1,600. On behalf of the Baptist Union of Great Britain and Ireland the first stone was laid by the Rev. D.J. Hiley, a Baptist Minister for 50 years, 'to the glory of God, for the up building of His Church, and for the salvation of the world.' Mr. A.R. Cleaver, of Northampton, laid a stone in the name of the Northants. Baptist Association, to which the New Bradwell church was connected, and Mr. A. Brown laid a stone in the name of the deacons and supporters 1925-36. The Rev. R. Williams and the Rev. F.H. Rollinson jointly laid a stone in the name of the ministers of the church 1925-36, and additional to their names were those of the Rev. E.F. Forsdike and the Rev. E.J.E. Briggs, of Dewsbury. Mrs. A.W. Leeming, of Stony Stratford, laid a stone in the name of the women workers, in recognition of their devotion and loyalty, and George Pollard and Nance Breeden laid a stone in the name of the Sunday School, they being the two scholars who had made the best attendances during the past three years. Of individual stones Audrey Clarke laid one in memory of her mother, who had assisted in the Sunday School and the church in other ways. William Sturgess, of Wolverton, laid a stone to the memory of his mother, whom he said had started the Baptist cause in the house in Middle Street where he was born. In fact he was oldest scholar of the Sunday School who was present that day. Mrs. Riddy of New Bradwell laid a stone in memory of her mother, Mrs. Wallace, who having joined the church in 1898 remained a member until her passing in June 1922. Mrs. Riddy's sister, Mrs. Hale, of London, laid a stone in memory of their father who joined the church in 1901. He had died last year having served for a long while on the diaconate. After the stone laying a tea was served by the lady members of the church to a company of some 150 in the Labour Hall. This was due to the limited accommodation at the Baptist schoolroom, and at the tea table ministerial greetings were voiced by the Rev. Claud M. Coltman MA B Litt, who congratulated the church from being an old Baptist Sunday School scholar, and also as the minister of Wolverton Congregational Church. The minister of Stony Stratford Baptist Church, the Rev. L. Curwood, said that many years ago there had only been the Stony Stratford Baptist Church in the district. Then others 'sprung up' and 70 members went from Stony Stratford to form a church at New Bradwell.

The new church duly opened in 1936 on Saturday, September 12th consisting of an entrance lobby, a minister's vestry, and a deacon's vestry. The sanctuary provided seating for 250 with the seats arranged in three groups with two aisles. Electricity was provided for lighting with heating by gas appliances under thermostatic control. As for the appearance, in later years this would be described in a survey by Milton Keynes Development Corporation as 'in an Art Deco style with cubist glazing bars in the large windows characteristically filled with pastel coloured textured glass.' Among gifts to the church was a green pulpit, or lectern cover, with the inscription 'I.H.S.', given by Miss Faulkner and Mr. Turnbull. The old church would now be used for the Sunday School and weekend meetings until such time as new schools could be built. Despite inclement weather a large company assembled outside the building for the opening, and for the dedication the service was conducted by the Rev. F.J. Walkey OBE, MC, of Chesham, the Area Superintendent. This opened with the hymn 'Thou, whose unmeasured temple stands,' with the singing lead by the choir. Then followed prayer and a dedication address by the Superintendent. As a former pastor of the church the Rev. F.H. Rollinson, of Chipping Norton, was handed a golden key, saying before he unlocked the church door how grateful he was to be present that afternoon. With the door opened a large congregation entered for a divine service conducted by the Rev. J.H. Rushbrooke MA, DD, who also preached the sermon. In the old church one of the largest gatherings ever assembled in the premises then had tea at which a former minister, the Rev. E.J.E. Briggs BA, BD, now of Dewsbury, presided. Several addresses were given and at a meeting in the evening Mr. A.R. Timson congratulated the people of New Bradwell on having remained steadfast in their ambition. The Rev. F. Everett Thomas BA of Mount Pleasant, Northampton, president of the County Baptist Association, remarked that the last time he preached in the old church was one of the coldest days of the year, and he had to keep his overcoat on in the pulpit! Albert Brown, the church secretary, visualised the time when they could build new Sunday Schools on the spare piece of land near the church. He then read a letter from Miss Robinson, aged 92, a daughter of the first minister in Bradwell. She was now in the Bethany Homestead, Northampton, and said her memory took her back to 1855, when the first cause of any kind in that neighbourhood was established. In giving the financial details Mr. Brown said the anticipated cost of the church together with that of the land would be about £3,700. At the stone laying over £200 had been contributed and a £1,000 loan had been secured from the Baptist Building Fund, free of interest for 10 years. Of this the church was committed to repay £100 per year. In the will of the late Alfred Richard Cleaver of A.R. & W. Cleaver Ltd., builders' merchants, Northampton, was a bequest to the New Bradwell Baptist Church of £350, this being in accordance with a promise that he made during his lifetime. On the Sunday morning a civic service took place at which as well as those of Wolverton Urban District Council members of the New Bradwell Company of Girl Guides and the British Legion were in attendance. Indeed such was the congregation that chairs had to be placed in the aisles. In the afternoon the Rev. R. Williams conducted a united children's service and a large congregation attended a service in the evening. In 1937 on Saturday and Sunday, September 11th and 12th, the anniversary of the church opening was celebrated. With the occasion being to erase the last £120 to settle the builders' account (the total cost of the building being £3,920) on the Saturday the pastor, the Rev. Williams, sat in the vestry to receive gifts. In the evening a special service of praise and thanksgiving took place and he then conducted well attended services on the Sunday, during the afternoon of which Frank Brooks and his Orchestra performed a concert in the church. A surprise visit was that of the Rev. James Leggatt, who had been the pastor 25 years ago.

In early 1940 Albert Brown completed 25 years as secretary of the church and at the annual gathering on the evening of Friday, January 26th remarked how he was always delighted to remember how in 1919 they as a church had decided to go into the sustentation scheme. Now with the blackout and the weather times were difficult, further compounded by the breakdown of the heating apparatus of the school buildings. £6 had been spent in repairs but now it had failed again and there was also an unexpected expenditure of installing gas radiators. On more warming matters, in the old church building there was a crowded audience for a variety concert arranged by men of the church in 1940 on Saturday, April 13th. The evening comprised musical, vocal and humorous items including a Hilly-billy scene, depicting a birthday party on a ranch. However the compere, Mr. W.J. Jones, said the Rev. R. Williams, the minister since July 1935, was absent due to illness. Then on Saturday, April 27th the Women's Own Effort, an annual event at the church, took place. The convener was Mrs. Kemp, Secretary of the Women's Own, and the concert's programme lasted the whole evening. Comprised of the ladies singing popular melodies this was based on a sketch entitled 'The Ladies' Effort' and with a further sketch 'Tea and Scandal' the evening raised £12. The membership of the church was now 81 and each year the Baptists set and achieved the task of raising £150 to reduce the debt on the new church building fund. By November 1940 this stood at £550 but it was realised that in time of war this would prove too much and was reduced to £100. Up to that month £70 had been raised and in place of the usual bazaar, or sale of work, an emergency effort was undertaken on Saturday, November 16th. Donations amounting to £15 11s 6d had been received and the event opened with a gift service followed by a tea and a social evening.

Having accepted the joint pastorate of the Middleton and Heywood churches, just outside Manchester, the Reverend Williams would leave in March 1941, and that month on Thursday 27th at the weekly meeting of the Women's Own he and his wife were afforded a surprise tea by the Committee. Mrs. Brice, a vice president, opened the presentation and referred to Mrs. Williams interest as president, and also that of the Rev. She then handed Mrs. Williams an electric table lamp and to the Rev. a Swan fountain pen. At the outset of the meeting the Rev. dedicated an oak book rest to the memory of the late Mrs. Adams who had died suddenly at a recent meeting. On Sunday, March 30th 1941 he then conducted his farewell services and at the close of that in the evening presentations were made to him and his wife by Mr. A. Brown, church secretary. On behalf of the church he handed the Rev. a watch together with a small albert, and to Mrs. Williams a case of cutlery.

The couple left that week, and in August 1941 it was announced that the Rev. E.J. Whitty had accepted the vacant pastorate, to begin in early September. Aged 33, married with two children, he was educated at Overdale College, Sellyoak, Birmingham, and would come from the Church of Christ, Leicester. This was a denomination closely applied to the Baptist cause, and having made application he expected to be accepted into the Baptist Union at a meeting in October. Presided over by Mr. A. Brown, a welcome meeting in the old church building was held in 1941 on the evening of Saturday, September 6th, at which the new minister told the assembly "I am not going to make any rash promises. You will know my worth by what I do. I have come here to preach the gospel. I am not going to preach fancy sermons nor preach over the heads of the people. You do not come to the church to be amused; you can be amused on the wireless. I am not going to try to be clever in my preaching; I shall try to be simple, so that I can preach to the heart and not to the head. I hope that in our work together we can build up a stronger church."

Both aged 82, in 1942 on May 29th Mr. and Mrs. William Sturgess, of 33, Jersey Road, Wolverton, celebrated their diamond wedding. Both natives of New Bradwell they were married at the church in 1882 on May 29th by the late Rev. J. Matthews and after their marriage continued to live in the town for many years. They then moved to Wolverton, as being closer to Mr. Sturgess' employment at Wolverton Works where he was apprenticed as a fitter. Indeed he would remain in railway employment until his retirement, having completed 54 years and 7 months of service. On the occasion of clearing the debt on the new church building the Rev. H.W. Janisch, of College Street, Northampton, preached at a service of thanksgiving on Sunday, September 13th 1942. This coincided with the anniversary of the church and in the afternoon the gathering was addressed by the visiting minister. The services were conducted by the Rev. Whitty, who in September 1943 received the sad news that his younger brother, 23 year old Private B. Whitty, of the Buffs, had been killed in action at Sicily.

In 1943 in the church schoolroom on Saturday, November 20th members and friends of the church performed a play for the Church Building Fund and the New Bradwell Forces Fund. As a two act comedy this was entitled 'Meet the Family,' 'concerning crooks planning a jewel theft and an escaped lion from a circus.' Then for the same cause in 1944 on Saturday, January 15th another play was presented in the church schoolroom. Written by the Rev. Whitty this was entitled 'The Child Looks Back,' and £10 was raised by the performance.

In May 1944 Albert Brown was made vice president of the Northants. Baptist Association. He had been deacon of the church since 1908, a superintendent of the Sunday School since 1922 and church secretary since 1915. Then in December 1918 he was appointed JP. He died in 1945 on Tuesday, January 16th. In 1945 at a church meeting on the evening of Wednesday, April 18th the Rev. Whitty announced having accepted a unanimous invitation from the members of the Hockliffe Road Baptist Church, Leighton Buzzard. He would succeed the Rev. W. Legassick (who left Leighton Buzzard the last September) and at New Bradwell conducted his final services in 1945 on Sunday, July 15th. In the schoolroom on Saturday, July 28th 1945 at 7.30pm he and his wife were then guests of the members of the church at a farewell social organised by the deacons and their wives. They would then take two weeks holiday before the Reverend began his new ministry.

In 1945 on the evening of Saturday, November 3rd a social was held in the schoolroom for the new minister, the Rev. H.M. Ray Smith, and his wife and family of two boys. He would conduct the services the following day and it was resulting from information from the Rev. F.H. Rollinson, of Chipping Norton, that he had first preached at New Bradwell. In consequence it was by a unanimous vote of their church meeting that he was invited to the pastorate at New Bradwell. Born in Surrey and educated at Kingston, for several years he was an accountant at Westminster but then trained for the ministry at Regent Park College, London, completing his course 10 years ago. His previous pastorates had been at Woodbridge and Witnesham, Suffolk, and at Blockley, Moreton in the Marsh, Glos., where he was Secretary of the Cotswold Sunday School Union and President of the North Cotswold Free Church Council. In April 1946 the Rev. R. Williams, the pastor at New Bradwell from 1935-1940, died at his home, Wingate, in County Durham. On leaving North Bucks he became pastor at Heywood and Middleton in Manchester and when completing five years oversight was offered a further stay at the church. He had recently been ill and his right arm had to be amputated.

In 1946 on November 29th a Yuletide bazaar was held in the schoolroom of the old church, this being in connection with the New Renovation Fund of the church. Yet in 1949 there would be further expense when the church was found to have serious defects in the roof. Repair work commenced last May had revealed serious deterioration of the timbers by damp by which a quarter of the existing joints and ceiling had to be condemned. With the cost of rebuilding the roof estimated at about £1,400 the Rev. Ray Smith, writing in the church news sheet for September 1949, said the project to build new Sunday school premises behind the church would now be delayed. Yet the school was outgrowing their present accommodation and it was therefore intended to proceed with a scheme for altering the old church to make an additional hall. £1,500 would need to be raised and in his article he stated; "A Church meeting on 3rd August, received a report from the Minister and Deacons. Repair work started in May disclosed serious deterioration of timbers by damp, condemning a quarter of the existing joists and ceiling and the discovery of fungus necessitated a change of design to facilitate ventilation between the joists. Advice has been sought from Mr. Paul I. Panter, FRIBA, Diocesan surveyor for Peterborough. He has submitted a proposal for rebuilding the roof in the more usual sloping fashion at an approximate estimate of between £1,400 and £1,500. The Church meeting resolved to have this work done, and it will be carried out as soon as permits and materials allow. A decision taken at the May Church meeting to adapt the Old Church to improve the Sunday School accommodation at a cost of £100 or so was reviewed in the light of these circumstances, and became clear that God was bidding us 'go ahead' with this too. The whole situation was faced and its issues accepted by the meeting with great courage." "A meeting of the congregation was called a week later, and the decisions of Church meeting were explained to it."

After a closure of about a year the church then re-opened in 1950 on Saturday, April 29th. The flat roof infected by dry rot had been dismantled and rebuilt with a gabled roof which, with the architect's fee and necessary redecoration, had entailed a cost of about £1,900.

In the afternoon the Area Superintendent gave an address to a large congregation and later at a tea in the schoolroom on the opposite side of the road tea table speeches were made. In April 1951 the Rev. H.M. Ray Smith informed his congregation that he had received a unanimous invitation to become the minister at Wokingham. Subsequently in July at a farewell gathering at the church many presentations to him and his wife and two boys, David and Malcolm, were made. The deacons and church members gave a monetary gift, to purchase a chair for his study in his new home at Wokingham, and his wife received a clock from the Women's Own.

Then on Saturday, September 15th 1951 over 60 members from the New Bradwell, Hanslope and Loughton churches travelled to Wokingham for his services of induction and recognition. In September 1951 the president of the Rutland Free Church Federal Council, the Rev. Garwood S. Tydeman, of Oakham, accepted the vacant pastorate of the New Bradwell church. Aged 41 he was born at Maldon and trained at the Irish Baptist College, Dublin, under the principal T. Harold Spurgeon MA BD. His past appointments had included that of minister at Martham, Norfolk, for 3½ years, Godmanchester, Hunts., for over 4 years, Chatteris, Cambs., for 6 years, and at Oakham since January 1950. At Godmanchester he had been president and treasurer of the Hunts. Association of Baptist and Congregational churches, and during the war served as a member of the ARP. While at Chatteris he was a Free Church Chaplain at Doddington Hospital and was now presently Chaplain to the Oakham Infirmary, the Rutland Memorial Hospital, and the Burley on the Hill Auxiliary Hospital. In October he became the father of a baby girl, a sister for his 6 year old daughter, and

additionally having charge of the Long Street Church at Hanslope began at New Bradwell in 1952 on Sunday, January 6th. The induction and recognition service took place on Saturday, January 19th at 3pm and at 4.30pm a tea and social evening was held. Then in 1953 such meetings would be enhanced by the welcome installation of electricity.

In August 1956 the Rev. Tydeman accepted the ministry of the church at Gamlingay, and at New

Rev. Tydeman

Bradwell on Saturday, August 25th a farewell party was held, at which he was presented with a cheque, and each of his three children were given savings certificates. Other presents were from the Sunday School etc., and in the evening a concert took place. He conducted his final services at New Bradwell on Sunday, August 26th and would begin at Gamlingay on Sunday, September 2nd. The church then remained without a pastor until in 1957 on Friday, June 21st the induction service of the Rev. Jonathan Victor Benson took place at 7.30pm. Born in 1919 on June 27th he had been in charge of churches at Millom and Dalton in Furness, Cumberland, and had married Marie Jean Sharpe at Millom on September 18th 1957. He was born in Dublin on June 27th 1919 but soon afterwards his parents moved to Belfast, where after an education at an elementary school he entered the Belfast Railway Academy. In 1936 he joined the Civil Service in London and in 1940 began duties in connection with the Ministry of Transport, remaining as such throughout the war. After applying to the Baptist Union for training as a minister he was accepted into Rawdon College, Leeds in 1946. His first church would be at Millom in 1950 with his work further increased three years later by the inclusion of Dalton in Furness, some 20 miles away. As for hobbies, with an interest in the local scenery he was keen on colour photography. Presently single he hoped to be married soon.

By September 1959 the church was free of all debt, and there was a profit only £10 short of their £200 target when members of the church held their annual thanksgiving bazaar in 1960 on Saturday, April 30th. With regard to the many repairs of the past few years Mr. A.G. Bavington, the church secretary, said "The debt is now paid and nowhere, I am certain, can a church boast of such a truly marvellous achievement." For opening the bazaar Dr. M. Coster, chairman, introduced Mrs. A. Johnson, of Swindon. A native of New Bradwell she had taught in the Sunday School for many years until she and her husband left the town 5 years ago. Also leaving would be the Rev. Benson, for in 1961 at the close of evening worship on Sunday, March 5th he announced having accepted a call to be pastor of the church at Sandy Lane near Bradford, Yorks. On the evening of Saturday, June 17th as a result of private donations and an ABC market the estimated cost of £300 for renovations to the organ was reduced. Yet this hardly concerned the Rev. Benson, for the following day he conducted his last services at New Bradwell. These were held at 10.30am and 6pm and on the Monday in the schoolroom at 7.30pm a farewell gathering was held. As for another former minister, on the afternoon of Monday, June 26th at Old Bradwell the Rev. Ernest J. Whitty, now of 278, St. John's Road, Hemel Hempstead, was travelling on a motorcycle with his wife when he collided with a van which skidded on the wet road. Fortunately only cuts and bruises were suffered.

In November 1961 a notice was posted stating that the Trustees of the Charity, with regard to certain Trust Property held in connection with the church, viz situated on the corner site of the junction of North Street and Bradwell Road and known as the Church Parlour,

Rev. Harris

proposed to sell the property for £250. Any higher offer was to be addressed to the Secretary, Charity Commissioners, London.

In June 1962 it was announced that a former president of the Baptist Student Federation, 26 year old Mr. David Malcolm Harris, presently at the Regents Park College, Oxford, was to be the new minister of the New Bradwell and Hanslope churches. Born in Coventry he became a member of Queen's Road Baptist Church and during National Service held the rank of lance corporal in the Royal Warwickshire Regiment. He attended courses at Coventry Technical School and on leaving the Army went to the University of Nottingham, where he obtained a BA in English, being also president of The William Carey Society, and chairman of the Hugh Stewart Hall Debating Society. In 1959 he went to Oxford University for 3 years where, occasionally playing rugger and cricket for his college, he gained an Hons. in Theology. He then gained a Baptist Union scholarship. At Coventry he married Ann Jones in August 1961, his wife being a teacher who trained at Coventry Training College and had been awarded the Diploma in Education. At the services of ordination and induction in September 1962 over a third of the congregation came from Coventry, many from Queen's Road Baptist Church, where he had been baptised and where for many years he had been a member. A tea then followed for some 200 in the Labour Hall. At New Bradwell he soon integrated into the community and within a few weeks had formed a youth club, which met every Wednesday.

In 1967 the deacons of the New Bradwell church submitted a resolution with regard to the relationship with the Baptist churches at Loughton and Stony Stratford. On December 27th a special meeting was held and at the meeting of New Bradwell church in February 1968 they placed their agreement on a 'Team Ministry.' Within this scheme the ministers would work closely together, each with a particular responsibility for his own church, with a 'new man' to be called to New Bradwell. Stipends would be paid by the individual churches, and the ministers would share any special gifts 'and would work together for the benefit of the group as a whole.' 'All churches would have a voice and a vote in the appointment of every member of the ministerial team.' A Senior Minister would be appointed and the other members of the team would be called Associate Ministers, having full pastoral responsibility for their own churches 'but sharing equally with the Senior Minister in the work

The Methodist Chapel, on the corner of North Street and Harwood Street.

and witness of the group as a whole.' The Deacons at New Bradwell feel that this is a preliminary step towards a SHARED MINISTRY for the group, in which two or more ministers would form a joint pastorate, the Ministers serving all the Churches equally, and whose stipends and expenses would be paid from a central fund. They would rotate around the Churches for Sunday worship, assisted by Lay Preachers or Lay Pastors. They feel that when a minister is settled at New Bradwell for a period of approximately six months, consultations should proceed immediately with this aim in view.' In other matters in February 1968 the secretary reported that in recent months there had been numerous enquiries from business men who wished to rent the school premises. However there was now a definite offer to purchase from a Mr. Addison of Luton, acting on behalf of Trident Chemicals Ltd., a firm which manufactured industrial cleaning materials for home and export. In final conversations with Mr. Bavington they had accepted a purchase price of £1,850, or £1,875 should occupation be required before April 6th. Planning permission had been applied for and a decision was now awaited from the Council. The financial position showed that a new hall with furniture could be built without incurring any foreseeable debt and a resolution was proposed and carried:-

> 'That the Special Church meeting, properly convened, agrees that if Planning Permission be given, the buildings known as the School Premises should be sold to Trident Chemicals Ltd. for the sum of £1,850, with the proviso that if occupation is required before March 31st, the sale price will be £1,875. Should the sale take place on the terms stated, the meeting authorises the Building Committee to meet at an early date and prepare plans for a new Church Hall adjacent to the Church.'

However it seems that in the autumn of 1968 the former Baptist Church schoolroom in Bradwell Road was taken over by Jehovah's Witness. Throughout 1968 the question of finding a new minister, 'the new man,' was considered and eventually the Rev. Basil Hill was invited, as stated at the meeting of March 11th 1969. However from his initially being 'in an unusual situation of a deferred or delayed ministry' Miss Rosemary Barrett offered the church a 'Summer Pastorate' which was accepted. At the annual general meeting in 1969 on October 23rd it was felt that the Rev. Hill's forthcoming ministry 'should bring a steadiness and a guiding influence.' Yet it was not to be, for having reflected on the state of the New Bradwell Church, 'and the lapse of time before any appreciable development could be achieved', he had decided (his estimate of the 'lapse' being 5 years) that this was not his calling (1970 January 8th).

Then in view of the decreasing congregations a special meeting was convened in 1970 on Thursday, March 12th to consider a suggestion from the Rev. Victor Taylor, Methodist Superintendent. This was that the Baptists and Methodists should work and worship together and after much discussion a resolution, with only voice of dissent, was proposed and carried 'That the deacons be authorised to explore arrangements of regular joint worship from October of this year, 1970; the position to be reviewed in March 1971.' Then at a meeting of the deacons in 1970 on November 20th consideration was given to the possible appointment of the Rev. Reginald Baker who, as reported in 1971 on January 15th, accepted the ministry. Plans for combined congregations were revived in 1971 and both denominations agreed to worship together alternately at each church for a period of 6 months from May 7th. The Rev. Baker and the Rev. F. Smith (Methodist) would share leading the services. The Manse had now been inspected by a Valuation Officer and at a figure of £3,250 it was resolved at the meeting on Friday, August 27th 1971 that it be firstly advertised. This was instead of placing with an estate agent, who would only be engaged in the event of a poor response. Also at the meeting it was stated that a recommendation had been made to the Baptist Union that a specialist Baptist Minister should be appointed in early 1973. Treated as an initial pastorate this position would be to have charge of the Church and the growing local community. Financial help would be given and 'It was envisaged at the moment that a "Shared" Church would be built in Stantonbury, perhaps to be used by the three denominations at New Bradwell and therefore it seemed essential that the Free Church witness should be strengthened by a closer working of the Methodist and Baptist Churches. The Deacons had considered this matter and had recommended that a letter be sent to the Methodist Supt. suggesting the holding of joint conversations, this to be sent in the first place through the Association Pastor. This policy was noted and agreed.'

Then in 1972 at the Church meeting on February 11th it was reported that the sale of the Manse had been completed. After meeting solicitors' fees £2,940 30p had been realised and following discussions it was resolved that the sum should be invested in the Baptist Union Loan Fund, where it would be easily available. In conclusion the congregation of the Baptist Church at New Bradwell gradually dwindled until only a few remained. They then continued to worship at the Methodist Church but the chapel building is now still in religious use by another denomination.

METHODIST CHURCH

At Mr. J. Wilson's at Linslade, in 1865 the plans and specifications for the new Primitive Methodist Chapel could be inspected until 6pm on Thursday evening August 10th. That year the foundation stones were laid and at a cost of £935 the building would accommodate seating for 300. Then on Sunday, January 14th 1866 the new Primitive Methodist Chapel was opened for Divine Service, at which the Rev. J. Langham, from Bedford, preached in the morning and the Rev. J. Minett in the afternoon. Anniversary celebrations would take place in the succeeding years such as in 1879 on Sunday, July 6th. During the afternoon an address was given to the children of the Sunday Schools and on the Monday afternoon the children's festival was held. Then in the evening a public meeting took place. By now the need had arisen for new buildings for the Sunday School, since the 140 children and 13 teachers all had to be accommodated in the chapel.

In consequence for the Sunday School Building Fund in 1891 on Friday, August 21st and Saturday 22nd a Loan Exhibition and Floral and Horticultural Bazaar was held in the LNWR schools. At the rear of the present chapel a piece of ground had been obtained and the event raised some £70. Then for the same intent on Saturday, November 28th a tea meeting was held, followed by an entertainment in the chapel. Fund raising events continued and in 1892 in the third week of August an exhibition and bazaar was held in the LNWR schools. So far £80 had been raised with the continuing need for a further £120. However with Mr. Tranfield as the architect plans and specifications had been prepared and the contract awarded to Mr. Adkins of Leighton Buzzard. The site was that at the rear of the chapel and with accommodation for 200 children the premises would consist of school rooms, two vestries, and offices.

Preceded by a brass band touring the streets, in bitterly cold weather in 1893 on Saturday, March 18th in the presence of a large company the ceremony of laying the foundation stones was commenced at 3pm. In the presence of a large company the Rev. G. Parkin said the purpose of building the school was to make the boys that came to the school reverent, 'and bring them up in the highest form of manhood.' The first stone was laid by Mr. Adams of Birmingham. Then on behalf of the Sunday School in laying another Mr. W.E. Thompson said he joined the school 23 years ago, and 20 years ago had become a teacher. A stone was laid by Mr. Geo. Barker and another by Mr. A. Barker on behalf of the choir. In the Baptist schoolroom, lent especially for the occasion, a public tea was provided and in the evening a public meeting took place with Mr. Tompkins in the chair. In speaking of the scheme the Rev. George Percy Maynard (d 1951) said the idea had originated some 17 years ago when a promise (which had now been fulfilled) of £20 was made by the LNWR. When he came to Stantonbury three years ago he was asked what he thought of building a new schoolroom and in response considered that firstly they should have a practical scheme. Then 12 months ago he was asked to stay on circuit for another year with the understanding that the schoolroom would be commenced. A meeting was held but it was too late to commence building before the winter. Thus it was early this year that tenders were sought, with that of Mr. Adkins accepted to build the school for £262 15s, excepting furniture. Presently there was a debt of £151 on the chapel but when that was cleared they intended to enhance the building with new seats and cushions. Towards funds for the new school up to January 1893 they had £115 in the bank and the collection that afternoon had raised £2 1s 7d.

In 1893 during the afternoon of Sunday, June 11th the new Primitive Methodist Sunday School was opened. A sermon was preached by the Rev. Barron of Northampton, and with several ladies of the congregation presiding a tea was served. In the evening a public meeting took place. The cost of the new addition had been £294 5s leaving a deficit of £102 7s 11d. As for other monetary needs, in aid of the renovation fund of the chapel in 1895 on August 27th and 28th a bazaar and exhibition of arms and armour was held in the National Schools.

Then in 1901 on Tuesday, October 29th the second in a series of lectures in aid of the Stantonbury Primitive Methodist Organ Fund was delivered by Mr. J.T. Whitmee of Castlethorpe. The venue was the Liberal Hall and entitled 'Bubbles' the session was illustrated by the fascination of various chemical and physical experiments.

In later financial requirements in 1922 on Wednesday, November 29th a sale of work was held at the chapel for the purchase of a new organ. Then for the costs of new heating apparatus in November 1924 a two day sale of work took place.

From a ministry at North Cave, Yorkshire, in 1927 the new pastor at New Bradwell became the Rev. Harold Henry Woodward MC. Born at York in 1878 to an Inland Revenue Officer and his wife, in early life he spent four years at sea, indeed being shipwrecked in the North Sea. Then at the age of 20 having come under the religious influence of the zealous Joseph Odell (born at Dunstable) he became a local preacher, and after serving 4 years as an evangelist was accepted as a 'special case' to train for the Ministry. In 1908 after 2 years at the faith's Hartley College he became a Primitive Methodist Minister at Bath. Subsequently Crowle in 1910, Lynn in 1912, and Wisbech in 1915. That year he joined the RAMC as a private but with the increasing need for chaplains he was appointed as such in 1916 on December 9th, and along with a group of new Primitive Methodist Chaplains crossed to France. Serving with great distinction he insisted on going 'over the top' with his men and it was by their recommendation that he was awarded the Military Cross. Having been wounded three times and gassed he would never recover from the effects and was invalided out of the Army in 1920. In the following year he took up the ministry at Howden, then in 1924 North Cave. Then Stantonbury, where in 1928 on the afternoon of Saturday, April 14th he conducted the service when following renovations the Primitive Methodist Church was re-opened.

The ceremony was performed by the Rev. J. Reeves of Northampton and after the service a tea was provided for some 70 persons. In the next year for the School Renovation Fund a two day sale of work began on the afternoon of Wednesday, February 20th.

From being a Primitive Methodist chapel, from the union that took place in 1932, the church became part of the Methodist Church and in the second week of August 1933 the New Bradwell Methodists met in the schoolroom for a farewell presentation to the Rev. Harold Woodward and his wife Margaret, nee Kermeen. (The couple had married at Douglas, Isle of Man, in 1912.) After six years he was leaving for the position at Wirksworth, Derbyshire, and with members of other denominations present Mr. F. Butcher presided. As a gift from the various organisations of the church a wallet of treasury notes was presented by Mrs. S. Biggs, one of the oldest members of the Methodist Church in New Bradwell, and via Mr. B. Betts the Band of Hope presented a fountain pen.

In September 1933 the New Bradwell Methodists purchased the property adjoining their church for an enlargement scheme. They would now sell their plot of land on Newport Road facing the parish church, and towards enlarging the church and school premises in 1934 the sum of £360 was made by the annual two day bazaar at the chapel on a Wednesday and Friday in April. The bazaar was entitled 'My Lady's Home' with the schoolroom representing a house with various rooms containing articles for sale relative to the purpose of those rooms. At a cost of about £1,100 the scheme was to extend the present church building into half of the present schoolroom and connect up the adjoining property, which would be made into two large classrooms, a kitchen, a bathroom and an entrance hall.

In 1938 in the early hours of Thursday, March 3rd Fred Rawlings Butcher died aged 58 at his home 23, King Edward Street, New Bradwell. His employment had been at Wolverton Works but as a local preacher he had a long connection with the New Bradwell Methodist Church, where he was a trustee and chapel steward. In 1939 a former pastor, the Rev. Harold Woodward, now of Wirksworth, Derbyshire, made a welcome visit to the New Bradwell Methodist Church for the Band of Hope prize distribution. (Due to the wounds from WW1 for the last 7 years of his life he would become a 'frail but radiant invalid' and having undergone several operations he died at Westcliffe on Sea in 1949 on October 17th.)

In 1941 on Thursday, November 13th the New Bradwell Methodist Women's Meeting held its 21st birthday gathering. No doubt making a joyful noise this was attended by some 200 ladies and in June 1945 the church acquired a reconditioned organ for the sum of £140. This came from the Bletchley Road Methodist Church and on Saturday, June 16th the opening took place when, preceded by a tea, Mr. C. Kenneth Garratt performed a recital. Regarding the purchase there was no debt due to special efforts and the sale of the old organ.

In February 1948 the New Bradwell Methodist Church took over the premises adjoining their building where each week the youth of the church would meet for recreational purposes. In fact this new youth organisation was open to members of all denominations, with organised programmes arranged to make the Tuesday evenings a success. In 1948 on Saturday, June 5th the church hosted a large audience for the first concert by the newly formed local Male Voice Choir. This was formed from members of all denominations and the collection of £7 2s was given to the Men's Section of the New Bradwell Methodist Church.

In November 1951 members of the church were at work on Saturday mornings building a surrounding wall. This was a replacement for the iron railings removed during the war and fortunately an expert brick layer was amongst their number.

In 1958 on Saturday, March 29th the opening took place of the church's new permanent stage. At 7.15pm a grand variety concert was performed by the Bletchley Spurgeon Memorial Concert Party with the proceeds applied for the church funds. Via the Bucks Association of Youth Clubs, in October 1961 the New Bradwell Methodist Youth Club applied for a grant from the Carnegie Trust. This was for additions and improvements to the building which they used for club nights four times a week, and although they would do most of the work themselves the cost of materials would be over £200. Then in 1966 the trustees of New Bradwell Methodist Church hoped to buy Bowyer Hall for youth work but at the annual meeting of Buckingham Conservative Association at Bletchley, on the evening of Friday, June 3rd, the treasurer, Mr. W.S. Johnson said the building had been sold to a higher offer made by Mr. C.P. Hiorns of New Bradwell for commercial purposes. A disappointment for the Methodists but such activities have now long been consigned to the past, for at New Bradwell the Methodist Church closed its doors for the last time on Sunday, May 28th 2006.

However in 2008 the congregation joined with that of St. James', and as a vestige of the old chapel two chairs and a small font were brought from the former premises to be placed in the chancel.

THE REVEREND ALLAN NEWMAN GUEST

'A big, burly, rotund man with a rolling gait and a happy, jovial face tanned by exposure to wind and rain.' (Although it seems recollections may have varied!)

Allan Newman Guest was born in 1867 on November 24th at Listowel, Kerry, Ireland. There he was baptised, and it was there that his parents, George Guest and Mary Ann Newman (born in

January 1846 at Listowel), had married in 1865 at the parish church on September 27th. After a private education, for six years Allan attended Trinity College, Dublin University, gaining a BA in Divinity in 1889 and an MA in 1893. He was ordained deacon in 1890 and at St. Patrick's Cathedral, Dublin, was admitted into holy orders as priest on November 29th 1891, being curate of Creagh Co. Galway 1891-

2, and Molyneux Chaplin, Dublin, 1892-4. From friendships in Ireland with renowned Protestant Loyalists he believed he was on an IRA 'hit list,' and in consequence moved to England in 1897 with his widowed mother. (His father had died in a workhouse but Allan, having contacted the Registrar, had the record amended whereby 'for workhouse read Union Infirmary a paying patient,' 'for commercial traveller read Gentleman.') Apparently he declined the first parish to be offered from objection to the name, Piddlehinton, in Dorset. Instead, resident at 53, Dynham Road, he came to the church of St. James', West Hampstead, London NW, where he remained until 1897. He then moved to St. John the Evangelist at Brighton. During 1899 he was appointed to the church of St. Paul, Brentford, and then in 1901 to the church of St. Philip at Kensington, being resident in April that year with his widowed mother at 97, Abingdon Road. In 1903 his next appointment was assistant priest at the church of St. Stephen's, Lewisham, and from 1904 he would be curate of St. John the Divine, Stamford Hill. The parish contained some very poor districts and he gained popularity amongst those in need from performing much good work in the slums of the Tewkesbury district. Aged 61 his mother died at Eastbourne in 1907 and it was whilst curate of St. John's, resident at 27, Vartry Road, that in 1908 he was offered and accepted the vicariate of Stantonbury. This was in the gift of Earl Spencer, and there was a large congregation at the church of St. James on the evening of Thursday, September 17th for his induction by the Archdeacon of Buckingham. As an excellent speaker and a great advocate of temperance, the Rev. Guest became immersed in his duties and around March 1909 began attempts to raise money for the building of a Working Men's Church Institute. The site had already been acquired, with £350 collected towards the necessary £1,700. Around this time he discovered the church of St. James had never been licensed for marriages. Thereby some 1,000 were technically invalid and he immediately communicated with the Registrar-General, who confirmed his findings. In fact the whole affair had arisen when the Rev. Guest wrote to the Registrar General for a new marriage register. He then noticed that it bore the name St. Peter's and having pointed this out to the latter began to examine the papers belonging to the church. Further correspondence took place between himself and the authorities at Somerset House, resulting in a notice that no further marriages were to take place at St. James' until an order of registration had been made. Thus causing great shock and disbelief on the evening of Sunday, March 28th 1909 in the course of his sermon the Rev. Guest revealed his investigations to the congregation. He explained that 'a flaw in the title of a document' had caused him to communicate with the Registrar General who, making consequent investigations at the Diocesan Registry, and also in his own archives at Somerset House, confirmed that seemingly no licence had ever been issued to solemnise marriages at the church. Therefore until an order was made legalising the past matrimonies he had no alternative but to sign an official notice prohibiting the vicar from solemnising any such marriages. In the meantime ceremonies were to take place at the old church of St. Peter's, Stantonbury, which was presently only in use for special occasions. Not surprisingly his announcement caused great dismay amongst the crowded congregation, for although it seemed there had been intimations during the morning it was only at the evening service that the facts were fully made known and confirmed. Since the opening of the church some 1,000 marriages had been conducted (the first groom being a lawyer!) with the Reverends C.P. Cotter, A.C Woodhouse, A.O. James and now Newman Guest as the successive incumbents. At the inception the church had been consecrated by the Bishop but this was insufficient to legalise the marriages contracted within it. The Rev. Guest also said that whilst it was locally known as St. James' he had found no trace of the church having been officially dedicated as such. However he later received a communication from the Diocesan Registry stating that a document of proof had been discovered. In remedy of the recent turmoil the Rev. Guest would receive a communication from the Registrar of Oxford Diocese, in which was stated that pursuant to the Ecclesiastical Commissioners consultation with the Law Officers of the Crown it had been decided to frame a special Act of Parliament. This would legalise all the marriages conducted since the date of consecration, while in the meantime three weddings would take place at St. Peter's on Easter Sunday. These couples, whose banns had been handed in before any knowledge of the illegality, had decided to be married by special licence, for which the usual fee was £2 15s. As a preliminary the young people journeyed to Newport Pagnell one Wednesday evening to arrange the necessary formality. The Reverend Guest accompanied them to the vicarage, the residence of the Rev. F. Gunnery, the commissary for marriage licences, and having each been called in to state the relevant particulars they emerged 'smiling and happy' from being told that the Easter weddings could take place. As for the response from one of the three brides, "I am so glad it has turned out well after all. I didn't know what would happen when they told me the banns could not be read at St. James' Church. I wrote to my boy, who is working in the north, and told him we could not be married the day we had arranged, and that it must be put off until the banns could be read on three Sundays all over again. When I heard the news about the special licence I could have jumped for joy, and I am writing to tell my sweetheart that he must be at the church in time." As for the notice to officially rectify the situation;

'Ecclesiastical Commissioners - Instrument dated July 1st 1909. Instrument substituting the new church of St. James, situate at New Bradwell within the parish of Stantonbury (sometimes described as Stantonbury with New Bradwell)), in the county of Buckingham and in the diocese of Oxford, for the old church of St. Peter, situate within and hitherto being the parish church of the same parish. The Bishop of Oxford, Earl Spencer and Rev Guest ' have by an Instrument under their hands, bearing date on or about the twenty-seventh day of May, in the year one thousand nine hundred and nine, certified to us, the said Ecclesiastical Commissioners for England, that it would be for the convenience of the said parish of Stantonbury that the said new church of St. James, situate at New Bradwell within such parish, should be substituted for the old parish church (dedicated to Saint Peter) of the same parish.' By their power the Ecclesiastical Commissioners decree 'that such new church shall henceforth be the parish church of the said parish of Stantonbury, in lieu of the old said parish church of Saint Peter, as fully in all respects as if the said new church of St. James, so hereby substituted, had been originally the parish church of the same parish; ... 'They 'do hereby transfer all the endowments, emoluments, and rights belonging to the old said parish church (dedicated to Saint Peter as aforesaid) of the said parish of Stantonbury, of or belonging to the

Vicar or Incumbent thereof, to the new said church of Saint James (now being by virtue of these presents the parish church of the said parish of Stantonbury) and to the Vicar or Incumbent thereof and his successors for ever.'

In 1909 on June 4th an Act of Parliament was duly presented to validate the marriages, being confirmed in the House of Lords on July 16th. Thus the matter was now settled, and on the domestic front in 1911 the Rev. Guest was settled at Stantonbury Vicarage with Charles Walter Seager, age 42, married, employed as 'a valet and general man,' and Elizabeth Seager, age 52, married, employed as a housekeeper.

However in ecclesiastical matters the year would begin a long decline in the relationship with his parishioners. Not least on Tuesday, November 14th, when correspondence was read from the Reverend at the monthly meeting of the Stantonbury Council School Managers. Therein he stated that by a deed poll dated November 8th 1858 the London & North West Railway Company had in consideration of 5s 'freely and voluntarily' granted and converted to the vicar and churchwardens the land on which the schools were built. Also he claimed discovery of an old deed wherein was stated that the schools were only intended for use by the Managers on certain nights in the week. Thereby he gave written notice that "after this day you will not be accorded the use of the schools until such time as you have the exclusive right with my permission." With Alderman Wylie in the chair this caused much discussion amongst the managers, who deemed that the deed referred to by the vicar had been cancelled. In fact by the present arrangement the vicar and his successors could only claim the use of the schools on Sundays, since as successors to the old School Board the Council School Authorities had leased the schools from the Church of England by an agreement dated October 8th 1896. However in his letter the Reverend stated that by the agreement of 1896, namely between the managers of the Stantonbury National School and the Bradwell School Board, the latter were only allowed the exclusive use of the school premises upon certain clearly defined occasions; 'the right to the use of the school (except the teachers' residence) at all other times to remain vested in the Church School Managers represented by the Vicar.'

Continuing he said, 'Now, it is quite clear that for the space of the last 15 years the Board School Managers and their successors have let the premises and continue to grant the use of the buildings at other times than they are allowed the exclusive use thereof; thus violating the said agreement of the 8th October, 1896, and usurping the powers of the Vicar and Churchwardens as representing the old managers.' Therefore from 'letting the schools when you had not the right to do so' he asked for the monies to be handed to him. 'Furthermore, I hereby give you notice that on and after this date you must not be accorded the use thereof at such times as you have not the exclusive right without my permission in writing, or give the use thereof at such times to any other person or persons.' In reply the chairman said a later agreement had empowered the managers to let the schools. They had a right to the buildings from Monday mornings until 10 o'clock on Saturday nights, and the only claim the vicar had was for their use on Sundays for religious instruction. The Rev. Guest then asked where this amendment was, to which the chairman said he knew were it was. The Reverend then argued that the schools were leased from the Church of England authorities and when the £3,000 had been paid, and he believed that had now been reduced to £1,000, and after he gave them notice the whole of the property reverted back to him as vicar of the parish. Alderman Wylie said it was no use bringing the matter before this meeting - "go to Aylesbury and put the case forward." Holding a document aloft the vicar said he'd been to Whitehall and the agreement was binding; "Have you another document in your possession?" The chairman said there was but he didn't have it; "We have a perfect right to do as we like. You have only the right to have your Sunday School classes there on Sundays." In clarification Mr. Sykes said the School Board had refused to take over the schools under the conditions of the first document, and so another had been drawn up allowing the schools to be used by the vicar only on Sundays. Another member, Mrs. Edwards, asked the chairman "Were you not present in London when the last deed was signed by the Rev. Woodhouse, Mr. Lawyer Powell, and the London & North Western Railway Company, that the parish should have the use of the schools for six days of the week?" The chairman affirmed that he was, at which the vicar said

"You never told me of the existence of any document such as you now suggest." The chairman said that he had, when the vicar called at his house about the matter. The vicar replied "My solicitor will see that deed …" Then when he said that through the instrumentality of the National Society and the Bishop they would become voluntary schools Mr. Sykes and Mrs. Edwards retorted "Never." Following further remonstrations Mr. Sykes said the best thing the vicar could do was to see the deed, to which on rising from his chair the Rev. Guest said "I don't care for any Manager nor anyone in Stantonbury; I shall go on with it. .." The chairman said "Just do as you like. You haven't got an atom of ground to stand on." At this the Rev. Guest wished the managers "Good night" and left the meeting.

Yet that wouldn't be the end of such dealings, for now in the vicar's absence a letter was read from the Superintendent of the Stantonbury Band of Hope. In this he asked if it was fair or just for the Rev. Guest to have removed the only musical instrument in the Boys' School (a harmonium) and take it to the Infants' Room, where was already a piano; "This is what happened on Tuesday evening, the 17th, when he demanded that the caretaker assist him to remove it, saying 'I am a Manager, and I mean to have it.'" In further details the Superintendent said the Band of Hope had commenced a fortnight ago, and used the instrument from having been allowed a room in the Boys' School. The Rev. Guest had started a group in opposition in the infants' large room, to where the instrument had been taken. Thus the Superintendent queried that even if the Reverend was a manager, did he have such authority; "I can say in all truthfulness that it has only been done for spitefulness." In answering the letter the Correspondent said he'd confirmed that the instrument should not have been removed. Indeed the vicar had received no authority from the managers to even use the room. Attention had also been drawn to the unruly character of the children. Some were standing on the desks thus causing obvious concerns about the school furniture being abused in that way. The chairman duly moved that a letter be sent to the vicar stating the harmonium must not be taken, that permission must be asked for the use of the room, and that any rowdy behaviour would not be tolerated. In fact according to one member it was hardly a 'Band of Hope.' The children were invited by the vicar, who another member said was a trespasser. Subsequently it was moved 'That the Rev. Guest be written to and informed that he must make application to the Managers before he uses any room in these schools for his Band of Hope.' This was seconded and carried unanimously. Further it was moved 'That the large room be locked up except on nights when permission is given by the Managers for its use.' This was also seconded and agreed. As regards the 'Band of Hope,' this seemed to be more of a club for the encouragement of developing 'moral well being and physical development.'

Perhaps not surprising, for of athletic physique the vicar could often be seen jogging barefoot around the local fields and vaulting five bar gates! Indeed he placed great importance on promoting sporting pursuits and had recently been forming a Boys' Club at Stantonbury, where meetings took place at the Vicarage. Having in younger days practised 'self defence' he encouraged the members to take an interest in 'manly games,' writing in January 1912; "I wish to say a few words on self defence in relation to the morals and physique of Englishmen. Now, it is evident that the whole range of the seven deadly sins - called "deadly" by the Church because of their effect on soul and body - are successfully resisted by the employment of Nature's own knuckledusters. ... " He then expounded the benefits, stating "In fact, there is nothing like boxing. It kills the seven deadly sins. The fighter - not necessarily the prize-fighter - becomes a kind father, a good husband, a friend to his boys, a good comrade, and a citizen who is a credit to the Union Jack. ..."

In fact during the month it was announced that a boxing match was to take place one Tuesday morning between himself and Joseph Hepworth. A soldier who had fought in the South African War, and during his military service had reached the Army finals for boxing, he was now an Army reservist and helped his mother in a shop at Stantonbury. Such was the interest in the proposed event that 500 men from Wolverton Works intended to have the morning off! As for the origins of the challenge, a while ago Mr. Hepworth's boxing exploits had come to the notice of the vicar, who in passing some criticism of his boxing style included "Can Mr. Hepworth feint with his left?" When made aware of this Joseph, who was under 30, jokingly said that he'd take the vicar on, and the Rev. Guest laughingly said he wouldn't object.

Thus it was arranged to take place at 11am on the appointed day on the vicarage lawn, to be fought under Queensberry rules of 14 rounds 3 minutes each - 1 minute between each. There was much excitement and such was the local fervour that wagers were seemingly being placed in the local pubs. However on hearing this the vicar called off the match, saying "For the benefit of the Boys' Club I wanted to have a little bit of a sparring exhibition. When I found out that there was betting going on in public houses over it I would have nothing more to do with it. To call it a prize fight is absurd. ... Had the contest been proceeded with all kinds of exaggerated rumours might have reached the Bishop of Oxford's ears. Consequently I felt it my duty to abandon the contest. I have not refused the challenge, and at some future time I will have a few friendly bouts with my opponent when everything is quiet."

As for Mr. Hepworth, he said he was still quite willing. Nevertheless there would be a local conflict a few weeks later, when many people in Stantonbury became increasingly disturbed by the Rev. Guest's apparent deviance from the doctrines of the Church of England. Not that he took any great measures to dispute this, for on a notice board placed in a corner of the churchyard at St. James', indeed overlooking the Newport road, was posted;

'JESU MERCY
MARY INTERCEDE
SERVICES MARCH III.
MASS 8a.m.
SOLEMN EVENSONG 6.30
HIGH ALTAR
2nd LESSON SEQUENCE
THE CATHOLIC CONFITEOR

Devotions from Rosary of Virgin Mary and Litany of Loretto with Adoration of JESUS and Intercession for souls in Purgatory.

Hail, Queen of Heaven, the Ocean Star!

Guide of the wanderer here below.

Thrown on life's surge we claim Thy care;

Save us from peril and from woe.

Mother of Christ, Star of the Sea.

Pray for the wanderer, pray for me!

A. NEWMAN GUEST.

Parish Priest.'

Of his intentions he made no secret, saying "We accept the teaching of the Undivided Church before the Reformation, and we pray to the Virgin Mary as head of the communion of saints, the Queen of Heaven." As was reported, "The Undivided Church is his ideal and he holds that the Pope is spiritual head of the Church of England. He says Protestantism is 'the cockle amongst the corn' and that he is one of 10,000 trying to restore the doctrines, the faith, and the creeds of the pre-Reformation period." When asked if he prayed to the Virgin Mary the Rev. Guest said; "I do, and on that point it should be remembered that there is nothing in the Bible about praying to the Holy Ghost. We accept the teaching of the Undivided Church before the Reformation, and we pray to the Virgin Mary as the head of the Communion of Saints, the Queen of Heaven." When asked if the man in the street might regard his service as Roman Catholic he replied; "That is the construction that the man in the street might put upon it. But it is all in the Prayer Book. I wear only the vestments ordered by the Prayer Book."

Yet for some his sermons appeared to have profound effect, with one attendee moved to write, "On Sunday the church was crowded to the door, and I was in a spell which I cannot explain. The service was Roman Catholic. ... The glorious sermon gripped me: but whether it was heaven or hell I don't know. He is the Pope's man. A lot of men who came in for fun were kneeling down praying. ... I know people who curse him, and yet cannot keep from the church. The vicar is a man of blameless life. I see children running up to him in the street to be blessed, even in Wolverton. He prays to the Virgin and has Mass. Married women go to the confession."

Amplifying his leanings the Rev. Guest announced that from 'a high official' he had received letters of introduction to the Vatican. Indeed that year he hoped to have an audience with the Pope, intending to ask him to come to London to the Albert Hall and speak on the "Reunion of Christendom." Inevitably such blatant views caused controversy with those parishioners of the established faith, and as equally inevitable they became more vociferous in their dissension.

Manifest not least on Sunday, March 3rd 1912 when during the morning and evening only the choir boys were in the choir stalls. As for the reason it seemed that on the last practice night, Thursday, at the close of the ordinary Sunday services 'special music' was put before the choir. Since the time was 9pm objections were raised about continuing for another hour or so, primarily since it would be too late for the boys to be out. Therefore the choir declined to stay. On leaving the church three of the men then came across the Rev. Guest, who on being informed that the special music had not been practised allegedly told them that on Sunday the choirmen would not be permitted to enter the church.

Nevertheless on the Sunday morning with a view to reaching a settlement the men waited outside the church vestry but the vicar remained adamant, and they were not permitted to enter. In consequence during the service the vicar informed the congregation that they didn't have the choir with them, and the members would have to return alone. In fact there had already been a previous dispute by which only three of the choir boys now remained. The choirmen continued their strike, and when the vicar said at a vestry meeting on Thursday, March 14th 1912 that he had nothing to withdraw and nothing to regret they told him they wouldn't return. In a further escalation the Wolverton members of the choir remained absent from their usual places in the stalls and Mr. Thorneycroft, the organist and choirmaster, handed in his notice!

More was to follow the next year, when unprecedented rowdy and tumultuous scenes erupted at the crowded vestry meeting on Wednesday, March 26th 1913. Even as chairman the Rev. Guest had little control over the mayhem, and had to repeatedly appeal to the people's warden to subdue the commotion. Seated at the desk near the door the Reverend had a mass of papers before him.

Also in the form of a big roll of paper several feet long a petition against him and some of his services which, extensively signed, the parishioners had sent to the Bishop of Oxford. On the right of the vicar were the two wardens. Also a man whom he'd asked to act as his amanuensis, and although the meeting had opened quietly this only served as a prelude to a gathering storm. The first rumbles were not long in coming, for in dealing with the allegations of the petition the Reverend began, "I am sorry to have to strike a discordant note at the very beginning about such matters. But I say if you are to behave like Englishmen, strike fair, don't hit below the belt. There are two statements in this petition. One is that 'the Litany is rarely if ever said in the church.' That is not true and I told the Bishop so. The Litany is said three times a week, on Sunday, Wednesday, and Friday, as ordered in the Prayer Book, but no one is present at the services, though the bell is rung." A voice; "It may as well not be said if no one comes." At this the vicar replied "That is where you show your ignorance; the fact that it is said makes that statement into a falsehood." The other statement, said the vicar, is "that the Rev. A. Newman Guest is in the habit of holding from time to time services which cannot be associated with the Book of Common Prayer, and which are most objectionable to all the worshippers." Countering this he said the services were not objectionable to all the worshippers. A voice; "Very nearly." The vicar; "Oh, no; there are people here who will hold up their hands and say that, and that will be sufficient to utterly damn that cause." Voices; "Tell them to put them up." No one did. A parishioner then urged that they get on with the business but rising hurriedly from his chair the Reverend said "Oh no; I am chairman here, and I shall conduct the meeting as I like." (Laughter and jeers.) The parishioner then continued "This meeting is for the election of sidesmen" - (Hear, hear, and continued booing) - and when the Reverend tried to speak his words were lost in the escalating disorder.

At length when a relative calm was restored he then read another clause from the petition, alleging that on Sunday, October 13th 1912 "the whole of the service after the second lesson was conducted from the communion table, the Vicar again wearing a cope, which could not be associated with the Book of Common Prayer." With regard to this the vicar said that every spoken word from the beginning of evensong to the end, except the hymns, was in the Book of Common Prayer. A voice; "The words were there but not your actions." Refuting this the vicar claimed to have a statement signed by four men to the contrary, which he had shown to the Bishop. He then threw the petition on the table saying "The petition, and everything connected with it, is ended." Voices, "Not yet, we are only just beginning." Indeed this proved just the start of several more altercations, the next of which came after the wardens' accounts had been presented. The vicar remarked that the amount of the church collections needn't be stated at the Vestry meeting, which resulted in loud cries of "Oh, oh." A parishioner asked if this was correct and when the vicar affirmed that it was his questioner said he hadn't heard of it. Mr. Tompkins, the people's warden, then read a statement which laid down that the collections should be made known at the Vestry meeting. However in reply the vicar read a ruling that the 'Vestry have no right to inspect the churchwardens' books; they can only be seen on special occasions.' Another member said "The churchwardens can present a true statement of accounts; it is silly to talk as if the books were to be handed round." Shouts then came of "We have gained a point," to which Mr. Guest retorted "Yes, Bradwell is always right." "But you are not," shouted a previously quiet bespectacled little lady in black who, seated facing him, continued to be one of his most outspoken critics. Other members then stood up and with fists clenched the vicar replied in kind to their derisive shouts.

Next came a third 'scene' - involving kneeling mats in the church! The vicar urged that the church could have done without them for 12 months and quoted the example of a church in Moscow, where the congregation knelt on bare bricks. Then having been silenced by shouts of disapproval he informed the Vestry that he had never authorised the churchwarden to purchase any kneelers. However this brought gales of laughter when Mr. Tompkins corrected "You ordered them and went so far as to write out a cheque for them." There followed a further dispute as to whether the organ was the property of the parish and not the vicar. The Reverend said he wasn't prepared to say until he knew more facts about the instrument. More confrontations ensued, not least regarding the Catholic nature of the services. Then perhaps the most amusing episode arose when the Reverend moved a vote of thanks to the choirmaster and the choir for their services. This prompted Mr. Betts to move an amendment that the matter should not be passed a vote. They weren't carrying out the services of the parish church, to which the lady in black shouted "No, they are blacklegs." As for the vicar, in an incredulous sight he stood head pushed forward with hands thrust deep in his side pockets while jumping all around him members of the meeting hurled insults. Then when he claimed he could get 400 people to sign a favourable petition there came cries of "Rats," "Chuck him out," "You could not get one." At this he seized the yards of petition and flung it to the floor, where it rolled under the piano against the wall.

In the aftermath of this chaotic meeting came further disturbances, when for several days towards the end of April two 'energetic preachers' in pursuing the policy of their movement's founder, the late John Kensit, aggressively attacked those practices and ceremonies introduced by the vicar into his services. This culminated at the visit by the Bishop for a confirmation service at New Bradwell on Sunday, April 27th, when with regard to the parishioners' petition he held a meeting in a schoolroom afterwards. The service proved orderly but outside in the street a vociferous crowd of several hundreds had gathered to hear an address from the two antagonists, who greeted the arrival of the Bishop and the vicar with loud insults and hooting. For the meeting an excitable crowd of some 1,000 people packed the schoolroom, and initially the Bishop's address was listened to in silence. Then matters became increasingly heated following the attention drawn by Mr. Tompkins, a churchwarden, to the vicar's alleged 'Romish practices.' In vain the Bishop appealed for the gathering not to applaud the warden's remarks, of which some of his own were received with hooting. As the fervour increased the more vociferous members launched into cries of "Chuck the vicar out," "Duck him in the river," and "Why should we be saddled with a parson when we don't want him?" However at the latter the Bishop said that whilst they might not have everything they wanted they had got a good many things. Not that the crowd were pacified, with ripostes of "The vicar has all his own way," "He's one by himself,"

"Why should we have all he wants." Causing further uproar a man waving his arms wildly stood on a form and questioned had they not met to pass a vote of censure on the vicar? The Bishop replied that wasn't the reason and announced that due to the approach of evensong he would not be able to answer any further questions. He then suggested that the meeting should end in prayer but this was greeted with shouts of "Rubbish," "Rats," and "It's no use praying when you do everything to drive people from church, and when Mr. Guest tells us to go to hell."

Standing motionless the Bishop awaited an opportunity to close the gathering, but in the continuing mayhem a lady rushed to the front of the platform and in forcing home an argument whacked the vicar with her umbrella. Since there seemed no chance of restoring stability the Bishop and the vicar then made their way from the platform, with chaos still erupting all around them. Little had changed the next morning, for when the Bishop attended a Communion service he was booed as he walked back from the church to the vicarage.

Indeed it seemed that at Stantonbury controversy was to be the Reverend's destiny, manifest yet again in 1913, when it was stated one Tuesday evening in June at the monthly meeting of the New Bradwell School Managers that he had attempted to obtain the use of a room at the school. This had been previously let to Mr. Betts but in a letter it seemed the County Authority had agreed to the Reverend's request. This lead one member to strongly protest that the Reverend had gone over their heads, and it was subsequently moved that the managers should express 'regret' to the committee at Aylesbury.

Unfazed by all the recent events, in pursuing his aim to return to 'the old time form of worship' the Reverend organised a 'pageant' for the celebration of St. Peter's Day at St. Peter's Church on Sunday, June 29th. Informing of this, for several days posters worded in crayon had been nailed to the church notice board, and on the appointed date following a service in the church the procession marshalled outside St. James at 2.30pm, prior to setting off on this annual 'pilgrimage.' Holding the church crucifix aloft a choirman clad in a red and white surplice headed the procession, and carrying richly woven banners three similarly clad choirmen plus three others in purple and white gowns completed the party of singers. Others in the procession included a brass band, and dressed in white a small number of little girls carrying roses. Wearing a yellow cope and black biretta the vicar brought up the rear. Of no surprise there was little reverence from the large crowd which followed, although despite rumours to the contrary there were no attempts to interfere. On a little knoll to the left of St. Peter's church a temporary altar had been erected, with the vicar's reading desk and two rows of seats for the congregation arranged just below. In the churchyard flags waved in the breeze although before the end of the service someone had cut the string and the bunting fell to the ground. Smoking cigars some members of the congregation were overtly unsympathetic, whilst others kept their hats on and talked. The service was unelaborate and when about to start the Magnificat the vicar exhorted the choir to sing; "We don't want you here to be dummies." Then turning to a man on his right he reprimanded "Thank you sir, don't talk here."

During the singing of the Magnificat incense was used before the altar. Also throughout the chanting of the psalms and some of the prayers, and during his sermon the vicar said this service in the field was simple and in keeping with the Christianity of 'Merrie England.' Afterwards the band played musical selections and collections were taken for Northampton Hospital.

As respite from the eruptions of the previous year, a period of relative calm returned to Stantonbury when during the summer the Rev. Guest took three months' vacation. His place was taken by the Rev. C.L. Redfearn, a well known Army chaplain, who one Saturday entertained over 100 children of the Church Sunday School to tea. This was held at the vicarage, in the grounds of which sports were indulged during the afternoon and evening.

Then in 1915 matters returned to normal, when arriving with a bundle of papers and a book on Church law the Rev. Guest attended the Easter Vestry meeting. This by his alteration was held on Thursday, April 1st at 11.30am instead of 8pm on Wednesday night, and as per previous occasions he refused entry to non ratepayers. Towards enforcement he stood at the school doors and as the first to arrive five women parishioners were asked "Are you ratepayers?"

When one made an inaudible reply he said "Then out you go!" and despite being a ratepayer she left! The four others were likewise questioned and also departed! He next carried out his threat to exclude the representatives of the Press. Two were asked the same question and after some discussion were shown to the door, with the vicar remarking, "If you do not go quietly I shall have to use violence. I know what I am doing and I take full responsibility."

In the continuing tension he was met at the door with hostile comments from the men, whilst one old lady said "Come out, you coward, and let us come to the meeting. You ought to be ashamed of yourself turning women out. Conduct your business properly and you will be well treated. It is a shame to see a man in your position acting like an overgrown schoolboy." On saying she was a ratepayer she was duly admitted. Also three others but to ever increasing laughter for 5 minutes or so he stood at bay from a crowd of hooting and jeering women. Then appeared his nemesis from previous encounters, 'the little lady in black.' Affording him a mock curtsy she entered and took up a prominent position in the passage leading to the vestry, appropriately where the criticism raged the most. Then supported by a number of men from Wolverton Works, who had come "just to see that the Vicar did not have the Vestry all his own way," the people's warden, Mr. Tompkins, appeared and challenged the vicar's right to debar anyone from entering the room, not least the Press. In reply the Reverend said "I will have no one who is not a ratepayer in this meeting and if anyone who is not so entitled forces his way in I will close the Vestry." On the understanding that Mr. Tompkins would move a resolution for the Press to be admitted the reporters then withdrew from their position in the doorway. Next the Vicar entered the room and closing the door drew up his chair against it, also placing himself and a table as reinforcement to prevent any intrusion. Meanwhile the exiled women hammered unceasingly on the door panels with their fists.

As for the Press, after a while through a forced open window a reporter managed to gain a view of the extraordinary goings on within. The vicar was standing in the midst of a gesticulating crowd, and above the commotion could be heard such phrases as "I know what I am doing," and "I declare the meeting closed." Then came more jeering, and taking up his hat and books the Reverend walked to the door to be met by more verbal onslaughts. "You coward", shouted one man, to which the vicar replied "I am not a coward. I shall not come tonight because I have done the business that was to be done." "Well," said the man, "if you are not a coward will you kindly take your place at the vestry tonight?" The vicar replied "Man, you know I am not a coward. You can elect your own chairman." As for the woman in black, "If you are not a coward go and fight the Germans." On the way back to the vicarage the Reverend told his version of the happenings to a reporter, saying he'd nominated Henry James Elliott as his warden; "Mr. Tompkins had moved that the meeting should be adjourned until 8pm and I agreed, but I shall not be there." However this version was disputed by Mr. Tompkins, who said that from deeming it unacceptable to keep the parishioners out he immediately moved an adjournment of the meeting; "Twice I moved that adjournment, and after the third attempt the Vicar put it to the meeting. He then nominated his warden and signed the minutes of the last Vestry. Both of these acts we consider illegal, because the adjournment proposal had been adopted."

The previous year at the equally rowdy meeting the vicar had said he wouldn't allow the church accounts to be presented at the next vestry, ie the present one. But countering this Mr. Tompkins as the people's warden said 'he would see about that,' and as the only churchwarden to have officiated during the year he now called a special vestry meeting for Wednesday night. This was held at the usual hour but although he had the right to be chairman the vicar didn't attend. In replacement Mr. Tompkins was unanimously voted to the position and in an orderly meeting the accounts were duly presented, discussed and adopted. Regarding the reason for the meeting Mr. Tompkins reminded the members about the vicar's previous statement that no churchwardens accounts should be presented this year. Mr. Tompkins had told him that as long as he was the churchwarden they would be presented, and thus they had gathered today. He then referred to some of the church services affecting the church accounts, specifically the 11.15 service on Sunday mornings. On looking through previous balance sheets he'd found that before the services were introduced the accounts were in a much better state than now.

As for other matters he protested against the attempt to produce a new Prayer Book, saying the teaching would be false and corrupt and if it was introduced the nation's accepted religion might become a thing of the past. In fact parents who sent their children to the Sunday School should attend one of these services, to witness what their children were being taught. As for the offertories he stated that the total taken during the financial year was £44 12s 2d. Of this £23 6s 10d had gone to 'Special Purposes,' and thereby they had to manage the church upkeep on £21 5s 4d. The balance sheet was then read and adopted, but in a footnote Mr. Tompkins marked the small amount contributed for church expenses. Partly this was due to the large number of parishioners who had deserted the church from the nature of many of the services. However another reason was the vicar's apparent motive to devote a large proportion of the offertories to 'Special Purposes,' with the intent to seemingly place the church wardens in difficulties.

Not that the Rev. Guest had any intent of obscuring his religious beliefs, for at the beginning of the week he issued the local residents with two documents. In one was stated; "Oh, for the day when English people, forsaking the German Protestantism of Martin Luther, which in the 17th century came, fought, and conquered over the true Catholic faith in England (the literature of that time swarms with un-English German names), will renounce Luther as they renounce the Kaiser today, and go to Mass, having been shriven in penance and absolution by their own lawful English clergy."

Thus hostilities continued to rage between the vicar and his ever dwindling flock, to even include Alderman Wylie, who had been a devoted church attendee for some 50 years. Yet with the ongoing world war there was now a much wider conflict, at the outbreak of which the Rev. Guest had volunteered to be a chaplain in the Royal Navy. However if he did the Ecclesiastical Commissioners said his living would be forfeit, and he thereby remained in Stantonbury to become the local representative of the Inns of Court Officers OTC.

Away from the domestic and wider hostilities, with the arrangements made by the vicar and the Sunday School teachers on the afternoon of Saturday, June 26th 1915 over 200 children enjoyed a tea at the vicarage, in the grounds of which attractions were provided to include swings, roundabouts, sports and games. Then doubtless to the relief of all the Reverend spent two months' holiday at Eastbourne, where every morning at his annual visits he would take a dip from the pier head and indulge in fancy diving. A regular spectacle watched with great interest by the early morning promenanders! As for the supposed benefits, the Reverend held that "Our school curriculum is all wrong. The attention given to the three R's and interior school work generally is all very well, but it does not help to overcome the Germans. Boys ought to be taught to drill at school as a preliminary to spending a couple of months in barracks or camp in the year, and they would learn the whole secret which open air life and exercise have to give. A man who develops his muscles makes the best citizen in every respect."

Apart from his swimming at Eastbourne in other athletics he ran Mr. J. Charnwood, a local cricketer, around the pavilion! Meanwhile at Stantonbury his duties were being undertaken by the Rev. Humphrey Vaughan Hughes.

However this harmony proved but temporary for in September at Newport Pagnell Petty Sessions the Reverend Guest was fined £3, or a month in prison, for having smacked a 14 year old girl, Gladys Scott, of 45, Bridge Street, on the eleventh of the month. Regarding the case in a crowded court it was stated that about 7.15pm she had been standing against her house with several friends. The Reverend came up to her and asked why she didn't come to church. He wanted her to attend a service that evening but she told him she attended the Primitive Methodist Sunday School. He said "Never mind that, you must come to church." However she said she wouldn't leave it, and following further words her mother came out. The Reverend asked "Why don't you let your daughter come to church" but she made no reply. He then repeated the question but the girl said forcefully "I shall not come to church." At this the Reverend retorted "don't begin arguing" and striking her on the cheek knocked her onto the path. In utter disbelief the mother questioned "What did you hit my daughter for?" to which he replied "Yes, and I will hit you too." "You come and do it then," she said, but saying "Yes, I will," the vicar walked away. The mark on the girl's cheek was still visible the next day, and when he returned to the house to express regret the door was slammed in his face.

Then in March the following year came another court appearance, when at the Petty Sessions he was fined 20s for having repeatedly said "You are a d***** slacker" to a married man with two children. This despite the man having attested for military service and wearing the armlet.

And so, dear readers, the Reverend continued his confrontational ways. Yet sometimes in a more sporting fashion, as per a letter read at the meeting of the parish council on Tuesday, July 4th 1916. Therein he wrote; "I have pleasure in subscribing one guinea towards the expenses of the bathing place at Stantonbury. The site chosen is alright. I hope when I return from vacation you will get the committee to arrange for a swimming competition, in which I shall enter on level terms for 100 yards against all comers ten years junior to myself." "The Parish Council must not be greedy" he said, "and if - say half - the charge of admission per head were given to Lady Pearson for the fund for keeping our soldiers blinded in the war, a very large sum could be despatched to headquarters. Besides, very little expense has been incurred in making the bathing place. The LNWR gave all the plant gratis, the site has been a gift by the Radcliffe Trustees, and the men did the work free - more power to 'em. The entire district, if not exactly flowing with milk and honey, is decidedly well off by reason of war work in the factories. Let us send a bumper cheque, and I will run a 100 yards soon after the swim with anyone ten years junior to your humble."

In consequence the council would receive a letter from Mr. O.H. Bull JP, of Newport Pagnell, stating that he would take up the challenge and bring a Newportonian to swim 100 yards at the opening of the baths. Further he would pay £1 to the funds of the bathing place if the Rev. Guest beat the contestant, and vice versa. Thus on Saturday, August 26th 1916 the Reverend arrived at the contest wearing a white felt hat with a coloured band, a rough tweed jacket, white trousers, and brown shoes, and his appearance was further enhanced by his physical fitness. A county councillor formally opened the bathing place (on the River Ouse at Stantonbury) and afterwards the vicar and his opponent, Sidney Cooke of Newport

Rev. Guest with his son Alan.

Pagnell, who had captained Newport Pagnell Swimming Club for several seasons, appeared and received a hearty reception from the large crowd of onlookers. Keeping well ahead from the start, to the cheers of the crowd Cooke proved the victor of the contest, by which about £450 was made. The Reverend had been training at Eastbourne, where whilst on vacation in August he wrote "I am prepared to accept the challenge of Private W.T. Evans (20736, 1st K.S.O.B., D19 Hut, E Division, Summerdown Camp) to swim 100 yards in the Devonshire Baths or elsewhere, my sole proviso being that the gate money must be given to the Lord Kitchener Memorial Fund." Thus on Wednesday, August 30th 1916 with the 6d admission fees for the Kitchener Memorial Fund this additional watery contest took place at 6.30pm over 100 yards at Park Baths, Eastbourne. However before completing half of the return the Reverend gave up and emerging from the water congratulated his opponent.

Perhaps he was conserving his energy, for on October 23rd at St. Saviour's Church, Eastbourne, by special license he married 25 year old Dorothy ('Dolly') Muriel Stella Cooke, "a smart well spoken women, quite a lady." A spinster of 91, South Street, Eastbourne, she was the daughter of George Cooke, of independent means, and in 1917 on September 10th a son, Castelfranc, was born.[18]

Yet it seems that neither marriage nor family had greatly mellowed the Reverend, for he remained absent from the Easter Vestry - that he had summoned - in 1917 and 1918. Possibly also in 1919, when on March 20th a daughter, Betty Guest, was born.[19]

In 1920 the vicar was again absent at the vestry meeting in April on Wednesday 14th. Mr. Styles presided and no names were forwarded for election either as churchwarden or sidesmen. Then the following day a meeting was held to elect a Parochial Council.

This time the vicar was present along with his wife, who when feelings began to run high restrained him from saying too much by chiding "Now, Vicar, be careful." Firstly he explained the working of the 'Enabling Act,' and consequent to asking for a secretary to the Council the appointment was made of Mr. Betts, with Mr. Tompkins as vice chairman. However on the grounds that he never went to church Mrs. Guest objected to the nomination of Mr. P. Styles as a member of the Council. According to the vicar his children attended the Baptist Chapel but Mr. Styles said that didn't account for his own action. In fact they had ceased attending some three years ago.

As for Mrs. Guest she was elected a member by common consent. Being inevitably lively at times, during the two hour meeting several references were made in the latter part to the use of vestments and the wearing of a biretta by the vicar. However later that month he had to suspend his duties through illness, with the preaching undertaken at St. James' by Canon Harnett. Yet not for long, for the Reverend was soon back to his usual self - not least when presiding at the Easter Vestry in 1921. The venue was the Girls' School and true to expectations the meeting again proved 'lively' with no business undertaken due to the several heated arguments. In opening the proceedings the vicar explained that its reason was to elect the churchwardens and sidesmen. However from the outset he was asked if he had any minutes of the previous meetings, and when he replied that he hadn't he refused to answer why. Then later he said that if there were any minutes he wouldn't sign them, so it would be pointless to produce them! Several times he asked for nominations for the office of churchwarden, and after several minutes of silence said if none were forthcoming he would leave. Mrs. Guest then rose to speak but he ruled her out of order from not being a ratepayer!

Also on the subject of controlling behaviour, for allowing a dog to run loose he was fined 10s in January 1922. The offence had occurred on December 17th and on the collar the name Guest had only been scratched on with a nail. In his defence the Reverend said the dog was needed to protect his property, as his fruit had been stolen.

As for a two legged addition to the family, that month on January 18th a son, Allan Newman Guest, was born.[20]

Despite the religious antagonisms, in 1923 on Saturday, June 16th members of St. James' Church Girls Club met in the presence of the churchwardens to present the vicar with a new processional Crucifix. Fashioned full length in brass this bore across the socket the inscription, 'Presented to Rev. A. Newman Guest, M.A., by members of S. James' Church, Stantonbury, Girls' Club.' and expressing pleasant surprise the Reverend said the first use was proposed to be on July 29th, when the Bishop came to dedicate the war memorial.

Also of surprise, in 1923 on Thursday, June 28th the vicar received a visit from the present head of the Elkins family at Yelvertoft. Some 300 years ago the family had farmed land at Stantonbury and their tombs were said to be the oldest in the churchyard. The visitor said his uncle had shown him an oil painting in which an Elkins figured who had lived in the shepherd's house close to St. Peter's Church. The visitor further told a rather fanciful story from the reign of King James, when a family member was allegedly apprehended in Stantonbury from implication in the Rye House Plot. Supposedly he concealed himself in the old wide chimney but was discovered, taken to London and beheaded. Interesting, but perhaps implausible?

More certain were the predictable antics in April 1923 at the evening meeting of the Easter Vestry and Parochial Church. After an orderly start matters again became 'lively' when a report on the work of the Parochial Church Council for the past year was requested. This sparked a heated exchange between the vicar and the parishioners and even between several of the parishioners themselves. However calm eventually prevailed and in the quieter parts of the meeting the vicar 'was most amusing with his witty remarks,' which created much good humour.

Also in 1923, on the afternoon of Sunday, July 29th there was a large congregation at St. James' for the Bishop of Buckingham's dedication of a handsome marble war memorial. This, affixed to a pillar of the north aisle, had been made possible by the efforts of a band of church workers led by the vicar and his wife, and bore the inscribed names of the 86 parishioners who had fallen.

Perhaps disappointingly in 1924 the vestry meeting proved orderly, and that year during the spring and summer a local newspaper published a series of historical articles on Stantonbury written by the vicar. Available at 1s a copy these he had printed in pamphlet form, with a review appearing in the Times Literary Supplement in October. Then in June 1925 he received a message from Lord Stamfordham stating that the King wished a copy! In regal compliance this was duly sent to him at Windsor Castle. Also the vicar had received a letter from Sir O. Stoll, to the effect that he had put the booklet aside with a view to it becoming the basis of an historical film. Also worthy of filming, in 1926 on Saturday, September 18th a children's pageant, 'Cries o' London', in which 60 children took part, was held in the vicarage gardens, with the proceeds for the restoration fund of St. James'. Then later that year the vicar would be absent from the church, having been confined to his room in November through an illness of such concern that prayers were offered in church.

However the following year after many years absence he attended a Ruri Decanal Conference at Wolverton, but in May was again ordered to rest on medical advice. This was intended for a month but he still remained indisposed in October and was stricken with pernicious anaemia from 1928 to 1930. Nevertheless attracting an appreciative congregation in the second of a series of recitals at St. James' on the afternoon of Sunday, February 9th he was the solo pianist, having engaged a removal firm to transport his prestigious Spencer grand piano to the church from the vicarage.

Also in 1930 on Sunday, August 10th at St. James' he performed the opening recital on the new two manual electrically blown organ, built and installed by Messrs. England and Roberts of Harlestone and Ringstead, Northants. Having been on holiday he had travelled especially from Bournemouth, although on the family's frequent trips there his musical talents proved of less appeal to his disgruntled mother in law. Not least from reputedly making a nuisance of himself by playing the piano into the early hours of the morning. The police were equally unimpressed, from having to be called out to stop him.

Indeed it seems the Reverend's wife had also had enough, for she now left him and took the eldest son, Castelfranc, to live with her at Bournemouth. In consequence in 1932 on Wednesday, January 6th at Newport Pagnell Police Court the Rev. Guest was ordered to pay his wife £11 18s. Applying for custody of the three children he had issued a summons but failed to appear at court. Mrs. Guest, now of 16, Waltham Road, Pokesdown, Bournemouth, sat at the back of the court with her brother in law and a maid, and when the case was called Mr. T. Faulkner Gammage, of Messrs. Groves and Gammage, of Northampton, said the reason that she and her witnesses had travelled from Bournemouth was from her anxiety to clarify her position. Since matters had become so difficult she was seeking a court directive as to the custody of the children, but having no notification from Mr. Guest that he wished to withdraw the summons Mr. Gammage said that under the circumstances it was impossible to go on with the case. If the magistrates consented to the summons being withdrawn it should be on the grounds that the costs for Mrs. Guest were paid.

This was not the first time it had happened, for Mr. Guest had taken out a summons in September last year and then casually withdrew it via a phone call to the magistrates' clerk. Fortunately on that occasion Mrs. Guest had received notice just before leaving Bournemouth. The chairman said "I don't think we can grant any costs of this kind unless the case is heard" and thus as far as the Bench was concerned the case was not withdrawn. Then after further consultation the Bench decided to refuse the application and when the chairman asked for the amount for the costs Mr. Gammage stated the train fares of Mrs. Guest and her brother in law and her maid. Also the expense of Mrs. Guest having to spend two nights in a hotel. The clerk asked for the total to which Mr. Gammage stated £9 16s plus the advocate's fee, making £11 18s. The chairman said the costs would be granted adding that it was very unfortunate that the application should be made at all. A great many people had gone to a good deal of unnecessary trouble and expense - "I hope it will not occur again."

Then in 1932 at Newport Pagnell Petty Sessions on Wednesday, January 20th the Rev. Guest stepped into the witness box and informed the chairman, Sir Walter Carlile, that he objected to some of the observations made at the last court (ie on January 6th.) Also the way in which his case had been dealt with, intimating that he was applying to the Home Secretary to revise the question of costs. The chairman said the time allowed for an appeal against decisions of the court was 7 days from the sitting, when an appeal could have been made to the Quarter Sessions. No appeal could be made to the Home Secretary but there was nothing to say that he couldn't write to him. After exchanging words with the chairman, to include "I refuse to stand down and if anyone touches me I shall summons them for assault", the Reverend asked whether he could appeal for damages against his wife - who he said had an income of £2,000pa as a furrier - for desertion and for her treatment against his children.

However the Bench considered the matter closed, to which on leaving the court the Reverend shouted "Good morning, sir, you will hear more about this." As for the mention of Dorothy being a furrier, in 1932 on March 23rd notice was posted that all persons having claims against the estate of Robert Turnbull, of 'Glengarth,' Waltham Road, Boscombe, Bournemouth, formerly of 461, Christchurch Road, Boscombe, Bournemouth, and 90, Old Christchurch Road, Bournemouth, furrier, who died on October 6th 1931, and whose will was proved on March 19th 1932 by Eva May Smith, Janet Luker, and Dorothy Muriel Stella Guest, were to contact the solicitors. As the outcome of the marital saga Castelfranc would stay with Dorothy.[21] Allan and Betty would remain at Stantonbury with the Reverend, who employed a housekeeper for their upbringing.

Being a well known sight in the locality the Reverend rode a bicycle distinctive from having a motorcycle saddle and wide handlebars. However one day in April 1932 when cycling down Old Bradwell canal bridge hill the front fork collapsed and he was thrown heavily onto his head. Dr. Harvey of Wolverton administered initial treatment and then conveyed him home in his car. Then one Monday evening in July the Reverend suffered another accident when cycling near Loughton. On this occasion he sustained an injury to his leg that entailed nine stitches and a period of two weeks rest.

On the morning of Sunday, October 16th 1932 Betty Guest was one of the candidates at a Confirmation service at St. James'. This was conducted by the Bishop of Buckingham, whose staff was carried by her brother, Allan. In their domestic routine both children had to have a music lesson every day. This was at 4.30pm and in evidence of their progress in 1934 on the afternoon of Sunday, February 11th they contributed to a programme of classical music at St. James.'

With a collection to be taken for Northampton Hospital this was performed by members of the church and congregation, with the Reverend Guest playing solo piano. Violin solos were performed by Betty and her brother Allan, who that year on the morning of June 17th was amongst those to be confirmed in a ceremony at St. James' church.

In June 1935 at a ruri decanal conference for the Wolverton Deanery, held at Stony Stratford, in the following discussion on Parochial Church Councils and Christian Witness the Rev. Guest said "To my mind Church Councils today have become a clique. They are officered chiefly by women. Men are conspicuous by their absence. I am of opinion that Parochial Church Councils are a ghastly failure and want abolishing in our parishes." However the Rev. Crosby of Loughton said there were undoubtedly times when a Church Council might be a source of irritation to the incumbent. Then on the other hand there were incumbents who were a source of irritation to Church Councils!

When bathing in the river, in 1936 on the evening of Tuesday, June 23rd 16 year old Max Nursaw was seized with cramp. Fortunately his plight was witnessed by Betty Guest who immediately dived in and brought him to the bank. Despite having gone under three times he was revived by artificial respiration. It seems Betty possessed the swimming prowess of her father, who in other talents had composed in five verses the words and music of 'Ode to Childhood,' a new carol sung for the first time in December 1936 at St. James' evensong.

Another cause for celebration came early the following year with the impending coronation of George VI. As with numerous communities, in preparation New Bradwell held a Coronation meeting - from which the Reverend Guest walked out! Mr. A. Brown JP had been suggesting the appointment of a chairman when the

Rev. Guest asked if the proceedings had anything to do with religion. Mr. Brown explained this was a residents' meeting to consider the Coronation Day programme, and when the vicar attempted to address the gathering Dr. P. Atkinson, an Urban Councillor, said Mr. Brown had successfully chaired the Jubilee celebrations. Indeed he had spoken about this to Mr. Guest, saying it would be beneficial for a councillor to be chairman on the grounds that a certain amount of money would be spent from the rates. Thereby the Council could monitor the expenditure. He therefore proposed the appointment of Mr. Brown and this was duly seconded. The vicar then said he had an amendment, and proceeded to ask if this was a definite Coronation meeting, or to ask for some co-operation in connection with the religious part - "If it has nothing to do with that I am an outsider at this meeting and shall thank you and retire." He said he required information and in the absence of such would call his own parishioners together on Wednesday evening next. Then repeating that the church would have its own meeting he said "Goodnight" and left the room!

In 1937 in the children's service at St. James' on the afternoon of Sunday, June 13th Master Allan Newman Guest took the part of a Bishop. Robed in red and yellow vestments with a red mitre (at the back of which was a Latin Cross) he conducted the service throughout, while his father sat in a pew behind the congregation. Yet Allan would soon leave New Bradwell for employment at Bedford with Barclays Bank in St. John's Street. Betty became a nurse at Bedford Hospital and thus at the outbreak of WW2 only the Rev. Guest remained at the Vicarage. That is until the arrival of some evacuees, who would soon find that their new accommodation was almost as hazardous as the dangerous zone from which they had fled!

This was all courtesy of the Rev. Guest, who in October 1942 was fined £2 at Stony Stratford Police Court for alleged assaults on evacuees at his home. Regarding the claimed inflictions on Israel Bloom, an elderly tailor, on September 25th, and Bloom's wife, Sarah, on September 24th, he pleaded not guilty. In court Israel Bloom of 156, Millfield Road, Acton, said that at the time of the alleged assault he and his wife were billeted at the vicarage. He was sitting having his tea when he heard some "messing about" with a padlock and found the vicar trying to lock them in. Israel tried to pull the door open but the vicar kicked him between the legs. Being elderly and a cripple he shouted for help and for the police, and then went "absolutely unconscious." He claimed the vicar would barricade the doors and said such actions were "paralysing my wife and terrorising her life away." In fact he had now moved out from the vicarage, too afraid to stay there any more. As for the vicar's version; "I asked you to close the door of your room because there was a brilliant light, and not for the first time." Bloom replied "You said if you won't close the door I will cut your throat." By the vicar; "I asked you to get out, as I am not going to get into trouble over the blazing light." Mrs. Bloom and a granddaughter said they saw Mr. Bloom being kicked, and when the vicar asked if they were committing perjury she said "No, I am telling the truth." The vicar said "The Germans have been over my house and wardens have been round my house complaining of light. I told him to keep his door closed. I told him it must stop. I suppose his leg must have been caught in the door." Mrs. Violet Grew of 12, East View, New Bradwell, and Mrs. Jane Faulkner, housekeeper at the vicarage, were then called for the defence. However they were unable to provide evidence of the assault, with the vicar saying they didn't know anything because there was no assault. Nevertheless with regard to this case the Bench decided to convict. Then when asked if he pleaded guilty to the second summons the Reverend retorted "Good gracious, no." In this incident Mrs. Bloom said the vicar was trying to lock her in, and when she tried to prevent it he hit her with his fist on the shoulder. She could still feel the pain. He then told her to clear out of the room, to which she said "That's nice for a Vicar." The granddaughter, Betty Sachs, said she was making tea when the vicar struck her grandmother. The vicar said he was about to have a bath and could not have her prowling about. On being sworn he said the old lady nearly always had the door open and he couldn't go upstairs to have his ablutions. He asked if a dossier of the case could be prepared for the Home Office. The chairman, Mr. S.F. Jones, advised him to consult his solicitor but the Reverend said "I don't want to pay unless I am forced to." He was then told by the magistrates' clerk that he would be forced to, at which he said "I tell you this case is only the beginning." However he paid the fines.

There were more altercations in 1944, when on Thursday, April 20th the Easter Vestry and Parochial meeting of St. James' was held. Only 16 people attended and with no propositions from the parishioners the vicar declared the former members duly elected to the Parochial Church Council and the Ruri- Decanal Conference. He then proposed to appoint a lady as his Warden but was informed that she was not on the electoral roll. Mr. Tapp declined re-appointment as People's Warden, a position that he'd held for 20 years, and when Mrs. Welch, the Superintendent of the Sunday School, reminded the vicar that he could not elect the People's Warden himself he retorted "Will you stop talking: when I want you to talk I will ask you." As for the matter of electing the Vicar's Warden he turned to Mr. May and alleged "You are only a mock churchwarden, as you have no status." "I appoint Mrs. Capel as my Churchwarden for the next twelve months." Mrs. Welch said she wasn't on the electoral roll but the vicar said she was; "If not, my son is, and I appoint him." (His son was serving in the Navy!) Then turning to Mr. May he said "You hand over those keys as soon as possible!" At this Mr. May and Mrs. Welch began to speak but the vicar interrupted with "Don't bawl," to which Mr. May replied likewise. Mrs. Welch gave the electoral roll as 98, and was in the course of saying it had been brought up to date when the vicar curtly interjected "Don't talk until I ask you." Additionally during the meeting there came a sharp exchange between the vicar and Mr. May, with the vicar saying "I will finish with you soon." "I have been trying to get the keys of my own Church for the past twelve months, and he (Mr. May) won't let me have them." "You give me my keys. You are no longer my warden. Give me my keys, do you hear?"

He then asked Mr. May for 14s 8d, as the sum he had paid to the Electric Light Company on behalf of the Church, and when Mr. May began talking he said "Stand up. If you brawl I will put you outside." Mr. May said he wasn't brawling but the vicar said "In a minute I will put you outside. The Home Guard has not done you much good." Voices - that's a threat, that's an insult. The vicar - "Get on with it." By Mr. May, "Not until you withdraw that." Nevertheless the meeting continued and Mr. May read the financial statement which by a letter from the auditors was certified correct.

Not surprisingly from thereon relations became ever more tense. Mrs. Welch left the church and 210 of the Sunday School children followed. The organist left. Then the choir of 3 men and 12 boys, and finally the congregation of 30 dwindled to 6 - the vestry councillors. Yet with complete disregard the vicar continued to ring the bell for services, play the organ, and read the prayers to empty pews! Then locking up the church he would return to the vicarage. No Easter Vestry was held in 1945 and in March 1946 following a visit by the Bishop there were rumours that the Rev. Guest might be leaving the parish in the near future. When asked if he was going to live at Eastbourne he said wouldn't say yes but he wouldn't say no.

Then a notice posted on the door of St. James' on Sunday, October 6th 1946 informed that he had resigned. With effect from October 3rd 1946 it was signed by E.A. Bacon, acting registrar to the Diocese of Oxford, and it was further stated that with William Thomas May and Thomas Robert Tapp as churchwardens the living had now been entrusted to the Reverend E.A. Steer, vicar of Stony Stratford and Rural Dean. During the following days a band of willing ladies cleaned the interior of the church, washed and polished the pews, and scrubbed the floors but until the appointment of a replacement vicar no Sunday services could be held.

Then on Sunday, November 3rd 1946 the services re-commenced,

Rev. Thomas Robert Trapp

conducted by Canon F.T. Howard. He was a former vicar of Aylesbury and having recently retired from the active ministry was presently resident at Wavendon. The church choir was now being reformed with quite a number of boys being trained by Mr. C.H. Scott, who had temporarily accepted the position of choirmaster and organist. A number of men had also volunteered their services. In 1946 the Rev. Guest died at a Bedford Nursing Home on Saturday, December 7th. He was 79.

Then in January 1947 it was

announced that the Rev. H. Thornton Trapp, whose cousin was the Bishop designate of Zululand, was to be the new vicar. Presently he was priest in charge of Clewer St. Agnes, Berks., but a notice in the porch of St. James' informed that the Bishop of Oxford proposed to collate him to the benefice. After training at Kilham Theological College he had been ordained at Canterbury in 1934 to a title at Whitstable. Later he served in West Ham and Clewer St. Agnes, before joining the RAF, in which he served for 4½ years in England, North Africa, Italy and Sicily. Following repairs to the vicarage he took up residence in March 1947 with the institution taking place on Saturday, March 22nd by the Bishop of Oxford. After the service Canon Howard, who had served interim, was presented with an illuminated shaving mirror and a cheque by Mrs. B. Welch, secretary of the PCC, on behalf of the parishioners. Additionally on behalf of the choir members he was presented by Mr. C.H. Scott, the organist and choirmaster, with a fountain pen and propelling pencil.

SALVATION ARMY

The Salvation Army in New Bradwell began in 1893 on December 7th, with a visiting band travelling from Olney to provide the musical accompaniment for the hymn singing and celebrations. Within the area of Thompson Street the accommodation was in the top floor of a building known as the Old Mill, the ground floor being in use as a bake house and a flour mill. Due to building operations the Corps had to move a number of times including to Wolverton and the temporary shelter of a loft in a shed.

However they soon became established and in 1899 on Saturday, July 22nd the 'junior soldiers' from the Stantonbury Salvation Army Sunday School held their annual treat at Leighton Buzzard. A tea was served in the barracks in Lake Street with games and amusements indulged in a meadow.

In February 1904 the resident officer was Captain Howes at 13, Glyn Street, who would be glad to receive donations for the Salvation Army Week of Self Denial, commencing that year on Saturday, February 27th. By 1910 with some 20 members a band had been formed, primarily to support the Sunday services by providing musical accompaniment for congregational singing.

Then in 1912 the Salvation Army moved to the 'Assembly Hall' in Newport Road, which nowadays accommodates the DIY store of Sid Telfers. Here Sunday services were held regularly and as the membership increased so came the need for a purpose built centre. With plans undertaken the cost would be £708, of which the local corps had been asked to raise £412. This they accomplished, and in a central position on the Newport Road the stone laying of the building took place on Saturday, June 19th, 1915 attended by a large company of local Salvationists and friends. Either side of the entrance two stones, fashioned by Messrs. Gurney Brothers, Stonemasons, Wolverton and Stantonbury, were laid by Mrs. Littleboy and Miss A.M. Coales. Both were residents of Newport Pagnell and the inscriptions read "Laid by Mrs. Littleboy, "I am come that they might have life," June 19th 1915." "Laid by Miss A.M. Coales, "Looking unto Jesus," June 19th, 1915." Brigadier Pointer presided at the ceremony with Northampton Number 1 Band providing accompaniments to the hymn singing. The proceedings closed with a hymn and the Benediction and in the evening in Church Street, Wolverton, the band played for a well attended open air meeting.

Afterwards they performed at a musical evening in the Assembly

Stone laying ceremony for the Salvation Army Hall in 1915.

The Salvation Army life saving guards, New Bradwell

Hall and also the following day, when for the special services they paraded around the town and, attracting a large gathering, gave an open air concert in Wolverton Park.

Then in 1915 on Saturday, August 28th the opening ceremony of the new centre was held. Salvationists from surrounding communities attended and also the band of the Buckingham corps, which had especially cycled to New Bradwell. On behalf of Central HQ, after a hymn and prayer Brigadier Pointer presented the key of the building to Mrs. J.M. Knapp of Little Linford, who, in the presence of a large assembly, unlocked the building saying "I declare the building open to the glory of God and for the salvation of the people." The large gathering then entered and a service of praise and thanksgiving was held. In conducting the service the Brigadier Pointer thanked all friends who had given assistance to the local corps, and Staff Captain Turner gave details of the financial costs. Addresses were given by Mr. and Mrs. Knapp and afterwards a tea was served in the Baptist Church schoolroom. During the weekend many well attended services were conducted by Adjutant Merrick of Northampton and Captain Watmore of Bradwell, and those attending were no doubt impressed by the rising platform at one end of the Hall, and the seating, the forms of which had been made by the Salvation Army Social Institution. As for heating this was by means of a slow combustion stove.

At this period with Len Healey as bandmaster (later the bandmaster at Bletchley) there were 12 members in the band which once a month visited Wolverton to conduct an open air service. After a stay at New Bradwell of about a year, in the first weekend of May 1920 the farewell services took place of Captain and Mrs. Lamplough. They were now going to take charge of the Banbury Corps, and special services were held in the Hall on Sunday and Monday.

In May 1921 Ensign Berry, late of West Green, London, became the new officer of the Corps but the following year he and his wife left on Thursday, May 26th for Potton. They would be succeeded by Capt. Vincent and Lt. Peake of Coventry III Corps.

Then in 1924 Ensign and Mrs. Groom took command. They left in 1926 on Thursday, May 27th for Rushden, to be succeeded by Capt. and Mrs. Feltwell of Abingdon.

Following their appointment to Belfast, in 1927 on Sunday, May 15th welcome meetings at the Hall were held for the two new officers, both ladies, Capt. Thurman and Lt. Pearce of Bradwell. Their duties had begun the previous Thursday, and on the Monday evening the newly formed Life Saving Guards made their first public appearance, comprised of a troop of 18 girls in two patrols and two leaders.

In 1928 on Saturday and Sunday, May 12th and 13th welcome meetings were held for the new officers Ensign Mayes and Lt. Johnson. They were late of Waterbeach and perhaps had extra duties when in 1929 on April 16th the Hall was registered for the solemnisation of marriages.

In May 1933 Capt. H. Mitson and Lt. L. Adams completed 12 months as officers in charge of the Corps. However owing to a period of illness Capt. Mitson would remain with the Corps for a further year to be joined by Lt. A. Booth, with this his first appointment after leaving the Salvation Army Training College at London. As for other moves, having been promoted to Capt., that month Lt. Adams left New Bradwell for an appointment at Dunvant, Swansea.

In 1933 on the evening of Friday, May 26th the Hall was crowded for a visit by the 'Musical Miriams.' These Army 'lassies' were making

Charles Daniels (left) selling the 'War Cry' for the Salvation Army.

a 1,000 mile tour of Britain, and being a speaking, praying and singing brigade of 25 lady officers of the Salvation Army performed an interesting programme, to include a visit to a Wolverton resident who was ill.

In 1934 on Saturday and Sunday, May 12th and 18th welcome meetings were held in the Hall for the new officer, Capt. Hutchinson, and it seems that the following month a wooden hall, built at a cost of £120 on brick piers between the Hall and the Ouse, for the use of the Sunday School, was opened. (There was also an old railway carriage which housed the infants' Sunday School.)

In 1936 on Saturday and Sunday, May 16th and 17th welcome meetings were held for the new officers Adjutant and Mrs. Bloom from St. Neots. They had taken up duty at New Bradwell on the Thursday following the transfer of Capt. Godwin to Kent and her Lt. to Sawston.

In continuing transfers in 1937 on Tuesday, June 1st farewell meetings were held for Adjutant and Mrs. E.A. Bloom. Indeed there would now be new accommodation for officers, for in January 1938 having occupied 13, Glyn Street, New Bradwell, for over 30 years the New Bradwell Salvation Army moved its officers' quarters to 62, Stanton Avenue, New Bradwell. However this only proved a short residence for Captain and Mrs. Fenwick for that year their farewell meetings were held on Sunday, March 27th and Wednesday, March 30th.

As a stalwart of the Corps, in 1938 on November 7th Sergeant Major Charles Daniels of 7, Harwood Street, New Bradwell, retired after 47 years of railway employment, all but two at Wolverton Works. On Tuesday, November 8th Adjutant and Mrs. George Jeffrey, the New Bradwell Salvation Officers, organised a supper to celebrate his birthday and to recognise his 40 years as a Salvationist, 30 of which had been as a local officer in the district. Three of his brothers and two of his sisters were among the 92 persons at the Hall, where many appreciative addresses were given. Formerly Adjutant but now Major (later Brigadier) and Mrs. Groom were presently in charge of the Men's Social Work in Belfast but at one time they had been stationed at New Bradwell. There a son was born and now at the age of 13 he proved a cause celebre at the large music festival of the Salvation Army held at the Albert Hall in December 1938. Over 10,000 people had gathered to listen to the Army's best talent in Bands, Songster Brigades, and other musical sections, and as was written in the War Cry, "One of the happiest sights was the schoolboy knees of thirteen year old soloist Young People's Band member Albert Groom, of Belfast, who tripped up and down the black notes on his copy with a skill and assurance which nine tenths of the Bandsmen present would have given much to acquire. Amid a furore of applause Bandmaster Twitchin, who wrote the solo, shook hands with the boy and the Chief brought the father, Major Groom (of the Men's Social Work), and son into the spotlight, where the General kissed the soloist!"

In 1941 having been in charge for the past 19 months Capt. Joyce Smith moved to Corby on May 22nd. Farewell services had been held the previous Sunday and she was succeeded by Capt. and Mrs. Emerson, who took up duty on Thursday, May 22nd.

In April 1942 the New Bradwell Corps achieved its highest target in its self denial effort, raising £148 1s 0d. Much of the credit was due to Sgt. Major Charles Daniels who for the 12th time gained the silver bar awarded to the highest collector in the Northants. Division. In 1942 on Sunday, June 7th welcome services were held for the new officers of the Corps, Capt. and Mrs. L.G. James, who had arrived from Chipping Norton. Then after 12 months in 1943 on Thursday, June 3rd they would leave for Wollaston, to be succeeded by Capt. and Mrs. Arthur Holliday from Bognor Regis.

In 1944 having been without officers for a few weeks on Thursday, June 22nd the Corps welcomed two lady officers - Adjutant E. Stephens and Capt. N. Sizeland. However there was a sad farewell when William Lindon, well known as a player of cymbals in the now defunct Corps band, died at Renny Lodge on Friday, December 22nd.

In 1948 on Sunday, May 9th farewell meetings took place at the Hall for Capt. E.W. Sutton, who after 12 months at New Bradwell would leave on the Thursday from having been appointed to the International Training College at London. He would be succeeded by Capt. and Mrs. Frank White from Stonesfield, near Banbury, who were welcomed on Saturday and Sunday, May 15th and 16th. At the anniversary services at the Hall in August 1948 a feature was the singing of the Songsters, a newly formed band of youngsters who were now making good progress.

On Thursday, December 1st 1949 a welcome was extended to Lt. Diana Woodward on behalf of the Corps by Mrs. Roberts, the Home League secretary.[22] She had transferred from Foleshill, Coventry, following the departure from New Bradwell of Lt. and Mrs. John Thornhill, who left for Irthlingborough. At a time when Mr. Cox was the newly appointed Sergeant Major of the Corps, in 1951 on Saturday, September 1st Mrs. Bottle of Sittingbourne, an ardent worker amongst young people in her home area, and mother of Lt. Bottle, CO of the New Bradwell Corps, re-opened the Young People's Hall at a ceremony held on the steps. After a short meeting inside she was presented with a bouquet by a primary member of the Sunday School, Stephanie Bandy, and in an address Lt. Bottle referred to the opening of the hall in 1934 on April 29th.

Having been one of the officers of the Corps for the past 12 months, in February 1952 Lt. A.W. Reeve moved to take charge of the Willingham (Cambs) Corps. Then the following month in succession to Lt. Bottle two lady officers, Capt. R. Johnson and Lt. Doreen Felstead, arrived from Wollaston, having previously been together in the Northants. Division at Willingham. Prior to this Capt. Johnson had been in the South Yorks division, going to Sawston when she transferred to Northants. They were welcomed at a special gathering at the Hall on the evening of Thursday, May 22nd and special services were held on the Sunday.

In 1955 on Saturday and Sunday, September 24th and 25th the Corps celebrated their 62nd anniversary and in paying a visit former Corps officers Col. and Mrs. Feltwell conducted the services. On the Saturday a programme was arranged by the Songsters and members of the local Corps, and on the Sunday services were held at the Hall. In 1956 on Saturday and Sunday, May 12th and 13th welcome services were held for the new second in command 2nd Lt. Jane Welsh, who had arrived from the Social Work. The CO, 1st Lt. Bessie Sanderson, would be remaining for a further period.

The Salvation Army band, New Bradwell

In May 1961 after 12 months as Commanding Officer of the Corps Lt. E. Whitehead and his wife left for an appointment at Corby. A native of Leicester he had arrived straight from college in London and would be succeeded by Lt. Miss D. Brown from St. Neots, who would take over on May 25th.

In 1962 the officer was Lt. Miss Esme Lewis but in the succeeding years the number of members dwindled, and with the building in need of renovations the Salvation Army decided that the cost for such a small attendance could not be justified. Eventually, in the summer of 1984 having once been the main centre in the area, with outposts at Newport Pagnell, Stony Stratford and Wolverton, the Salvation Army left New Bradwell, with the remaining members transferred to the newly opened Milton Keynes Central Corps in Conniburrow. The wooden hall had burnt down in 1983 and having been sold the building now accommodates the Faith Tabernacle United Pentecostal Church.

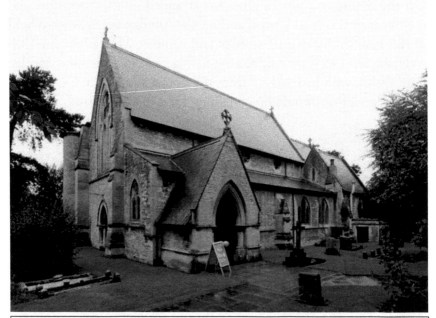

The church at New Bradwell, dedicated to St. James and completed in 1860. It was designed by the architect G. E. Street.

ST. JAMES' CHURCH

In February 1857 the Rev. Henry Brancker MA of Wadham College, Oxford, was instituted by the Bishop of Oxford to the vicarage of Stantonbury, value £54. However in June 1857 he was appointed to the Perpetual Curacy of Thursley, Surrey, value £85, and would remain there as vicar until 1886. Then in July 1857 it was announced that the Rev. Charles Purcell Cotter was to be vicar of Stantonbury with New Bradwell, an order in council having been made for a new ecclesiastical parish called Stantonbury with New Bradwell, carved out from the adjacent parishes. A son of the Rev. Joseph Rogerson Cotter and his wife Mary (nee Purcell) he was born at Castlemagna, County Cork, in 1826 on February 17th, and graduating MA from Trinity College, Dublin, was made a deacon in 1849, then priest in 1850. In 1851 he was the curate at Tincleton, Dorset, residing with his sister Catherine, but in 1852 when resident as a clergyman at Trowbridge, Wilts., on July 13th at Holy Trinity Church, Dorchester, he married 19 year old Mary Anne Caroline Gaitskell. She was the only daughter of a Bengal Civil Servant, and in May 1853 a daughter, Alice Harriet, was born at Dorchester (d 1927 Nov. 27th.) Then in 1855 on August 16th a son Charles Plunkett Rogerson Cotter, with the family residence as Hadlow Parsonage, Kent.

Designed by G.E. Street the vicarage at Stantonbury was built between 1858 and 1860 and it would be on Monday, May 24th 1858 that the laying of the foundation stones of the new church, St. James', was performed. Bearing their respective banners and emblems, the members of the various benefit clubs, together with the school children, were assembled on the turnpike road to receive the arrival of the varied dignitaries shortly after noon. The Marquis of Stafford, MP; Lord Alfred Paget, MP; and Messrs. Earle, Thompson, Moore, and Lawrence, directors of the company, and the Marquis of Chandos, chairman of the LNWR, accompanied by his wife, were greeted by a large number of clergymen and the locomotive superintendent, and churchwarden of the parish, Mr. McConnell. He then gave an address to the Marquis and his wife in which he expressed the acknowledgments of the parishioners for having accepted the request to perform the ceremony. The Marquis then laid the foundation stone of the church and his wife that of the school, being afterwards addressed by the Rev. Cotter in an appropriate speech. The company then retired to a marquee in an adjoining field for refreshments, and at the same venue with Mr. McConnell presiding, the workmen of the company, with Mr. Rowland as chief foreman, were provided with a substantial dinner.

Yet the completion of the church, and to meet the remaining expenses, would now entail a further expense of some £3,000. In

January 1859 a son, Edmond Ludlow Purcell Cotter, was born at Stantonbury to the Rev. Cotter and his wife and the following year on Thursday, December 6th the consecration of the new church and burial ground was performed by the Bishop of Oxford, J.G. Hubbard. However with the cost presently £4,430, of which the shareholders had contributed about £2,560, and local persons and other sources about £1,870, it would still be necessary to complete the spire and the upper part of the tower, with a north aisle also proposed. With Mr. Street of London as the architect, and Joseph Mills of Stratford on Avon as the builder, the church of 'Decorated Gothic' style had accommodation for some 500 persons with the open timbered roof some 50 feet in height. The construction was of Cosgrove stone with Ancaster tracings, and also of Ancaster stone was the pulpit inscribed 'Presented by the foremen and workmen in the engine factory at Wolverton.' Of octagonal form the font was the gift of the Marchioness of Chandos, and was used for the first time for the baptism of Ronald Stafford McConnell, the son of the locomotive superintendent. Having been received at the entrance at 11am by Lord Chandos, Mr. McConnell, the churchwardens, and the clergy in their robes, the Bishop proceeded to the consecration of the burial ground adjoining the church reciting the proper Psalms for the occasion. A procession having been formed he was followed by a numerous body of the clergy, the churchwardens and others, and entering the western door of the church proceeded along the nave towards the Communion table. £210 was collected in aid of the funds and after the service some 200 guests sat down to a repast in the large schoolroom, at which the Bishop presided.

In 1861 the Reverend Cotter and his wife were resident at the vicarage with sons Charles and Edmond, daughter Alice, and the Reverend's widowed mother in law Harriett Gaitskell.

With the church now established, in 1870 on Saturday, February 5th a public meeting and tea was held in the church schoolroom in aid of funds for the Wolverton and Stantonbury Protestant Association. With the benefit of free fuel in winter the room had been lent by the Rev. Cotter for the weekly discussion classes, over which he provided, and the Association had been formed after a visit to Wolverton and Stantonbury the last autumn by Mr. Murphy,

Mary Cotter and her daughter Alice Harriet.

the anti Popery lecturer. It had been a short while ago that the committee contemplated organising this public tea meeting at which nearly 300 attended including Mr. Richard Bore and his family. After the tea the meeting was held at 7pm and as chairman Mr. Bore said in his address "It is the first time I have visited Stantonbury, to attend a public meeting since I have resided at Wolverton, but it will not be so long before I come again. The subject upon which the lecturer will dilate I am quite ignorant of, save that it is in connection with the Stantonbury Protestant Association. That savours very much of another side to the question. There is a Protestant side and there is the other side; you will quite understand what I mean by the other. I may say something about our good old Protestantism; what it has cost our forefathers, how much they suffered and what they underwent that we may enjoy the blessings which we have so quietly, and I may say peacefully, enjoyed." The Rev. Cotter said he fully reciprocated those feelings and since this was the first religious tea meeting he had been unable to perceive any possible connection between theology and teacups! In explaining his main support for the extinction of Popery he said this rested on the advance of education, which he held to be wholly incompatible with a permanent belief "in the childish absurdities of Rome." Mr. Smith as the secretary of the Society said the origin might be dated to the time when Mr. Flanagan came to Stantonbury in 1867 and lectured upon "Luther, the solitary monk who shook the world." This prompted the origin of the association but only 12 people attended the first meeting. In fact it would be 6 weeks before any definite arrangement was made or a discussion was brought forward, "for there had been some crotchety men to deal with."

However the society now had 46 members. Mr. Flanagan then delivered his address and the meeting concluded with the singing of the National Anthem. Manufactured by Messrs. Beavington's of Soho Square, London, in 1870 on Sunday, November 20th the new church organ of 8 stops was opened with a sermon preached by the Rev. Charles Francis Luttrel West, rector of Shenley Church End. The cost of £120 had been mostly borne by those connected with the railway company and also the congregation and there was no outstanding debt.

In April 1872 Charles Plunkett Rogerson Cotter, son of the Rev. C.P. Cotter, vicar of Stantonbury, was appointed to a lieutenancy in the Queen's Own Light Infantry Militia, London. This was on the recommendation of Sir J.L. Cotter who had been a captain in the corps. As the third such occasion of his incumbency, in 1873 on Tuesday, January 28th the Rev. Cotter was presented with a testimonial by the parishioners in the National Schoolroom. This had been contemplated for some time with his recent temporary absence taken as the opportunity to finalise the plans. As the chairman, Mr. Gilbert said to loud cheers "we have met tonight to offer this testimony of our sincere love and respect to our good and worthy vicar. ... His quiet and unassuming manner, his extreme affability and condescension, his own ready kindness to all, have won him the love and affection of his parishioners." From being deputed to present the testimonial Mr. Mundy said a short while ago two young ladies had canvassed the village for donations. With this achieved a meeting as to how to apply the proceeds was called, with it duly decided to purchase a large handsome piece of ornamental tableware on which a gilt shield was inscribed "Presented to the Rev. C.P. Cotter by friends and parishioners of Stantonbury. January 28th, 1873." On rising to hearty cheers the Reverend expressed his profuse appreciation, saying "I have had opportunities of removing from among you by offers that I have had of other parishes, including one from our late bishop, but I have preferred to remain among you. My esteem for you is a real sentiment, founded on solid grounds, on the kind and friendly feeling I have uniformly met with; on the good sense, good order, and intelligence that I have seen among you.

I have not looked anxiously to see whether you were Churchmen, Wesleyans, Baptists, or Independents, but there is one thing I have looked for - I have looked for the spirit of Christ among you; that feeling of kindness and of sympathy for others which brought Jesus into our world for our welfare. I say I have looked for the spirit of Christ in Stantobury and in Wolverton, and I have found it." The evening included singing and musical selections, and the wish for health, long life and happiness was expressed for Mrs. Cotter.

Indeed in October 1874 the Rev. Cotter was offered a deanery in a colonial cathedral, and subsequently the archdeaconry of the same diocese, but he declined both and despite having tentatively accepted another appointment then cast 'some lingering looks behind,' and resolved to stay at Stantonbury.

Appreciation of his loyalty was recognised in 1882 on Friday, March 24th when he was presented by a deputation on behalf of the congregation with new canonicals. The gifts comprised two surplices, college cap, and MA hood, and had been supplied by Ede and Son, of London, robe makers to the Queen. However it seems a religious occupation was not the destiny for the Rev. Cotter's son Charles, for he became a marine engineer and in 1885 at Birkenhead on June 24th married Eleanor Grace, the only child of the late Major J.F. Garstin. Yet sadly Charles died in 1887 on October 18th, his brother having died the previous year at Stantonbury on August 3rd. Then in 1889 on March 21st at the age of 56 the death occurred of the Reverend's wife, and thus as a widower in 1891 he was resident at the vicarage with his daughter, Alice, and widowed daughter in law Eleanor. Then having been confined to bed he died after a short illness in 1891 on the morning of Saturday, May 16th from congestion on the lungs and other complications. On the afternoon of Thursday, May 21st in inclement weather his body was interred in the churchyard and of subsequent appreciations was written; "Mr. Cotter has been described as a meticulous man who in his lifetime maintained the records of the parish with great care. Any records that the church has for the period before 1836 are largely due to his work. The remarkable thing about Mr. Cotter is that his handwriting never varied.'

In July 1891 it was announced that in succession to the late Rev.

Cotter the Rev. Arthur Chorley Woodhouse MA, vicar of St. Marks, Battersea Rise, had been appointed as vicar of Stantonbury. The living was in the gift of Earl Spencer, value £220pa, with residence and 2 acres of glebe. He was born at New Shoreham, Sussex, in 1854 on May 3rd and in 1861 the family were resident in Parsonage Street, Manchester, where his father, Frederick, was rector of St. Mary's, Hulme. After attending Lancing School he entered St. John's College, Cambridge, gaining a BA in 1876 and later an MA in 1880. In 1878 he was ordained deacon by the Bishop of Rochester and that year became curate of Battersea. The following year he was ordained priest and remained at Battersea until appointed as curate of St. Anne's, Brookfield, Highgate Rise, in 1882, in which year on June 8th when resident in Lewisham Road, Highgate, he married at St. Mary's, Hulme, 24 year old Margaret Helen Morris. Of St. Mary's Rectory, Hulme, she was the daughter of William Barton Morris, gent. In 1883 the Rev. Woodhouse accepted the offer of Canon Clarke to became vicar of St. Mark's, Battersea Rise, and in 1883 on November 18th a son, Disney Charles Woodhouse, was born. (The Rev. Woodhouse was a godson of Mrs. Disney Thorp of Lyppiatt Lodge, Cheltenham). Then in 1886 a daughter, Esther Margaret, was born. At this time the family were resident at 19, Leathwaite Road, Battersea, but in July 1891 it was announced that the Rev. had been appointed to Stantonbury. In consequence on the evening of Monday, October 5th 1891 at a large gathering at St. Mark's Vestry Hall, Battersea Rise, after his 8 years at the church he was bade farewell by the parishioners. With many having subscribed to the leaving fund he was presented with an illuminated address and a purse (for his wife) containing a cheque for £80.

Then on the evening of Tuesday, October 6th at a public service he was inducted by the Bishop of Reading into the living at Stantonbury, to begin his duties at the morning service on Sunday, October 11th. A large congregation attended and in the evening such were the numbers that many could not be accommodated. The Reverend soon began to assess his new parish and on the evening of Thursday, October 29th held a meeting of the church attendants towards the more efficient conduct of the service, and the cleaning of the church. Also that collections would be taken once a month for the Church Restoration Fund.

Following the death of the Rev. Cotter by 1892 his only daughter, Alice, had moved to 27, Kildare Terrace, Paddington, and on April 23rd at St. Stephen's Church, Paddington, married Charles Henry Miles, physician and surgeon, LRCP Lond. 'etc,' of The Laurels, Stantonbury. The memory of the Rev. Cotter was still greatly cherished and in August 1892 a memorial window was placed at the east end of the chancel aisle. As the work of Mr. J. Davies of Shrewsbury this comprised three lancet shaped lights, the figures of which represented the parable of the Good Samaritan.

Presided over by the Rev. Woodhouse, in 1894 on the evening of Monday, August 27th a public meeting was held in the schoolroom to discuss the best means of forming a branch of the National Anti Gambling League. In his opening remarks he pointed out the need to take steps to prevent the problem of betting and gambling becoming prevalent in the district. Also to adopt some means of rescuing the young from such peril, and with deputations from various denominations present the Rev. J. Mathews, the Baptist minister, resolved "That this meeting having duly considered the subject feel it desirable to form a united society, including Wolverton, Stantonbury, and Stony Stratford." It was suggested that the chairman should be the representative, and as such write to those places to ask that a joint meeting might be held at Wolverton.

In 1895 in January the Rev. E. Marshall was licensed to the curacy of Stantonbury. As for the Rev. Woodhouse (whose father was now vicar of Holy Trinity, Folkestone, and hon. Canon of Canterbury) in May 1901 with his son now at Winchester College, and his daughter at Cheltenham Ladies' College, he accepted the offer from Mrs. Nevile Wyatt to the living of St. Philip and St. James at Leckhampton, Gloucs.[23] This had been vacant since the death of Canon Hutchinson.

In September 1901 it was announced that the Rev. Arthur Oswel James, formerly rector of Bugbrooke, and Rural Dean of Weedon, was to be the new vicar of Stantonbury. A graduate of Lincoln College, Oxford, taking an MA in 1875, he had been ordained in 1872, being that year appointed curate at Stoney Stanton and later to Narborough and Hinckley. In 1879 he was made vicar of Long

Buckby and in 1891 was at Leicester as vicar of All Saints Church. Born at Liverpool in 1850 he came from a religious family, his father being the Rev. David James, rector of Pantag, in Wales, and his brother of ecclesiastical renown. He remained at Stantonbury until 1908 when Lady Augusta Palmer presented him to the Rectory of Wanlip. When Leicester was made a Bishopric he was made an Honorary Canon and for 9 years until 1928 he would be Rural Dean of Goscote II. He died in 1932 at The Rectory, Wanlip, on August 3rd.

St. James Church Choir c.1948.

At Stantonbury in succession to the Rev. James the induction by the Archdeacon of Buckingham took place of the Rev. Allan Newman Guest. Attended by a large congregation the ceremony took place on the evening of Thursday, September 17th 1908 and the story of his successive years of tribulation and torment is deservedly told in a separate chapter! Suffice to say that consequent to a visit by the Bishop in March 1946 it was rumoured that the Rev. Guest might soon be leaving the parish. Then on Sunday, October 6th 1946 a notice posted on the door of St. James' informed that he had resigned and that the living was now entrusted to the Reverend E.A. Steer, vicar of Stony Stratford and Rural Dean. A replacement vicar had yet to be appointed and for the meanwhile no Sunday services would be held.

Then on Sunday, November 3rd 1946 the services re-commenced, conducted by Canon F.T. Howard. He was a former vicar of Aylesbury and having recently retired from the active ministry was now resident at Wavendon. In January 1947 it was announced that the Rev. Hubert Thornton Trapp, presently priest in charge of Clewer St. Agnes, Berks., was to be the new vicar, a notice in the porch of St. James' having informed that the Bishop of Oxford proposed to collate him to the benefice. Following repairs to the vicarage he took up residence in March 1947. His father had died in 1946 on February 18th at 146, Clewer Road, Windsor, and so the Reverend's mother moved with him to Stantonbury Vicarage, where she died in 1948 on October 22nd. The institution took place on Saturday, March 22nd 1947 by the Bishop of Oxford and after the service Canon Howard, who had served interim, was presented on behalf of the parishioners with an electric shaving set and a cheque by Mrs. B. Welch. She was secretary of the Parochial Parish Council, and on behalf of the members of the choir Mr. C.H. Scott, the organist and choirmaster, presented him with a fountain pen and propelling pencil. Born at Penrhiwceiber, Glamorgan, the son of Albert Henry Trapp, a fruiterer, and his wife Amy, the new vicar had trained at Kilham Theological College and from being a former member of St. Alban's Church, South Norwood, was ordained a deacon at Canterbury Cathedral on Sunday, May 27th 1934. He was appointed to a curacy at Whitstable and later served in West Ham and Clewer St. Agnes, before joining the RAF, in which he served for 4½ years in England, North Africa, Italy and Sicily. A keen motor cycle rider in May 1949 he spent his vacation touring in Italy! In 1951 he sung the Mass at a ceremony at which a new east window at St. James' was dedicated on Saturday, February 3rd to the memory of former priests and parishioners in the 91 years existence of the church.

Yet he would soon be a former priest, for in March he informed members of the Parochial Church Council that he would be vacating the parish for a living at Paddington. Thus with clergy and servers present from the surrounding district, on the afternoon of Saturday, May 26th in a tea after the service of Corpus Christi he was presented by Mrs. B. Welch with a cheque and autograph book signed by the donors. Then on the Thursday evening two bus loads of members from New Bradwell travelled to Paddington for his induction service at St. Mary's and were afterwards entertained to supper by the members of the church. In fact in some ways the Rev. Thornton Trapp invoked memories of the Rev. Guest from having at times 'alarmist views,' not least from banning any members of the clergy who were Freemasons from preaching in his church. Also warning his parishioners against purchasing South African produce, due to his views on apartheid. Then in 1956 when vicar of the London Anglo-Catholic Church of St. Mary Magdalene, Woodchester Street, Paddington, he was received into the Roman Catholic Church on Tuesday 3rd and intended to become a Catholic priest!

Rev. Fallows.

At New Bradwell in the wake of his departure the vicar for the past 12 years of Holy Trinity Church, Prestwood, near Great Missenden, the Rev. Harold Fallows, became the new incumbent in July 1951. Before going to Prestwood he had lived in New Zealand for 15 years, and having trained at St. John College, Auckland, was an MA and Licentiate of theology of the University of New Zealand. During WW2 he had been Chaplain to the Troops at Peterley Camp and there he was later Chaplain to the Jugoslavs. His interests included painting and music and he was also a talented metal worker. At New Bradwell he made arrangements for the Norman arch at St. Peter's Church to be incorporated at St. James' but having been a patient at Radcliffe Infirmary, Oxford, for two months died on Tuesday, April 8th. At the funeral on the Saturday at St. James' the Bishop of Buckingham performed the last rites, with interment in the churchyard. The Rev. Roy Rendell, of Wolverton, had taken oversight of the parish during his illness and although the new incumbent was to have been the Rev. Herbert John Sutters, a minor canon at Ripon Cathedral, in July 1952 he instead accepted the chaplaincy of Wells Theological College.

Thus in November 1952 the new vicar became the Rev. James O. Snell, from a position as vicar of Dawley Parva, Wellington, Shropshire. Born at Dartford in 1913 on May 5th (his mother's maiden name was Osborne) he was educated at Dartford Grammar School and Cambridge and Ely Theological College. He was ordained deacon in 1936 and went as curate to St. Michael's Church, in Summertown, Oxford. In 1938 he was appointed priest in charge of St. Margaret's Mission Church at Bletchley and in 1940 on Tuesday, December 31st at the church of St. Michael and All Angels at Oxford married shop assistant Miss Jean Barbara Le Conte of 3, Harbord Road, North Oxford, second daughter of Mr. C. Le Conte, a hairdresser, of Summertown. The couple would then make their home at 24, Lennox Road, Bletchley, and in 1942 a son, Christopher James Le Conte Snell, was born.

Rev. Snell.

Then in February 1943 the Vicar announced to the annual meeting of St. Martin's Church Council that the Reverend J. O. Snell would be leaving Bletchley after Easter. At a farewell address by the Reverend Wheeler, at the beginning of May he was presented with a cheque and a book token at a gathering in St. Martin's Hall. He was now moving to Rugeley, and in 1947, the year in which a son, Nicholas, was born, would be appointed as vicar of Dawley Parva, in Shropshire, being instituted on St. Martin's Day in recognition of his association with Fenny Stratford. In 1947 at Wellington, Shropshire, a daughter, Helen, was born.

Yet the Rev. Snell would be reacquainted with the area in November, 1952, when collated as the vicar designate of St. James', New Bradwell. A daughter, Mary, was born in 1955 and the family were still at the vicarage in 1961. However resident at Winterstoke Way, Ramsgate, he later became the rector of Holy Trinity Church, Ramsgate, where on May 1st 1971 his daughter Helen married Ian Ulrich of Weston Super Mare. However it seems the officiating minister, the Rev. Peter Collins, failed to turn up, apparently being 'miles away' at a garden party, and so her father had to don his robes and conduct the ceremony! The Rev. Snell died in 2005 on October 8th at Canterbury, his son, Nicholas, also commemorated on the gravestone. His widow died in 2014 on March 28th at Ramsgate.

With the coming of the New City of Milton Keynes religion in the Stantonbury area has become more inclusive of the various denominations, and as per the message on their website, "We are partners with other Churches in the Stantonbury area and enjoy worship in the Anglican, Methodist, Baptist and United Reform Church traditions."

ST. PETER'S CHURCH

Saint Peter's Church is said to have at one time been held by the priories of Goring and of Bradwell. Indeed it formed part of the endowment of Goring Priory in Oxfordshire, as apparent from a confirmation charter of 1181, when said to be in the gift of the brothers William and Ralph Barry.

The church dates from the early 12th century or possibly earlier, with a 13th century chancel and north aisle, the latter apparently demolished in the 16th century, when a porch was added. The church featured a timber clad western bell turret with a tiled roof, the west nave wall being a rebuild of the 15th century. As reported by a visitor in the mid 19th century;

"You continue the Newport road to the canal bridge, and then proceed along the towing path for a short distance, when, crossing a stile to the left, you see a small church, without spire or tower, standing within a stone enclosure of no great dimensions. Very deserted and desolate it looks just now; the churchyard is knee deep in grass, and white with "Devil's oatmeal." You climb over the gate, and make your way through the weeds which obliterate the pathway, to the porch. It is protected by a wooden gate. Before we enter let us take a glance at the exterior of the edifice. There is, as we have said, no spire or tower. The building consists of a nave, and chancel of much larger dimensions. Its architectural features have nothing remarkable, and only tell the old patchwork story. The only trace of Norman work is in a very small window in the very peak of the gable (not the original pitch) at the west end. Entering the building through an Early English doorway, we find a small nave much dilapidated and neglected. In the eastern corner opposite is a pulpit of James the First's time; in the western an early font much defaced; a highly enriched Norman chancel arch, with chevron and beak head mouldings; the latter alternating with other grotesque heads and ornaments will attract attention. The shafts of the pillars are also highly enriched, and the whole work is apparently in good and perfect condition, preserved and choked with centuries of white wash. (An interesting and perhaps contemporary photograph of the arch in position at St. Peter's church may be seen in the Victoria County History of Bucks, volume 4 between pages 464/5.) The chancel as we have said, is very large in comparison with the rest of the church, and more dilapidated than the rest. The walls are grimed and stained with mouldy fungi; and part of the roof is falling in. There is a piscina and no less than three aumbrys, in one of which lies a gauntlet of mail, and a broken sword. On the wall above is a helmet in situ, and what seems a dummy for feathers. There has been no service in the old church since the completion of the schools in the new Stantonbury, and we believe the total abandonment of the venerable edifice is contemplated. Of the wisdom of the transfer we do not pretend to judge, but we trust that the ancient edifice will not be demolished, nor suffered to become a ruin through neglect. Not many pounds are needed to put it into a state of cleanliness and weather-tight repair. ... It is a relic which new Stantonbury should be proud of and cherish."

Then in September 1886 came the comment;

"What a pity that the old church at Stanton Low should be left uncared for, and that dirt and damp should be allowed to work their way towards the destruction of this ancient edifice. The Church is worth keeping in order for the sake of past memories."

However for the first time for nearly 30 years on Sunday, May 12th 1895 a service was held in the church, which had been cleaned by willing workers and made as presentable as possible. Indeed there was a great crush to get in, with some 194 persons in the congregation. The chancel was nearly filled by the harmonium and the choir, and on the altar, above which was hung a floral cross, were placed vases of flowers. The Rev. E. Marshall, curate of Stantonbury with New Bradwell, conducted the service which consisted of a shortened evensong, followed by the administration of holy baptism and a short sermon. Then on the afternoon of Sunday, September

29th the last service for the year was held to a good attendance.

In 1898 on the evening of Wednesday, June 22nd some 25 teachers of St. James' Sunday School attended a service at the church. This they had especially requested, and apart from conducting a shortened evensong the Rev. A.C. Woodhouse gave a discourse upon the fabric of the church and the surroundings.

The following year, with a collection to be taken for Northampton Infirmary, the church, subject to the weather, would be opened for service at 3pm by the Rev. Merrin on the afternoon of May 21st; 'Cycles may be stored near and will be carefully guarded.' Then subject again to 'weather permitting,' and with an offertory to be taken for Northampton Infirmary, the Rev. E. Marshall, now formerly curate of Stantonbury, would conduct a service on Sunday, July 16th.

In 1907 on the afternoon of Saturday, June 29th the church was crowded for the festival of dedication, with a sermon preached by the Rev. J.R. Vincent of Shenley.

In 1908 came the arrival of the Rev. Newman Guest as vicar, inducted on September 11th, who in 1909 caused great consternation when he announced from the pulpit of St. James' Church at New Bradwell that the transfer of the rights and privileges from St.

On April 10th. 1909 a large crowd turned out to witness the wedding at the Stanton Low church, following the sensational revelation that St. James' had not been licenced for weddings. Here are George Pedder and Edith Townsend leaving the church as newlyweds.

Peter's had never been 'perfected.' Thereby since St. James' hadn't been licensed for weddings more than one thousand 'marriages' were deemed officially illegal. In consequence many couples wishing to plight their troth endured the hike to St. Peter's, including that year on Saturday, April 10th Walter Bull and Clara Hawkins, and George Pedder and Edith Townsend. In fact it had been more than 50 years since the last occasion and some 1,000 spectators had come to witness the spectacle and as was reported, "The two brides and bridegrooms plighted their troth under a Saxon doorway, kneeling on flagstones of Saxon fashioning, facing the tombs of knights and Templars, on each side of which are tablets of departed county squires, and above them, hung on the wall of the chancel, the helmet, gauntlets, spurs, and sword of a long departed manorial lord." Eventually a special Act of Parliament was passed to resolve the situation.

Some nine months after his arrival as vicar the Rev. Newman Guest had approached Lord Spencer, as patron of the living, and asked him to re-roof the church and arrange much needed exterior repairs. In June 1910 the work was put in hand, and at this time towards restoring the interior the vicar sought the services of Mr. Kemp, a builder of wide experience in work on local churches. Together they set about removing the crumbling mortar of the walls, in the hope of perhaps uncovering some frescoes. Should none be found then to re-point the stones.

However on the morning of Tuesday, June 7th 1910 a discovery was made that 'the slightly embossed fringes that draw towards the chancel in curves' rested on magnificent moulded pedestals, grouped in the centre upon four Roman pillars of enormous girth. It was found to actually traverse the wall from the outside to the inside, which at that point was 3½ft thick. The discovery had been made by Mr. Kemp, who when requested by the vicar tapped the visible base of the arch in order to discover any ornamentation. Two arches ran along the whole north wall, one, springing beneath the ancient arch of the doorway, was probably of the 11th century, being supported upon carved corbals and having a rounded pier; 'Already there have been exposed stone engravings of two monks apparently of the period of the preaching friars for the birettas are of the John Wycliff period of the church of England.' In fact from interest in the work Earl Spencer and Lord Althorp motored to Stantonbury on Wednesday, June 9th.

From a community in 1736 of four cottages, only a farm remained in 1910 together with the church, where a service was held that year on Sunday, November 6th. The Bradwell Band played as the procession crossed the fields to the church, which became so crowded that the bandsmen had to stand outside. With the St. James' choir in attendance the vicar, the Rev. Newman Guest, conducted a shortened form of evensong, and afterwards having mounted the stone sedilia Mr. T.N. Blagg FSA gave an informative address on the architecture and the history of the church. As for the restoration work in progress, removal of the lath and plaster from the rood loft had exposed an oak beam 5½ inches thick, interlaced with jet black oak struts. This spanned the entire nave, and when whitewash was scraped from the oak in the nave and the chancel it was revealed that the purpose of the original builder had been to make a contrast of the white oak in the nave and the black timber in the chancel. During the proceedings two very wide Norman windows in the interior, with the usual ashlar stonework, were revealed, and also there was evidence that the church had been used not only as a place of worship but also as a fortification.

In 1913 on Sunday, June 29th (St. Peter's Day) towards reviving the worship of olden times, namely in the open air, the Rev. Newman Guest conducted a religious pageant between the two churches. Having gathered outside St. James' Church at 2.30pm many people - albeit 'not many in sympathy with the Vicar' - followed the procession along the mile and a half length of the route. At the head the cross bearer was followed successively by the Newport Excelsior Band, the choristers in red and purple cassocks, a dozen little girls carrying roses, and then the vicar, replete in biretta and cope. Along the way the band's rendition of a lively march infused such a sprightly pace that having climbed the steep canal hill a large number of participants took a more direct cut across the fields. A halt was called outside the old church, where on the grassy wall an altar had been erected upon which had been placed candles and vases of flowers. From the many persons present no 'hostile demonstration' was made, excepting that during the alfresco prayers the Vicar rebuked one of his audience with the remark, "Thank you, Sir, don't talk here." Nevertheless 'The attitude of the congregation which had gathered around, numbering several hundreds, could scarcely be called reverent.' Being simple and plain the service was in the traditions of 'Merrie England, as pointed out by the vicar, who after the singing of 'Fight the Good Fight' proceeded to the church where the Te Deum was sung. This was followed by the Benedictus, with the band playing musical selections. Collections for Northampton General Hospital were taken, and before the close the vicar announced that he would hold a further open air service for the harvest thanksgiving. As a place of much mystery, there were many rumours of the presence of a tunnel in the vicinity, supposedly leading from the church, and intriguingly in the early 1920s the Rev. Guest wrote that if anyone wished to help in the excavation could they contact Mr. Alfred Bullard; "In 1911 I placed a large slab across the entrance. It is already dug for 10 feet by Tom Pain, an experienced man of that period, and is so lofty that a person can walk along it."

Towards providing a musical instrument to accompany the summer services, in April 1923 a resident of Stony Stratford donated two guineas to the vicar and churchwardens. However rather more immediate was the need to raise about £20 to repair the roof, an examination of which had revealed serious defects. A pressing requirement since services were still being held, to include at 3pm on Sunday, May 6th 1923 the administering by the vicar of the Sacrament of Baptism. In fact this would be the first occasion for many generations that the 12th century font, cut from solid rock, would be used. A harvest festival was held at St. Peter's in 1926 on the afternoon of Sunday, October 3rd.

Then in 1928 with the assistance of the New Bradwell branch of the British Legion he organised a digging party to investigate the alleged old tunnel at the church. Anyone wishing to help was asked to bring a spade and be at the church at 2.30pm on Saturday, September 29th. The following month to a crowded congregation he conducted a harvest thanksgiving on the afternoon of Sunday, October 21st. Harvest hymns were featured and under the direction of the organist, Mr. C.H. Scott, the choir of St. James Church led the unaccompanied singing. Having been thoroughly cleaned by the churchwardens of St. James, Messrs. Ellis and Tapp, the church had been decorated by Mrs. S. Ellis and Mrs. T. Tapp. In 1931 the harvest thanksgiving was held to a large congregation on Sunday, October 11th, and again under the direction of the organist and choirmaster, Mr. C.H. Scott, the singing was lead unaccompanied by the 28 boy choristers of St. James' Church, New Bradwell. The Rev. Newman Guest conducted the service, with the church having been decorated by Mr. and Mrs. Tapp and Mr. W. Robinson. Also Mr. S. Ellis, the vicar's warden, from whom for interested visitors the church keys could be obtained from 69, Newport Road, New Bradwell.

In 1933 on the afternoon of Sunday, April 23rd a sizeable crowd visited the church of St. Peter, when the first service of the present series was held. The vicar, the Rev. Newman Guest, gave a sermon-lecture with regard to the windows, and pointed out that the bell dated to 1216. Easter hymns were sung unaccompanied by the choir of St. James, and since there was otherwise no seating the churchwardens, Messrs. S. Ellis and T. Tapp, had brought a few chairs. Then on the afternoon of Sunday, June 11th a christening took place at St. Peter's. The water was taken from the nearby river and in officiating the Rev. Newman Guest said that in his 25 years of ministry he had only christened 10 babies there. Then during the same year on the afternoon of Saturday, August 26th he conducted an adult baptism, being namely that of Victor Verral of Queen Anne Street, New Bradwell.

In April 1934 the silver wedding of Mr. and Mrs. T. Bull was celebrated, of additional significance since they had been the first couple to be married by the Rev. Newman Guest. The ceremony had taken place at St. Peter's, where in 1934 the first service of the present summer series was held on the afternoon of Sunday, June 3rd. The church and the churchyard had been cleared by the Wardens of St. James' Church, New Bradwell (Messrs. T. Tapp and S. Ellis) and in conducting the service the vicar, the Rev. Newman Guest, made an appeal for a harmonium, as the previous one had now "gone past repair." Chairs had been taken from the church of St. James' as there was otherwise no seating. That year the harvest thanksgiving service was held on the afternoon of Sunday, August 16th, with the church having been decorated on the previous Saturday afternoon by members of St. James. During the recent high winds several roof tiles had been loosened, and raising £1 a collection was taken towards the repair of the damage. Later in the month a service was conducted on the afternoon of Sunday, August 26th, at which the Rev. Guest included historical information about the church. Consequent to his recent appeal Miss Layton of Newport Pagnell had presented a harmonium, and with Mr. C.H. Scott presiding at the instrument the choir boys of St. James' lead the singing of the hymns and canticles. Pleasingly from having an interest in the church several visitors on holiday in the district were amongst the congregation.

Also of interest had been the discovery earlier in the century of an underground tunnel which, supposedly extending northerly from the church, was again investigated in 1938. In August 1944 investigations were also made when wilful and malicious damage was discovered at the church. As stated by the Rev. Guest, "The west window sill of the porch has been broken so as to allow a person to climb through, and a stained glass window smashed. The windows situate before you enter the church which are protected with iron grills are practically broken, including priceless pre Reformation glass. The font, cut out of solid rock and reputed to be erected on Roman bricks, has been thrown off its pedestal. The best funeral regalia in England (14th century) which hung on the chancel walls lies on the ground broken to pieces, and the fourteenth century pulpit has been partly smashed." Having inspected the church he understood that several youths had been recently pursued in the direction of Newport Pagnell, and in consequence of a complaint being made an identification parade of boys took place at a local school. However the evidence proved insufficient.

In 1947 on Thursday, April 10th the Rev. H.T. Trapp, as the new vicar of St. James', presided in the Church Hall over his first vestry and parochial meetings. Some 60 parishioners were present and Mrs. G. Barton asked if it might be possible to hold - as they always used to, especially at harvest festivals - a service at St. Peter's. In reply the vicar said "Thank you for mentioning it, but I haven't even seen my chapel at ease yet. I have read about it, and it is unfortunate that a really beautiful church is let to go to rack and ruin." "Unfortunately we haven't a key, and unfortunately I am told a key will be necessary to get in." "I hope we shall be able to have a service there during the summer. I have got plans, but I understand windows have been broken." At this a voice interjected "Gipsies have stayed the night in it." Mr. May said that on four occasions both he and Mr. Tapp had gone to clean the church but on each Sunday it rained and no service was held. However that year at 3pm on St. James' day of prayer, Sunday, July 6th, a service took place with the Rev. K. Joyce as preacher.

Then in 1948 a service was arranged for the afternoon of Sunday, July 11th but again due to continuous rain it had to be postponed. Nevertheless in August a service was conducted by the Rev. Trapp, at which Vespers was sung by the choir of St. James', with the hymns accompanied by the New Bradwell band. In 1949 the future of St. Peter's was the subject for discussion at the meeting of Newport Pagnell RDC on Wednesday, January 5th. In reply to a letter from the Rural Council, a letter from the clerk of Bucks County Council stated that a member of the County Planning Office had interviewed the Rev. H.T. Trapp, and from this he understood that a Pilgrimage and service was held at the old church annually, generally arranged during August. Thereby the church remained in ecclesiastical use and because of this it seemed that the County Council, as the local planning authority, couldn't intervene. The vicar had informed the County Council's representative that on various occasions he had discussed the question of the old church with both the Bishop of Oxford and the Bishop of Buckingham. As for the Ancient Monuments Ministry of Works Inspector, he had notified the Planning Officer that the church was one of an increasing number not in use for their original purpose, and was thereby falling into ruin. The Ministry hoped that the whole matter would be dealt with comprehensively, and from being in touch with the ecclesiastical authorities they would keep the matter in mind. Mr. G. Uthwatt said he'd been told that the church was last used in September 1947. Also that about a year ago having broken into the church through a window some miscreants had not only turned the font upside down but had also set fire to the harmonium. Last September it had been arranged to hold a harvest festival at the church but when the day arrived it had rained too hard. Col. Williams asked if they could write to the Bishop of Oxford stating that since it was in their area they had a particular interest in the church. In consequence it was decided to write to the Church Commissioners on the matter.

In 1950 with special services having commenced at St. James' on the previous Wednesday, on Sunday, July 2nd the Lord Bishop of Oxford, Dr. Kenneth Kirk, gave the address at a service held in connection with the Patronal Festival at St. Peter's. With the only access being along a field footpath he, the Rev. Thornton Trapp, and the choir robed outside the church, which the previous day had been cleaned and decorated with flowers by a band of church workers. With the Bradwell United Silver Prize Band playing for hymns the vicar conducted the service, and since the only chair in the church was used by the Lord Bishop the congregation remained standing, prior to kneeling for his blessing.

During his incumbency the Rev. H. Fallows had obtained permission from the Bishop to remove certain masonry from St. Peter's, and by November 1951 this was safely in store awaiting installation at St. James' Church. An appeal would then be made for funds to carry out the work of preserving St. Peter's, for it was found that even a wall tablet had been smashed, with signs that the Norman arch had been pelted with bricks. In fact at a visit to the church some months before the vicar and churchwardens had discovered the windows smashed, the stone tracery damaged, the railings around the sanctuary pulled down, and the bell missing, although it had been in situ at a previous visit. Also there was evidence of tunnelling in progress under the west wall and under a tomb. In view of the ongoing vandalism before he died in May 1952 the Rev. Fallows took personal responsibility for rescuing the Norman chancel arch from complete collapse, and by July of that year the removal had been completed by local masons. Seemingly none too soon, for during the past year considerable damage had been done to the church, with tombstones ripped up from the floor and smashed, and memorial tablets pulled off the wall. As for the rescued arch, St. James' Parochial Church Council had opened a fund towards the estimated £200 cost of its installation, and donations could be sent to Mr. H. Baines of 34, St. Mary's Street, New Bradwell. Indeed a faculty for the work had been obtained, but only after a six month legal battle due to a single objection from a resident in the parish. Some of the other stonework from St. Peter's would be used to repair the wall of St. James' churchyard, whilst as for the situation with St. Peter's, in a letter to the local press in October 1952 John Inskip wrote;

"I was deeply moved to see in your edition of 11th July of the vandalism perpetrated on the old and historic church at Stanton Low. When I was a boy (60 years ago), and through later years, it was always a 'show place' for us to take our visitors or friends from distant parts of the country. The recollection of my last visit is a memory of uncut grass, at least two feet high: and after obtaining the key from a neighbouring house we went into the church where, we used to be told, Cromwell stabled his horse during the Civil War: and I used to imagine that "Oliver" would not be able to stable many horses in that small church! Why was this vandalism permitted? Was there no one locally of sufficient public spirit or interest to have sought to prevent this? Surely this should not have been allowed to have suffered this desecration. Some years ago I was told the local Vicar had removed the old oaken benches or seats we used when the annual service was held there, and I wondered then that he was allowed to do this. One is forced to come to the conclusion there must have been some ecclesiastical lack of interest. ..."

Adding that a faculty had been obtained for removing things from the old church and placing them in St. James', the Rev. J.O. Snell reported at the parochial church meeting in March 1954 that the church had got to be pulled down, saying "They can spend £800 on a windmill which has neither historic value nor interest - you can see plenty of windmills anywhere. Yet they are prepared to let a church go to rack and ruin which is at least 600 years old." However regarding his comments about spending £800 on a windmill, Ray Bellchambers felt compelled to clarify the position, pointing out that the condition of Stanton Low church had been brought to the attention of Newport Pagnell RDC in November 1948. In consequence the council brought the matter to the attention of the County Planning Department, who took the trouble to inspect the building and make a report. The planning department were then anxious to do all that was possible, but since the contemporary vicar claimed the church was still in use the County Council were powerless to act in any way. In the hope that action could be taken under the Ancient Monuments Act the matter was reported to the Ministry of Town and Country Planning, but again the same problem was encountered. Had the church authorities been prepared to forego the use of the church (it was then in use only on one day a year) there was no doubt that action to preserve the church would have been taken at a fairly high level. Indeed with this in mind the matter had been reported to the Church Commissioners and the Bishop of Oxford. The former replied that it was not a matter in which they were competent to take action, and the latter acknowledged the letter, and said it would receive attention. Presumably said Mr. Bellchambers it was still receiving attention, for the council had yet to be notified of any action. In the meantime a priceless example of Norman architecture was demolished; "The church can neither be used for services nor serve as an architectural example, and the "they" get the blame." It was now far too late to save the building, and it could only be hoped that archaeological interests would be allowed to inspect the demolition, and if necessary to carry out excavations (particularly the western end of the church) in the optimism that that some of the Stanton Low 'mysteries' might be solved.

Yet there was cause for some optimism since the Norman arch from St. Peter's was still in store under the care of Mr. A.W. Gurney, stonemason of New Bradwell. In August 1955 archaeological investigations at St. Peter's were led by Mr. G. Tull of Bletchley. He was hoping to form an Archaeological Society in Wolverton, and during the excavations fragments of green tiles were recovered, indicating a probable use as roof cladding. The work had the support of the vicar of New Bradwell, the Rev. J.O. Snell, and in September 1955 at the first meeting of the newly formed Wolverton and District Archaeological Society, held at St. James' Church Hall, Mr. W. May, the vicar's warden, showed the members the register of St. Peter's, dating from the 16th century. Meanwhile the church continued to decline, and in 1956 with a roar that could be heard at Haversham the roof crashed to the floor at about 8.30pm on Tuesday, May 1st. On hearing the commotion a Haversham resident saw a cloud of dust rising from that vicinity, and having been notified police officers then went to the scene.

In 1960 the last person to be married at St. Peter's, Mr. Leonard S. Dixon, died suddenly on March 22nd at his home, 59, St. Mary

Roof collapse at St. Peter's 1st. May 1956

Street, New Bradwell. He was 74 and had only been ill for 2 weeks. A native of Islington he moved to New Bradwell as a boy and entered Wolverton Works as an apprentice. He was a coach painter by trade and during WW1 had been wounded in the leg and taken prisoner in France. In WW2 he served in the Home Guard, and in sports activities joined the New Bradwell St. Peter's football club at its formation, playing for them on Red Bridge field. After 49 years of employment he had retired 9 years ago and in 1959 he and his wife Adelaide celebrated their golden wedding, having lived at 59, St. Mary Street for 50 years. Of their family there was a son, Lewis Dixon, and a grandson. The funeral took place at St. James' Church on the Saturday, with interment in New Bradwell cemetery.

In October 1960, when asked about grants for churches Sir Frank Markham said St. Peter's could almost certainly have been saved had it not been consecrated. However since the Church Authorities refused its release the Ministry were unable to make a grant, as these were only issued for disused churches. Nevertheless there was some preservation, when it was stated at the annual church meeting of

The Last Service at St. Peter's 29th. June 1963

St. James' in 1962 that the memorial slabs transferred 5 or 6 years ago had been installed, with £12 received towards the costs from the Council for the Care of Churches.

Then in 1963 under leaden skies on the morning of Saturday, June 29th what transpired to be the last service at St. Peter's took place. Of the 30 or so people attending some had made their way along the traditional route of the canal tow path and across the field, and at the isolated location the vicar, the Rev. R. Russell, ended Mass by reciting the last Gospel in Latin. The church was now without a roof and derelict but as a vestige during a communion and confirmation service on Whit Sunday 1969 the recently installed Norman arch, around the west door of St. James', was re-hallowed by the Bishop of Buckingham, the Rt. Rev. Christopher Pepys. The cost had totalled £400, with it having been 17 years since the then vicar, the Rev. Harold Fallows, had the stones removed from St. Peter's, to be carefully numbered and stored. The vicar, the Rev. R. Russell, said the stones were in perfect condition, and in remembrance of the Rev. Fallows flowers were placed near the arch.

In January 1974 an announcement in an Oxford Diocesan

magazine stated that St. Peter's had now been officially declared redundant, to which the vicar, the Rev. R. Russell, said "It is a long overdue statement of affairs. It means that the church will no longer be used for anything whatever." Due not least to the condition of the central arch the Church Authorities no longer wanted to accept responsibility for any harm to people wandering in the ruins, and the redundancy meant that although the area was still consecrated (the last burial was in 1934) the ruins would no longer be considered of historical interest. Indeed they might possibly be demolished. The Church still owned the land but although Mr. Russell said there were plans for its use he was unable to say what they were, or when they might be effected.

Then in May 1975 it was announced that Milton Keynes Borough Council had been given permission to buy the ruins from the Church Commissioners. The annual maintenance for the building was expected to be about £40pa, with the cost of immediate repairs estimated at up to £1,400. In 2012 volunteers formed a Save St. Peter's Church group to prevent further ruin, and in August 2014 persuaded Milton Keynes Council to fund a protective fence around the building. Today the Grade 11 remains are under the care of the Parks Trust, having been transferred to their custodianship in 2016.

The Norman arch from St. Peter's was rescued from the ruin and re-installed in St. James Church.

WEAPONS AND WAR

THE RIFLE BUTTS AT STANTON LOW

In November 1860 it was reported that 'a man holding a responsible situation at Wolverton' had been making great exertions at Stantonbury to recruit volunteers for the Rifle Volunteer Movement. However although within a few days there were apparently 30 members it seems that little came of it. More certainly in August 1877 'a gentleman in the neighbourhood' offered to become captain and promised the sum of £50 towards the expense of forming a Rifle Volunteer Corps. When this became known others came forward to act as officers, and from noting this enthusiasm Mr. Richard Bore, carriage superintendent at the Wolverton Works of the London & North Western Railway, engaged the interest of the railway company, with notices posted inviting men to join.

Subsequently in 1877 on October 22nd a public meeting was held at the Science & Art Institute at Wolverton. Here Mr. G.M. Fitzsimmons presided, supported by amongst others Col. Wethered, Capt. Rev. F.W. Short of St. Paul's School, Stony Stratford, the Rev. C.P. Cotter, vicar of Stantonbury, and J.G.V.F. Johnson, of Wolverton Mills.[24] A committee was formed and a second meeting took place at Wolverton on November 26th. This time the venue was the new dining hall of Wolverton Works in Stratford Road, with it realised that for the necessary funds the introduction of subscription would be needed. In the evening of the following Thursday the first drill for the recruits was held in the Work's large paint shop, which until the building of the Drill Hall at Wolverton in 1914 would also suffice as the headquarters of the Wolverton Company. Becoming No. 6 (Wolverton) Company of the battalion the Wolverton Company gained the relevant approval in January 1878, to be initially commanded by Captain Short.

Thus with a start underway in 1878 on Saturday, May 24th 'the 6th Company (Wolverton) of the 1st Bucks Rifle Volunteer Corps', composed of some 100 members, mustered for drill and lead by the band marched to a field at Stanton Low in the occupation of Lt. J.G.V.F. Johnson. There to include blank cartridge firing they were put through various exercises. (As a means to enforce discipline in the new company, since the men were predominantly employees of the L&NWR any contravention would also mean dismissal from their railway employment.)

The field was again the venue on Saturday, July 5th 1879 when under the command of Lt. Johnson they were put through a course of military field exercise, being afterwards regaled at his lodge. In further progress there were now proposals to establish a rifle range, with the necessary approval given by the Secretary of State for War in August 1879. On the 23rd of that month since the members were predominantly their employees the L&NWR Company contributed £100 towards the cost of building the practice butts. Completion was scheduled for mid September, to be ready for that year's class firing, and adjacent to St. Peter's Church at Stanton Low the location, being the property of Earl Spencer, was in the occupation of JGVF Johnson. From being a lieutenant he had been gazetted that year on September 13th to Captain. As such for the Volunteer Church Parade he was in command when, presenting quite a spectacle to the unaccustomed populace, No. 6 Company of the 1st Bucks Rifle Volunteer Corps, numbering some 80, assembled in fine weather on the morning of Sunday, April 25th 1880. Headed by the band they then proceeded to St. James' Church.

It seems the new butts were soon ready and on Saturday, November 6th 1880 the first competition for a challenge cup given by Captain Johnson took place. A four times winner would qualify to keep the trophy, and a marksman winning on two consecutive occasions would be awarded a silver medal, presented by Mr. Mudon of London. In the dull light, and with the wind blowing from the right and from the rear, the four highest scores were Corporal Thompson 55; Sgt. Hayman 43; Colour Sgt. Fry 42; and Sgt. Howes 40.

Then in 1881 the competition for the challenge cup was held on the afternoon of Saturday, May 7th, with Private H. Downing keeping the cup for the month. The following month the competition took place on Saturday 11th, with Corporal Mudon and Private Downing chosen to represent the company at Wimbeldon. With a score of 69 points Private Downing again featured in 1882 on

June 3rd, winning the monthly challenge cup presented by Lt. H. Williams. In fact Private Cadwallader had scored 70 points, but was disqualified from not wearing his uniform!

That year on Saturday, September 30th the annual prize shooting competition of No. 6 Company, 1st Bucks Rifle Volunteers took place at the Butts. Usually the tradesmen and inhabitants subscribed in money and kind to the prize fund, and Corporal Mudon was the winner of the 1st prize with 58 points for shooting, and 41 for drill. In view of its regular use extensive alterations to the range would be ordered and defrayed from the funds of the Company. The cost totalled more than £130 and with the work complete by January 1885 the range when inspected and passed by the authorities would again be available for practice. At this period in accordance with a recent order from the War Office the Volunteer Force, no doubt for consistency, would now be issued with the Martini-Henry rifle, as used by the regular troops. The Bucks Volunteers would be amongst the first to benefit, and with their Sniders having been sent to Birmingham, for the usual overhauling, the Martinis would be issued as replacements.

Perhaps they used this new issue when on Saturday, May 7th 1887 the competition was held for the monthly challenge cup presented by Mr. F.W. Bignell. The occasion would also decide the representatives of the Company at Wimbledon for the Queen's Prize, with Private H. Downing, Private G. Sandwell, and Sgt. T. Sandles being those chosen. Intriguingly the occasion in 1887 on Saturday, October 29th was stated as the first practice of the 'newly established shooting club' of the 1st Bucks Rifle Volunteer No. 6 Company, with this being the last opportunity for shooting in the Volunteer year. Many members were present and despite the light the shooting was good. Then in 1888 on Saturday, January 21st the monthly cup competition took place under Wimbledon rules albeit in inadequate light and with the wind blowing across the range. The schedule was 7 shots at 200, 400, and 600 yards, with the scores being Private G. Sandwell, 78; Private W. Mottram 72; Private H. Whitney 70; Private H. Wildman 60; Private G.F. Masters 55; Private J. Brown 44; Private A. Jeffrey 44; Private W.R. Fossey 34. From being a three times winner Private Sandwell now required just one additional win to keep possession of

Wolverton and New Bradwell territorials on parade, either at the outset or the end of the First World War.

During the Second World War the Home Guard comprised volunteers from Wolverton and New Bradwell and the surrounding villages.

the cup. For the same competition in 1889 in May it was resolved that Private Whitney, Sgt. Thompson, and Private A. Wootton would represent the company at the forthcoming Wimbledon meeting, this being the third.

However there might be a lapse in practice on Saturday, October 26th when John Jones, who acted as flag man when the Volunteers were shooting at the Stanton Low butts, broke his thigh when the pole fell as he was climbing up to raise the flag. This was near the canal side and with first aid rendered by members of the Ambulance Corps he was taken to his home at Stantonbury, where Dr. Miles set the limb.

For the Wolverton Company the range continued in use into the new century, and on the general military scene regarding the South African war in the school log book on February 28th 1900 was recorded 'Just after playtime, we heard of the relief of Ladysmith. The children were most enthusiastic. They gave three cheers for General Butler, General White etc., and then sang the National Anthem and Rule Brittannia. The boys went in procession after school to the Chairman and several members of the Board, and begged for a half day holiday. It was readily granted.'

It had been in December 1899 that Lord Chesham with reference to the Yeomanry issued a notice to the Royal Bucks Hussars, 'and all who wish to have the honour of going to the front in South Africa to serve the Queen.' 'Her Majesty's Government has decided to call out a force of mounted men to enrol themselves for the above service. ... Horse, arms, clothing, and equipment will be provided free, and pay and allowances given at the rates specified by the Government. Candidates must be from twenty to thirty five years of age, and of good character. Ships will be ready to take the first thousand men and horses in three weeks. 'Let us be ready before the ships!'" One of those who was ready was Trooper H. Fisher of Stantonbury, who that year in June as a 'trained soldier' had attended the Royal Bucks Hussars annual prize shooting and dinner of the first squadron at Stowe Park. At Stantonbury he had for many years assisted Dr. Miles, to whom, having joined the Imperial Yeomanry as dispenser and compounder of medicines, he wrote from Kimberley Camp in 1900 on April 5th;

Dear Dr. Miles.

I have much pleasure in again recording some more of my experiences of a soldier's life in South Africa. Many and various have been the things which have happened since writing to you last. First of all, I must tell you that we have been for an eight day's march with Lord Methuen's column. We have with us twelve big guns, two Maxims, two regiments of Infantry, one of Cape Mounted Police, two companies of Bucks Yeomanry, together with companies from the Berks, Oxfordshire, and Yorkshire Yeomanry: also the Sherwood Rangers. We went all around the other side of Barkley West, about fifty miles, so as to clear the district of some stray parties of rebels, but unfortunately we did not get near enough to fire upon them. The doctor having been ill, and not well enough now to accompany us, we had to get another doctor from the R.A.M.C.

I have to dispense every morning, take down the name, disease, and treatment of every patient, and get out a sick report every day for Lord Chesham's inspection. I also have charge of the medicine chest. I rather enjoyed the march, especially when it was fine, but unfortunately it rained nearly half the time, which made it most uncomfortable, as we had no shelter night or day. Wherever we found ourselves at dusk, there we tied up our horses, lighted our fires, and boiled water to make tea or coffee, to was down the bully beef and biscuits. I am getting quite used to the Veldt for a bed, a boulder for a pillow, and a blanket to cover me. One does not suffer much from insomnia, whatever the bed may be, after a hard day's march, such as we have. I had a little diarrhoea and sickness the other day, which lasted but a few hours; however the doctor said I had better have a few days' rest in camp. The column is starting for Boshof, where we expect to join it in a few days, with all the remounts, &c.

We have been supplied with Basuto ponies; they are about the size of your grey, but not so thick set, very hardy and surefooted, and pick their way anywhere; in fact, they could not fall down if they tried. I must tell you that the other day I found such a fine dog straying amongst the bushes; he is nearly as big as a lion, but only a pup. I have named him "Marcus," and gave him some bully beef. He has kept near the hospital tent ever since. If I can I intend to keep him and bring him home, as I feel sure you will like him very much. I believe we are working round so as to finally join Lord

Roberts. Yesterday I gained permission to go into Kimberley, so I went and found Mr. Brooks, and spent the time with him, or rather with both of them. They seem to be doing well, but of course the siege was a great drawback to their business. You would smile at the shop and premise; they are all built of galvanised iron, and, like, all other buildings out here, they have no second floor. They keep a general store, drapery, grocery, and almost everything combined. It is situated just out of the town, close to the native settlement, so that they do more business with the natives than with the whites. One of the natives came in for a pair of boots while I was there., and I was surprised to find how particular they are, and because the leather was a little bit rough the man brought them back. Mr. Brooks tells me that he purchased the whole business right out, and that it is answering extremely well. During the siege hundreds of shells came over the place, but fortunately not one touched it. He has several shells which he picked up; amongst them is one still loaded, which fell but did not burst. He says that he will try and get one for me to bring home to you. They had many questions to ask about Stantonbury, and things which had happened since they left. I therefore gave them a brief history up to the date of my leaving. They made kind enquiries about yourself, and wished me to send their kindest remembrances to you; also to Mr. Pidgen and Mr. Trodd.

You will be sorry to hear that we have lost one man of the Bucks from dysentery; another man belonging to the Berks was drowned when watering his horse in the Vale river. There seems to be a lot of dysentery and fever, but I think half of it is due to carelessness, such as drinking large quantities of bad water during the heat of the day. I feel sure I got my diarrhoea and sickness from this source. We were marching in the heat of the sun, and having been relieved of my water bottle by some kind friend before starting in the morning, I came over very thirsty, so I had a drink from the water cart. The water in the cart of course was supposed to be good, but I had not had it half an hour before diarrhoea and sickness commenced, and was very bad for a time.

I trust you are all well at Stantonbury. We often go to bed before you attend your Wolverton surgery in the evening, and I think to myself that the doctor at home is just starting for Wolverton by now. I hope Dr. Linsay is well, and getting on nicely. Please give my regards to him. Mr. Brooks says that if you come out here you would make your fortune in no time; he says the lowest fee is 10s 6d. I like the climate much myself, and the country very well, but the great drawback is the absence of life. You may travel thirty miles or more in any direction and not see a single person or a house; and, besides, wherever I have been yet I have not seen a tree worthy of the name, when compared with, say, an elm tree at home.

The feeling at Kimberley is that the war will soon be over, and I believe the soldiers will not be sorry; they do not like marching all over the country for nothing. Still, we may see a bit of fighting yet round Blomfontein, so as to gratify their wishes.

Please give my kind regards to all a home, and also to all other kind enquirers. Goodbye, Sir. With my very best wishes, trusting that you are well.

Believe me, yours sincerely,

H. FISHER,

37 Company, 10 Battalion, Imperial Yeomanry,

Field Force, S.A.

More locally on Saturday, December 8th 1900 a match was held between the Volunteers and the 2nd Cheshires (Crewe). Then in 1903 on Saturday, April 4th the 1st Bucks Rifle Volunteers Second Bisley and Spoon Competition was shot for in less than ideal weather. The following year and again in unfavourable weather the 1st Bucks Volunteer Rifle Corps handicap prize shooting competition took place on Saturday, September 24th. The 1st prize was £2, the 2nd £1 10s, 3rd & 4th £1, 5th breakfast cruet, 6th 15s, 7th 12s 5d, 8th 10s, and 9-20 'prizes.' Shortly afterwards on Saturday, October 8th the Wolverton Volunteers were the winners by 52 points in a competition with the London Irish. This was their first meeting and afterwards the teams spent a pleasant evening at the County Arms. In 1907 the Territorial and Reserve Forces Act of Parliament was passed, whereby the existing Volunteer and Yeomanry units were transferred to a new Territorial Force. In consequence in 1908 on March 31st the 1st Buckinghamshire Rifle Volunteer Corps became the 1st Buckinghamshire Battalion, the Oxon and Bucks Light Infantry, with Numbers 6 and 7 Companies at Wolverton becoming

To the Glory of God
and in memory of the brave men
of the parish of Bradwell
who fell in the Great War 1914-1918

F and G Companies, with Capt. L.C. Hawkins taking the dual command. Thus in November 1909 it was as the Bucks Battalion Territorial Force (Wolverton Detachment) that the 'Trained Men's Competition' was fired on the Stanton Low range.

The Rifle Butts were pulled down around 1926 by Taylor's steam traction engines of Little Linford. However The Butts remained as the name of the location, where including 1937 there was a popular Lido during the bathing season. As for the sounds of military action during WW2 a stick of 7 bombs fell across the meadow from Stanton Low in a line straight towards the Black Horse.

TO THE GLORY OF GOD
AND IN MEMORY OF THE BRAVE MEN
OF THE PARISH OF BRADWELL
WHO FELL IN THE GREAT WAR · 1914-1918

2ND LIEUT C.L.SHERWOOD.	PTE C.A.FRENCH.
SERGT R.ADAMS.	W.J.FOXFORD.
A.CRISGROOKE.	F.FOOLKES.
C.A.HOLLOWAY.	H.CALTRESS.
D.JOHNSON.	C.E.CALTRESS.
R.A.KETTLE.	W.GILLARD.
H.WILLIS.	R.W.GUNTRIP.
G.SYRETT.	H.GREEN.
CORPL J.G.T.CARTER.	A.G.HALL.
F.GILTROW.	L.F.HOWES.
A.V.FINCHER.	C.A.HENSMAN.
R.G.KIGHTLEY.	F.G.HARDWICK.
W.NABBUTT.	L.J.ILLING.
W.F.WINDSOR.	E.W.KNIGHT.
L.CORPL A.J.BRANSON.	J.H.KNIGHT.
B.J.COMPTON.	W.J.LENNARD.
W.C.HOLLIS.	J.H.MORBY.
L.V.KENT.	F.H.MCKAY.
J.POLLARD.	J.MORBY.
J.M.THOMPSON.	F.H.MEAD.
J.WILLIS.	C.NASH.
J.E.WILLIS.	E.ODELL.
PTE A.ADAMS.	W.OLDHAM.
F.H.ANDREWS.	A.V.PLANT.
A.BRANDOM.	L.POWELL.
H.BARNES.	C.H.PURTEN.
S.B.BISSELL.	H.RILEY.
J.BOWLES.	S.H.SAYELL.
W.H.BAKER.	W.SYRATT.
W.G.BIRD.	W.A.L.STEWART.
J.BERREL.	J.W.STREGARD.
W.J.BURNHAM.	J.J.STALLARD.
W.J.CARROLL.	W.G.STARES.
J.R.CASEMORE.	H.SEAR.
W.C.CROSS.	L.H.SHILLINGLAW.
J.T.CROSS.	H.SMITH.
P.C.JARVIS.	A.F.C.SAPWELL.
E.E.WHITFIELD.	J.THOMAS.
W.WOOD.	A.WICKS.
P.J.WALTERS.	A.WILLETT.
A.WALTERS.	WITT.
B.WOOD.	A.W.CHILD.
C.J.COOK.	F.G.WRIGHT.

1939 – 1945.

J.BAINES.	A.E.MOSELEY.
V.C.BODDY.	A.K.PARKER.
M.COOKE.	C.S.RATCLIFFE.
G.CRANE.	A.T.ROGERS.
H.HALL.	F.E.STONTON.
G.L.HOLLAND.	H.WATSON.
W.C.JERROM.	K.WOOLHEAD.
G.LAMKIN.	

THE LITTLE SOLDIER
A Memorial to the Fallen of both World Wars

In the aftermath of the First World War communities throughout the country made plans to commemorate the fallen, and at New Bradwell a War Memorial scheme was launched, to raise monies through donations and various events. This met with initial enthusiasm but soon interest began to wane and at a public meeting of subscribers, held in the Assembly Hall on Tuesday, November 2nd 1920, it was decided to abandon the intent. The public meetings had attracted only small and unrepresentative attendances of the townspeople, and since only £171 10s of the necessary £800 had been raised the committee felt it pointless to go on. Therefore it was decided at the public meeting to refund the donations and after a deduction for the committee's expenses send the surplus money raised by social functions to the Northampton General Hospital. Thus at the presentation of cheques to the Hospital on Saturday, February 5th 1921 that for £28 10s has handed in by Mr. Tompkins. Apathy was also apparent at the monthly meeting of Wolverton UDC on the evening of Tuesday, April 27th 1920, when with regard to war trophies the clerk read a letter from Mr. A.W. Wilson. This stated that by the instruction of the New Bradwell War Memorial Committee he was to inform the council that the residents of New Bradwell didn't wish to accept the war trophy promised to them. In consequence it was decided to notify the War Office that the German gun offered to New Bradwell was not required. However having probably known and employed many of the men Alderman Robert Wylie determined that a commemoration to the fallen should be made. He died in 1919 on April 10th and bequeathed means for an impressive monument to be fashioned. This comprised the 3 foot figure of a uniformed private of the Oxon. & Bucks. Light Infantry standing to attention with rifle on top of the 12 feet high memorial. On the face of the memorial were inscribed the names of those who had died, and on the front of the base;

TO FULFIL THE PROMISE OF THE LATE
ROBERT WYLIE J.P. C.A.

THIS MONUMENT WAS ERECTED BY HIS FAMILY

On the left side of the memorial were the words 'Our Glorious Dead' and on the right 'For Country'.

An unveiling by Mr. W.W. Carlile was performed at a ceremony held on Saturday, May 1st 1920 which, as reported by the local press, consisted of a procession marshalled by Mr. G. Tapp and headed by the Bradwell Prize Band followed by the relatives, the NFDDS, the Boy Scouts under Scoutmaster W. Holloway, the Girl Guides under the Misses Harnett, members of the Urban Council, and many representatives of town organisations. The procession entered the cemetery on the Newport Road to the music of the Dead March with the Burial Service read by the Reverends E.F. Forsdike of Bradwell, and E.R. Sill of Little Linford. Several hymns were sung and Mr. Carlile expressed the parishioners gratitude to the family of Mr. Wylie for the generosity of the late Alderman. The undraping of the Union Jack from the memorial then proved the signal for wreaths to be placed by the relatives and many others, with the base covered by beautiful flowers. Mr. B.M. Wylie as the eldest son then presented the memorial to the parish. He said it was a sacred gift for all time, and the ceremony was brought to a close by the sounding of the Last Post.[25] As for other commemorations, in 1922 as a result of an instrumental and vocal recital, held at St. James' Church on Sunday, September 24th, the sum of £10 was realised for the Church War Memorial. Hopefully debt free this it was hoped to have in place on a pillar in the north aisle by Christmas, and being a handsome marble war memorial it bore the inscribed names of those parishioners who had fallen. It had been made possible by the efforts of a band of church workers led by the vicar and his wife, and in 1923 on the afternoon of Sunday, July 29th there was a large congregation for the dedication by the Bishop of Buckingham.

BOMBS ON NEW BRADWELL

The inevitability of a second world war had long been anticipated and as recorded in a school log book before the outbreak the school emergency preparations were being practised; 'September 29th

1938. Practice was given today in the rapid evacuation of the school premises. All classes took part.' 'September 30th 1938. The staff wore gas masks at intervals during the day, to accustom the children to their appearance.' Indeed such measures proved necessary for in 1939 on September 9th the entry reads. 'School re-opened this morning at the usual time after the mid-summer holidays. As a state of war exists, no instruction is to be given to any children, but the premises are to be used for evacuated people.'

Then on September 22nd, 'School re-opened this morning for instruction. 2 rooms were used for the children who have been evacuated from Leopold St. School, Willesden. I have admitted 46 other children who are privately evacuated. We could not work entirely to the timetable, as I have had to fit the new children into the classes.' Yet even for evacuees the town was not immune to enemy action and regarding the Girls' School the entry for October 21st reads, 'Schools closed as the result of extensive damage caused by enemy action. Mr. Leonard came and inspected the damage caused. The schools are to be closed until further notice.'

The 'enemy action' had occurred the previous day, when on the evening of Sunday, October 20th 1940 not only was a basket of flares dropped at the western end of Bridge Street, falling on the allotments, but also bombs. Two (after the war two unexploded bombs were additionally discovered) fell at the western end of the High Street. One caused a 30ft crater in the road outside a doctor's house, and the other demolished 71, 73 and 75 High Street. Down from London and staying for the weekend, Mrs. O'Rourke and her three children were killed at number 75. At number 73 Mr. and Mrs. G. Bardell when sitting by their fireside were trapped by falling debris. Aged 82 Mr. Bardell was killed and his wife, Sarah Ann, seriously injured. After nursing in Aylesbury hospital she returned to New Bradwell to be cared for by her daughter in law, Mrs. A. Bardell, at 46, King Edward Street. Then later at the home of her youngest son at 76, Spencer Street. Yet she never fully recovered and after four months being bed ridden died aged 83.

SHOT BY THE HOME GUARD

In June 1941 an intensive hunt was made for a man in the uniform of a Scottish officer who fired a revolver at a police constable at Woughton. During the heightened alert a girl passenger in a car was wounded in the back when a member of the Home Guard fired when the vehicle failed to stop. She was Miss Jane Strittles aged 20, the eldest daughter of Mr. and Mrs. G. Sprittles of, 4 West View, New Bradwell. Soon after midnight she and Miss Daphne Eldred of Spencer Street, New Bradwell, were returning from a dance at St. Martin's Hall, Bletchley, in the rear of a car driven by Reginald Jackson of 16, Wood Street, New Bradwell. Having been stopped twice to show their identity cards, on passing through Loughton the driver failed to notice another instruction to stop and the Home Guard fired, with the bullet striking Miss Strittles just below the shoulder blade. She passed into a dead faint and with the car pulled up on the verge the occupants brought her onto the side and bandaged the wound as best they could. She was then driven to Stony Stratford where after attention by Dr. Douglas Bull she was conveyed by the Wolverton Works ambulance to Northampton Hospital.

MEMORIAL CLOCK TOWER

In 1946 the Bradwell branch of the British Legion held a discussion to decide the form of a memorial for the fallen of WW2. The initial choice was to build a Memorial Hall, towards the cost of which dances and whist drives were held. However no appropriate site could be found and it was instead resolved to erect a clock tower. An approach was made to Wolverton UDC and as a result a strip of land between the old and new Newport Roads was made available for a tower and memorial gardens. The flower beds were prepared by the council, the rose bushes were given by the British Legion, and the two teak seats donated by the Bradwell Band were quickly erected by the firm of Tarrant. Towards the total cost of some £1,700 the British Legion gave a cheque for £200 for the council to invest towards the expenses of maintenance. A lectern made by pupils of New Bradwell County Secondary School would be installed in the tower to hold the roll of honour containing the names of the fallen.

Then in 1962 on the afternoon of Sunday, September 2nd a parade numbering almost 400 persons with over 30 standards was lead by the New Bradwell Silver Band to join the large crowd assembled before the service of dedication. This was conducted by the vicar, the Rev. R. Russell, assisted by the Rev. D. Harris, the Rev. A. Bidnell as the Methodist minister, and Miss Esme Lewis of the Salvation Army. During the ceremony the plaque was unveiled by Dr. J. Love as president of the British Legion Branch, and his wife as president of the women's section. Mr. S. Teagle as chairman of the branch recited the exhortation and as members of the original committee Mr. S. Gascoyne and Mrs. C. Bardell placed wreaths either side of the tower door. Bandsmen Bert Tilley and Bill Campbell of the New Bradwell Silver Band played the Last Post and Reveille and afterwards a tea was held in the Social Club.

The Duchess of Marlborough acquired the manor of Stantonbury in the early 18th century and at her death bequeathed it to her grandson, later the 1st Earl Spencer.

Apart from the Grand Junction Canal in 1800 there was little development on the manor until the 4th Earl Spencer sold land to the L&NWR.

The Spencer name is honoured in Spencer Street and Althorp Crescent.

The phtograph shows the 7th Earl Spencer entertaining King George V and his wife at Althorp.

Endnotes

1   It is likely that the mansion was at least partly restored after the fire. Thomas Harrison, land agent for Earl Spencer, and his family lived there until 1773. The house is also shown on the Jeffreys' map of 1768.

2   In 1862 at Stony Stratford on November 5th the death occurred of Mary Scrivener, daughter of the late John Scrivener of Stantonbury, aged 61.

3   It stood to the east of the church, and built of local limestone with a tiled roof probably dated from the 17th century, with development in the late 18th century into a three bay two storey house.

4   At the age of 79, in August 1886 the death occurred of Richard Dunkley at Alby Rectory, Norwich. Formerly of The Lowndes, Blisworth, Northants., he was well known as a major contractor in the Midlands, his connection with the railway having commenced when the London and Birmingham line was constructed. In consequence he built most of the railway workshops, mills, and sheds at Wolverton and also 72 cottages for railway workers at Stantonbury. His life and work is copiously told on line at www.blisworth.org.uk 'Richard Dunkley, Railway Builder and Businessman..

5   Robert's siblings were John, born at Dailly, Ayrshire in 1818; William, born at Dailly, Ayrshire, in 1821; Jane, born at Dailly, Ayrshire, in 1825; Ann, born at Dailly, Ayrshire, in 1827; Marion Cochrane born in 1831 on August 27th at Gallowlee, Ochiltree, Ayrshire, 1831; and Agnes, born in 1835 on January 12th at Gallowlee, Ochiltree, Ayrshire.

6   See the volume in this series 'Loughton, Shenley & Tattenhoe.'

7   John Munday

As recorded in the register of births for Haddenham Baptist Church, John Munday was born to John Munday and his wife Martha at Haddenham in 1815 on February 13th. In early life he moved to Buckingham, where for some years his home was in Elm Street. Then in 1839 on the morning of Sunday, September 29th at Buckingham parish church he married Sarah White, born at Buckingham in 1811 and baptised that year on June 14th. She was the daughter of Catherine (Kitty) White (nee Mitchell) and Reginald White, and as a widow Kitty would live with her daughter and son in law. Their home would be in Chandos Road where John was the first to commence building operations - both his own and the adjoining houses. Afterwards several more houses in Chandos Road would be built by him. He was a member of the Town Council, School Board, and Board of Guardians and in his younger days was keen on cricket. When too old to play he then umpired local matches. In politics he was a Liberal whilst 'In religious matters he was far from orthodox, but being fond of singing, and having a good bass voice, he was often found in a place of worship and paid due reverence to the service.' Also he was tee total and a worker in the Band of Hope. In 1872 on Sunday, April 21st at their home in Chandos Road when about to go upstairs for some reason Kitty fell backwards into the kitchen, sustaining serious injuries about her head and face. Medical advice was hurriedly sought and she lingered until the evening of Friday, May 3rd. She was 85. An inquest into the cause of death took place at the New Inn, Buckingham, on Saturday May 4th at which John Munday, builder, said she was his mother in law and had lived with them for about 20 years. He gave an account of the day and said that on hearing his wife scream he found Kitty at the bottom of the stairs in a heap. A verdict in accordance with the medical evidence was returned. In another tragedy his only daughter Esther died in 1883 on September 15th at Buckingham aged 32. In September 1889 John and his wife celebrated their Golden Wedding. He had remained in good health but having become increasingly feeble his wife died in 1890 on May 1st aged 78. The funeral was held at Buckingham on the afternoon of Tuesday, May 6th. With his occupation now stated as 'farmer,' in 1891 John was living at 6, Chandos Road, with Elizabeth Franklin, servant. Yet it was at 7, Chandos Road, that by his direction an auction was conducted in February of household furniture, garden tools, carpenters tools etc. He was now leaving the town and would move to Haddenham. However on business matters he often returned to Buckingham, where he still possessed 4 of his houses in Chandos Road. In 1901, being visited at the time of the census by his widowed daughter in law, Elizabeth, he was living at Haddenham with Amos George aged 70, a retired blacksmith, and his 70 year old wife Elizabeth. (Nee Munday, she had been born at Haddenham, and the couple had married in 1852 on May 19th at Cuddington, Bucks., the home village of Amos). Aged 87 John Munday died in 1902 on Monday, March 17th at The Yews, Haddenham, where the funeral was held on Friday, March 21st.

8   William Beard Lake was born in 1869 on June 23rd, the son of Frederick Crompton Lake. He commenced his working life at Messrs. Barnard and Lakes Foundry at Rayne, where his father was a partner. Then in 1896 he moved to Braintree, starting a small business in a machine shop in New Street with one man and a boy. As such in 1901 he was in operation at Rayne Road, Braintree, as a tool manufacturer, his family comprised of himself, his wife and 2 children. Resident with his wife and now 5 children, the 1911 census records him of Tollgate House, Braintree, as director of a company manufacturing motor and cycle accessories, iron and steel castings. His several patents, including one to put spokes in wheels, made him sufficient money to build the Albion Works at Rayne Road, Braintree. This was for the manufacture of components and during WW1 he built a large foundry at Chapel Hill, Braintree, joined in partnership by Mr. E.F. Elliot. The business expanded whilst in public life in 1926 he was made a JP for Essex. From its founding he remained as chairman and managing director of Messrs. Lake & Elliot until his health failed. For some time he would be a patient at the William Julien Courtauld Hospital but he returned to his home at Mount Place, Braintree, just a few weeks before his death. This occurred at the age of 76 on Saturday, December 29th 1945 with the funeral held on the Tuesday at Braintree parish church. His widow, Martha, of Mount Place, Braintree, died in 1947 on October 22nd, with administration granted to Crompton John Lake, company chairman. Both she and her husband are commemorated in Braintree cemetery.

9   After an illness of some 9 weeks, at his home of 6, Bury Street, Newport Pagnell, Jesse Gregory died aged 75 in 1933 on Thursday, November 16th. He had been 'mine host' at the Morning Star for 19 years, having previously been licensee for 6 years at the Wheatsheaf at Loughton, and for a similar period at the Prince

Albert, Old Bradwell. He served on the committee of the North Bucks Licensed Victuallers' and Beersellers' Protection Society. He left the Morning Star in 1913 to live at Milton Keynes and then at Newport Pagnell, where he was keen bell ringer. His first wife had died several years ago on a visit to a married daughter at Chesham, and he was survived by his second wife, formerly a Miss Garrett of Milton Keynes. Hs funeral was held at New Bradwell, where he was buried in the churchyard.

10   The 'bungalow' in Newport Road, New Bradwell, was actually built in 1923 from four railway carriages to the design of Mr. Billingham and Mr. Edwards, a retired baker from New Bradwell. Previously Mr. and Mrs. Billingham and their four children had lived in Bridge Street, New Bradwell, where for two years Mr. Edwards lived with them. He owned a site in the town and for £100 at the beginning of 1923 bought the four carriages from Wolverton Works - two first class, one second, and one third. However prior to being removed from the Works by lorry they had to be cut in two! The building firm of Gurney then carried out the construction which was complete by November of that year. However Mr. Edwards died before the family moved into the accommodation which he left them in his will. The layout comprised a pantry, kitchen, bathroom, and coal place, and at the rear a long room overlooked the garden. Also there were five bedrooms but once the children had grown up and left home Mr. and Mrs. Billingham had two in one of the first class carriages converted into one large bedroom. After her husband's death, when moving to a small flat on the ground floor of The Gables, at Wolverton, Mrs. Billingham sold the unique bungalow to the Willowdene Garage. It would not be occupied again and was pulled down in 1968.

11   Number 8, Althorpe Cresent was definitely complete, for this was the home of 21 year old Brian Hayes who in 1947 on the evening of October 4th featured in the In Town Tonight programme, on the BBC Home Service, talking about his experiences in building his own television set and his activities in the world of short wave radio. He was employed by the Industrial Magneto Co. Ltd., of Bletchley.

12   In 1891 Arthur was a pupil teacher at Stantonbury. Then in 1911 as an elementary schoolmaster at Stockport he was resident at 73, Kensington Road, Cheadle Heath, Stockport, with Edith Ratcliffe, single, of private means. By 1916 he had been appointed as headmaster of St. George's Senior School, Stockport. However at the outbreak of WW2 as 'an independent gentleman' he was resident with an unmarried female servant at the Manor House, Pomphlett, Plymouth. There he died in 1962 on December 25th with the funeral held on the Thursday at Wolverton.

13   In 1872 Heber began as an apprentice at Wolverton Works, and in 1877 on the formation of the Wolverton Works Company of the 1st Bucks Rifle Volunteer Corps he joined as a private. He married in 1883 and in 1891 was living at Morland Terrace, Wolverton, with his wife, Mary, and children. In 1898 he was appointed as Outdoor Assistant Carriage Superintendent, and in 1911 was living with his family at 'Yiewsley', Wolverton. With the outbreak of the Boer

War, in January 1900 at a meeting at the Science and Art Institute, Wolverton, 86 men of the Wolverton Company of the Volunteers signed up for service in South Africa. Now with the rank of lieutenant Heber would command the detachment, and during his military career he would be mentioned in despatches during WW1, and reach the rank of Lt. Col. He retired from his railway position in April 1927 and moved with his wife to 'The Elms' at Newport Pagnell. That year his health deteriorated due to an internal complaint, and despite an operation he died that year on May 17th at Battlesden nursing home. He left a widow, a son, and a daughter. Another son, Harry Varney Williams, had died in 1883 on November 2nd aged 7.

14   The road known as Belle Vue in 1881 is now part of Portland Road (the north end) in modern Worthing. The road was known locally as Belle Vue between the 1850s and 1880s, although it was always recorded on maps as Chapel Street before being renamed in the 1890s as Portland Road.

15   (see History of Red House School, by Derek Mellor.)

16   In 1931 his namesake son married Ellen Minshull, born in 1901 on March 8th, and at the outbreak of WW2 they were in occupation in the trade of a grocer and confectionary dealer at 132, Connaught Road, Luton. Ellen died in 1946, and in 1947 John married a widow, Doris May Jarvis. Resident at Lon Teify, Swansea, John died in 1952 on October 19th, with probate granted to Doris.

17   Born in Ireland, Dr. Delahunty qualified at Dublin University. He had been an assistant hospital officer with the Ministry of Health in the North of England prior to coming to Wolverton, where his home was 'Yiewsley,' Western Road. Aged 58 he died in 1959 on Tuesday, May 5th.

18   **Castelfranc Guest**

Castelfranc was born to the Reverend Allan Newman Guest and his wife Dorothy in 1917 on September 10th. In 1931 when his parents separated he and his mother went to live at Bournemouth and in 1933 at the age of 16 he joined the Merchant Service, voyaging several times around the world. As a 3rd Officer in August 1939 it was announced that on the completion of Admiralty gunnery trials on the Clyde he was to be appointed as second in command of the Cunard liner 'Port Townsville,' his old ship on the Anglo Australian service. In 1940 he wrote to his father about an incident in which he and his ship were involved, recounting that on sighting a German ship the gunner in charge began to fire at it. The enemy crew attempted to scuttle their vessel but were overpowered by a boarding party and the ship was beached. Castelfranc (known in maritime service as Peter!) said that afterwards he went sea bathing, and regarding the incident had more trouble fighting the sharks! Then after another encounter in March 1941 he was hospitalised in Britain with his side riddled with bullets. He had been aboard a merchant vessel as third officer and was engaged in target practice (smashing the target with his third shot) when the periscope of a submarine was spotted. Seconds later a torpedo hit amidships, and being in charge of the gun crew he kept the ship's gun firing at the submarine until his vessel was almost awash. In a subsequent report to the ship's owners the captain paid tribute to his heroism, saying "the reason that there was not more casualties was due to the heroic action of C. Guest in directing the gun crew, whose firing caused the shots from the submarine to be erratic." Then in June Castlefranc received a letter from Cunard House, informing him that by the Admiralty's commendation he was to be mentioned in the London Gazette. By August 1941 he had recovered from his wounds and having passed his first mates exam would be going to sea again on a liner. The following year in November in an airgraph he wrote to his father of his subsequent travels;

"I had to leave my ship in New Zealand. I flew to Australia in a flying boat, and joined a new ship as second officer. She is a lovely ship, and I am very happy. I have been in India for a few weeks, and it is certainly very interesting. There are a few riots, but the situation is in hand now. It seems funny to see the sacred cows wandering about the streets, and camels drawing carts instead of horses. But apart from everything else, the thing that strikes you most is the awful stink everywhere. It's putrid. It soon vetoes the glamour of the East."

Of other adventures he endured a narrow escape when during an enemy attack on a convoy in the Atlantic bombs shattered the wheelhouse and pantry of his ship. He was unhurt but three members of the crew were killed. Fortunately a cruiser then came into view. In early 1944 he began three months' of study for his Master's Ticket as captain in the Cunard service. At this time he was engaged to an American girl who he met in the United States, where the Rev. Guest had a first cousin married to State Attorney Hodkins of New Jersey. While still in maritime service in 1951 his UK address was 13, Bridle Crescent, Bournemouth. However in 1958 he was resident at 32, Upper Tooting Park, Wandsworth, SW17, with Patricia L. Guest, William H. Neuff, and Katherine A.M. Neuff. Then the following year came the additions of Roger A. Fuller, and Eileen P. Fuller. In 1960 and 1961 at the same address were Castelfranc Guest, Dorothy Guest, Roger A. Fuller, and Eileen P. Fuller. Then in 1962 the names are listed as Castelfranc Guest, Dorothy Guest, John C. Hannaby, and Elizabeth M. Hannaby. Castelfranc died at Poole in 1973.

As for the usual name of Castelfranc, this explanation has been kindly forwarded by Brian Newman;

"George Guest, husband of Mary Anne Newman, was from Portarlington in Queen's County, Southern Ireland (now County Laois). His grandmother was a member of the Castlefranc family, whose family can be traced back to the 16th century. During this period of history it was very dangerous for Huguenots, or French Protestants, because the Catholics thought them to be heretics and despised them. Many were brutally killed, imprisoned or sold as slaves. This was the fate of many of the Castelfrancs. Their chateau was burnt to the ground as the result of an alliance with the Duke of Kohan - against the Catholics. Many of the women were taken from their family and imprisoned as children where they died. Others were sold as slaves and worked in appalling conditions until their escape to England. Rev. Guest traced his Castlefranc family back to the 16th century and acquired several 17th century wills, which are now held by the daughter of Castelfranc Guest, Diana. The Rev. Guest had an elder brother, Joseph de Nautonnier de Castlefranc Guest, born in Listowel, County Kerry, as was the Rev. Guest. He was born in 1866 on August 18th but died of TB aged 9. See Wikipedia for an explanation of Joseph's middle names - ie the 16th century castle is named after Guillaume de Nautonnier de Castelfranc. He was King Henry IVs geographer and astronomer and created the first observatory in France on the site of the Château de Castelfranc. It is to him that we owe the method of the magnetised compass which allows us to measure latitude and longitude. The site can only be visited from the outside as it is now a private property."

19   Betty Guest

Betty Guest (the name seems to have been Betty and not as an abbreviation of Elizabeth) was born in 1919 on March 20th. With her brother Allan Newman Guest she remained with her father at New Bradwell after their parent's separation, but in 1939 both were in adult occupation at Bedford, where Betty was a nurse at Bedford Hospital. There one of her patients was Pilot Officer Robert Morse Cooper RAF, who in flying operations had crashed in the 'ditch.' He had been born in London in 1919 on May 22nd but it seems the family emigrated to Canada. Indeed, although the in depth details are the province of the family members, in 1928 on July 6th aboard the Canadian Pacific Line vessel SS Montrose, he and his brother Alex, age 4, and their mother Ada, age 38, arrived at Southampton from Montreal. Canada was listed as the country of their last permanent residence but 20, Burton Road, Kilburn, London, was the address to which they were going. However at the time of his enlistment Robert was a draughtsman in Montreal, his record sheet for the Royal Canadian Air Force showing it was completed at Toronto in 1939 on October 16th, with service number 10792, rank AC2. The next of kin was entered as his mother, Ada Florence Cooper, of 610, Champagneur Avenue, Montreal, which was also his address. Robert and Betty married at Bournemouth in 1943 on June 19th and in 1944 Betty transferred to Boscombe Hospital. Then in October that year news was received that aged 27 Robert, service number J/17156, had been posted missing on an operational flight. It seems that attached to 547 Squadron RAF, operating from Leuchars, his B24 Liberator was lost without trace on October 28th. This was during an anti submarine patrol off the Norwegian coast, from Bergen to the Skagerrak Area, and with no body recovered he was presumed dead, being commemorated on the Runnymede Memorial. In 1946 Betty went to Canada to meet her in laws, Ada and Robert Cooper, and on settling there in her nursing career she aspired to Matron in a major hospital in Montreal. She died aged 68.

20   Allan Newman Guest

The namesake of his father, Allan Newman Guest was born in 1922 on January 18th. After his parent's separation he and his sister Betty lived with their father at New Bradwell. Allan was educated at Wolverton Secondary School and in 1939 began employment at Bedford with Barclays Bank in St. John's Street. With the outbreak of war he became a cadet in the Fleet Air Arm but in 1940 on the afternoon of Sunday, June 2nd performed together with his father, the Rev. Guest, in a piano and violin recital at New Bradwell. Included in the programme was a lament for the crews of lost submarines. Then in November 1942 the Rev.

Guest received news that Allan (often known as Newman), who had seen much active service on convoy work, had been commissioned in the RNVR. During his subsequent service two of his ships would be the Ganges in March 1943 and the Chinkara in March 1945. In November of the latter year it was announced that Sub. Lt. Allan Newman Guest RNVR had been appointed as an expert on aircraft carrier work in Cochin, China. However after the war in 1946 he resumed employment with Barclays Bank but would remain as an active RNVR until 1968. During naval service he had met Jean Diana Turner, born in 1918 in Fulham, the daughter of Charles Turner and Lena Graves. She was an educationalist (MA Oxon) and served in the WRNS chiefly at Bletchley Park, which was where the couple met. They married on February 21st 1947 at Kensington being resident at 15, Victoria Grove. In 1948 on October 23rd a daughter, Diana Jane Guest, was born in Hammersmith. Then in 1958 the family were living at 36, Hornton Court, and later at St. Mary House, Polstead Hill, Colchester, CO6 5AH. In his banking career Allan was employed in the City branches, later transferring to Newcastle Direct as a Local Director. He was offered a Local Director position in Milton Keynes but, retiring in 1979, the thought of returning to the scene of an alleged unhappy childhood contributed to an enduring period of stress. This lead to him being committed, and he spent his final years in a nursing home with dementia. He died at Colchester in 2013 on April 13th.

21   In 1932 Dorothy (Dolly), qualified to act as a juror, was resident with Phyllis Penman at 'Glengarth,' 16, Waltham Road, Bournemouth. Also from 1933 to 1937, but not mentioned in 1938. In 1939 she was a furrier at Tudor House, Stour Way, Iford, Christchurch. She died in November 1985 at Hindhead, Surrey.

22   From information kindly provided from Graham Crisp, who was born at 9, Harwood Street, New Bradwell, in the house where he still lives, with regard to Mrs. Roberts he recalls that she was his great aunt, Ethel Roberts, who told him that she had once been Home League secretary and the local agent for the Salvation Army Insurance Company. She married Johann Roberts, a Salvation Army officer from Bristol, whose son by his first marriage, Edwin Roberts, became Lord Mayor of Bristol in 1972, of which she was immensely proud. Mrs. Roberts had two sisters, Eva and Florence. Their maiden name was Rainbow and the family originated in Hanslope. Graham recalls that the premises now occupied by the Sid Telfer store was the Bowyer Hall, where he would take harvest produce from school and give it to Mr. and Mrs. Blunt. They ran the old peoples' 'Ivy League' and sat on the stage behind a large table; "There is still an upwards slope at the back of what is now Telfers where the stage once was, and I often think about that visit when I'm in the shop!"

23   The Rev. Woodhouse would remain at Leckhampton until 1911, with subsequent appointments as rector of Winterbourne Monkton, Dorset, and Pampisford, Cambs. Hs daughter married Alfred James Woodhouse in 1914 on August 10th at the church of Rusthall, Kent. His son, Disney, became a Chaplain to the Forces attached to the 12th Battalion Royal Sussex but died of dysentery at Boulogne in 1916 on October 6th. The Rev. Woodhouse died at 24, Milton Road, Bournemouth, in 1944 on August 19th.

24   **John George Ventris Field Johnson.**

Baptised at Cosgrove on September 12th 1847, John George Ventris Field Johnson (for obvious reasons usually known as JGVF Johnson) was born at Old Stratford on August 26th 1846 to William Johnson (1806-1877), a cattle dealer, and his wife Mary Ann (1810-1882). With the household attended by two servants, in 1861 as a 'landed proprietor' and farmer, employing 24 men and 6 boys, William was resident at Deanshanger, near Stony Stratford, with his wife Mary, and - all born at Old Stratford - daughter Sarah, age 22, John, age 15, and daughter Mary, age 11. Seemingly John gained early farming experience in Canada, writing in his later years, "I have been intimately acquainted with Canada for nigh upon 20 years, and was North-westward in 1869, prior to the so called Red River rebellion ..." Then employing 7 men and one boy, in April 1871 he was farming 285 acres at Wolverton Mill. However that year on May 23rd at London, Ontario, Canada, he married Canadian born Helen Macfie (1848-1884). He was described as being of 'The Mills, Wolverton, Buckinghamshire, son of William Johnson Esq., of Deanshanger House, Northants.', with the marriage conducted by the Venerable Archdeacon Brough. Helen was the only surviving daughter of Daniel Macfie Esq., of 'Ardaven,' London, Ontario.

Daniel Macfie was born on the Isle of Bute, Firth of Clyde, West of Scotland, in 1819 on October 10th. He was the 6th son (of 10 children) of Daniel Macfie, a cooper by trade, and his wife Isabel, and in his early years worked in a cotton factory. At the age of 18 he spent 3 years in a haberdasher warehouse but on being advised of an advertisement of Peter Buchanan & Co., of Glasgow, for the need of a salesman in Canada he successfully applied, being contracted for 3 years. His expenses for the voyage were paid and in 1841 he arrived in Toronto where Isaac Buchanan, MP of the united Provinces of Quebec and Ontario, and brother of Peter Buchanan, advised him to enter the business of John McKay at St. Thomas. When travelling there he passed through London, Ontario, to where following his 3 years engagement he returned. Then in 1845 he married Glasgow born Jean McKay, sister of the late John McKay, Registrar of the County of Elgin, and of the marriage three children - Isobel, Helen & Robert - would be born. In 1849 he began a dry goods business on the corner of Dundas and Talbot Streets and for some 20 years conducted a substantial trade. He also gained a social standing, being elected in 1860 to represent his ward in the City Council. The following year he was elected by the Council as Chairman of the finance committee. This position he held for 5 years, moving to London South in 1866, in which year around May for $9,000 he is said to have purchased from the former resident, John Mackenzie Esq., the family mansion 'Ardaven' (high above the river). Apart from the grounds this included 7 acres of adjoining pasture land, 11 acres in total. Originally built as a cottage in 1834 it was held to be a prime residence in the neighbourhood, having seemingly been contemplated as a residence for the Bishop of Huron had the sale not taken place. In 1867 Daniel became a candidate for a seat in Parliament, standing as a Liberal, but was narrowly defeated. Being made its first president, in 1871 he was involved in establishing the Dominion

Savings and Investment Society of London. From this he retired after some 10 years, and in 1885 was elected President of the Carling Brewery and Malting Company. That year his wife, Jean, died, and Daniel died 5 years later. Their son Robert Cathcart Macfie inherited Ardaven and lived there with his wife Lily and their 4 daughters and a son. As a furrier he was in business as R.C. Macfie & Co., selling wholesale hats, caps and furs. As for Ardaven, in March 1961 this was demolished to make way for a new development.

John then returned to England with his bride and in 1873 was mentioned as a miller of Wolverton Mills. As for his father, William, since he was relinquishing occupancy of the farm he instructed Geo. Wigley to auction at Deanshanger House Farm on Thursday, October 26th 1876, 100 shorthorn dairy cattle, 50 hogs, 3 cart horses, 4 cart and nag horses, 50 tons of old hay, and 220 acres of grass keeping. Then also on his instructions, from relinquishing the occupancy at Michaelmas next Geo. Wigley auctioned in 1877 on Monday, April 9th 230 acres of grass keeping, 6 cart mares, 40 sheep, 20 hogs 'etc.' William died at Deanshanger in 1877 on April 20th and in 1877 on Friday, September 21st at 1pm Geo. Wigley on instruction from the executors auctioned at Deanshanger House Farm the farm stock of animals and implements, to include agricultural steam machinery for corn grinding, chaff cutting, pulping and churning. As for John, apart from his business activities in 1878 on February 6th he was appointed as a 2nd Lt. in the Buckinghamshire Rifle Volunteer Corps, being promoted to Captain in 1879 on September 13th. At this period on the instructions of the executrix of his late father, William, Geo. Wigley was to auction at Stanton Low Pastures 120 cattle, 200 sheep and lambs, and 16 cart colts etc. For his daily occupation John carried on business as Johnson & Co., millers at Wolverton, advertising in October 1880 'American pig spice, American calf spice, Johnson's prairie sheep spice, Wolverton Mills.' Meanwhile in the continued disposal of his late father's assets on Monday, November 29th 1880 Geo. Wigley auctioned cattle and pigs at Stanton Low Pastures. In April 1881 the partnership of 'JGVF Johnson and Wallace William Cragg Johnson & Co., condiment and spice merchants, Wolverton,' was dissolved, and that month as a 'spice manufacturer and farmer, employing 8 men and 1 boy,' John was resident at Wolverton Mills with his wife Helen, their 2 sons and 2 daughters, and two servants. In 1881 on May 11th at 'Stanton Low and Great Linford, between Wolverton and Newport Pagnell,' Geo. Wigley on the continuing instructions of the executors auctioned at the Swan Hotel, Newport Pagnell, 250 acres of grass keeping; 'The grass is proverbial for its rich feeding quality, and several of the grounds have not been stocked since October last.' 'The watering and fences are good. A shepherd will be provided. Barnett at Stanton Low will show the lots' (b*). Subsequent to the aforementioned dissolution, with Mr. W.R. Bull as solicitor in 1881 the first meeting of the creditors of 'JGVF Johnson of Wolverton Mills,' 'farmer, miller, and American spice merchant,' was held at the Park Hotel, Bletchley, at noon on August 23rd, and in December John resigned his commission as a Captain. Then in 1882 at Stony Stratford Petty Session on April 6th his appointment as surveyor of Wolverton was opposed by Mr. Worley. This was from being unqualified, for although formerly the occupier of 'mill and land' at Wolverton he had ceased such occupation at Michaelmas last. However Mr. Johnson said he now occupied Wolverton Mill and thereby qualified as occupier. The case was adjourned for a fortnight to allow him to produce sufficient evidence. As for other concerns, in December 1882 a bankruptcy notice was posted regarding 'John George Ventris Field Johnson farmer, miller, and American spice merchant, Wolverton.' The estate was now in liquidation, with the second and final dividend at 6d payable at Messrs. Bull's offices, Newport Pagnell. Nevertheless in September 1883 he was appointed liquidator for the purpose of the voluntary winding up of the Wolverton and Stony Stratford Tramways Company Ltd. Not surprisingly John had now decided to emigrate with his family to Canada, where In 1884 on December 15th his wife, Helen, died at London, Ontario. It seems he then moved to Kinalmeaky Farm, Winnipeg, 'near Rosser and Headingley Stations,' where in February 1885 tenders were requested to erect a cattle shed for 100 milch cows. Indeed it was whilst resident at the farm that in 1886 on November 24th he married Frances Amy Sandwith (b1867). She was the second daughter of the late J. Sandwith of Preston, England, with the ceremony conducted by the Rev. E. Pentreath at the Christchurch Anglian Church, Winnipeg, Manitoba. It seems that John's fortunes had now greatly improved, and with regard to agriculture in Canada in writing from Kinalmeaky Farm in May 1887 he included; "Few persons in England have any idea of the immensity of this country or the vastness of its resources. ... We have herds of magnificent cattle, which may be counted in hundreds of thousands roaming over the prairie, and living entirely, both winter and summer, on its succulent grasses. ... To those who have adopted agriculture as a mode of livelihood, and whose lines of late years in England have not fallen in pleasant places, I would ask them to pause and consider whether it will not be to their advantage to abandon that which seems almost a hopeless task - viz., making a respectable living in England, to say nothing of providing a competency against old age, and turn their attention to other lands where the freehold will be their own, and all improvements thereon. ... The land in this country is cultivated in a rough and ready fashion, which can scarcely be called farming, but if taken hold of by practical men, who understand their business, results would be very different. ... A man can purchase 300 acres of any good land here for £300, whereas it takes nigh upon £3,000 to stock a farm of the same average in England. I am farming on a large scale myself, and know whereof I speak. ... This is a grand country for dairy farming, for which purpose I consider it, as a whole, the best adapted in consequence of the almost limitless range and abundant pasturage. The cheese and butter made in this country are excellent." With several children born of his marriage to Frances, in 1891 he was living as a grain merchant with his family at Assiniboia, Manitoba. Aged 63 he died after an illness of 3 months at the General Hospital in Vancouver on the night of Monday, November 23rd 1908, being buried at Mountain View Cemetery, Vancouver. Remembered as a public spirited man and an ardent sportsman he had formerly been secretary of the Vancouver Exhibition Association. His passing bereaved his widow and, from his two marriages, eight children. Two sons, both of the Canadian Pacific Railway telegraphs, resided with their mother and sister at 122, Lansdowne Avenue.

Another son, Ernest William Johnson, was a real estate broker in Winnipeg. Mr. Kenneth D. Johnson was manager of the Molsons Bank at Lethbridge. Mr. Daniel Macfie Johnson was farming near Toronto, and two daughters, one married, were living in England.

Timothy Barnett was for many years bailiff of the Stanton Low Farm but left around 1880 to live on a small dairy farm just outside Great Linford. His niece, Miss Martin, kept house for him, and after dinner at about 2pm on Thursday, February 6th 1890 she saw him fall forward in his arm chair, having suddenly died at the age of 76.

25   As a new burial ground for Stantonbury the cemetery had origins in April 1911, when with a previous location having been abandoned the Parish Council began investigating the field adjoining the railway midway between Rogues' Lane and the Black Horse Inn. Trial holes were dug with it found that the ground was easy to work, dry, and free from rock obstructions. Additionally no levelling would be required and convenient access was afforded by a frontage to the main road. Following satisfactory reports from the Medical Officer of Health and the Surveyor the location was duly confirmed.

JOHN TAYLOR'S VILLAGE STORIES

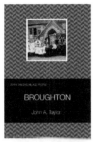

Prior to the creation of the new city of Milton Keynes over 50 years ago, the area was mostly rural, comprising villages that had their own history of self government. In several volumes, John Taylor has recorded in detail the former history of these communities.

1 **Broughton**
978-1-909054-94-3

2 **Great Linford**
978-1-909054-96-7

3 **Loughton, Shenley and Tattenhoe**
978-1-909054-97-4

4 **The Woolstones and Willen**
978-1-915166-02-9

5 **Woughton and Simpson**
978-1-915166-09-8

6 **Stantonbury and New Bradwell**
978-1-915166-13-5

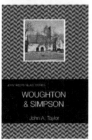

7 **Middleton Keynes**
Forthcoming.

Available at all bookstores and online retailers and direct from the publisher at **www. magicflutepublishing.com**